WHERE
THE HEART IS

WHERE
THE HEART IS

&⸹ ELIZABETH BORTON de TREVIÑO

Doubleday & Company, Inc.
Garden City, New York
1962

917.2
T

*To my husband
who shares these memories with me*

APOLOGIA

With all due apologies, I would like here to tell why I have written this book, in case any one might ask why I should assume that there could be any special interest in my family and my home.

About ten years ago I published a book called *My Heart Lies South*, which recounted my gradual integration into a provincial Mexican family as the wife of one of the sons of the house. In telling how I learned to appreciate and to love the country which became my home, I spoke often of Mamacita and Papacito, my husband's parents, the two people who taught me most. The whole book was, besides an attempt to show the life of a middle-class Mexican family, a tribute to my parents-in-law, and to the traditions and precepts by which they lived.

A few months ago there occurred yet one more in a series of incidents which encouraged me to write more about my adopted country as I have come to know it. A woman telephoned me and said, "You do not know me, but I know you, because I have read your book *My Heart Lies South*. Your book brought me to Mexico because I wanted to know people like your Mexican family. I stopped in Monterrey to visit the little house on Morelos Street where you used to live, and the people who are there now showed it to me, with great hospitality. And I went to find Papacito's grave, to lay some flowers on it." I was deeply touched—as who would not be?—but I was not surprised, for ever since the publication of *My*

8   APOLOGIA

Heart Lies South I have been receiving letters and visits and telephone calls asking for more about Mamacita, for news of my children and of my husband's family. Not taking any credit to myself, but through some undeserved grace of God, I had been permitted to reveal the personalities of people like Mamacita and Papacito and Luis, my husband, and Tia Rosa and many others, so that many Americans came to feel a sort of kinship with my Mexican family, and a reflection of my own deep love for them.

That is why I have continued my modest and very personal story. If this book contributes to a strengthening of that moving kinship readers have felt with my husband's people, I will be more than rewarded, for myself, for Mexican families like mine, and for Americans like me.

Elizabeth Borton de Treviño

CONTENTS

Home is where the heart is.

—ELBERT HUBBARD

I ❧

ADIOS, MONTERREY

Rancho alegre, mi nidito . . .
—SONG

My children have never called me Mama or Mom or Mommy.
They have always called me Mima.

One day in 1944 my two little boys came home from their
Mexican school in San Angel and stood on the carpet before
me to interrogate me.

"Mima," they said, "what are you? Are you a German,
or a Jap, or a gringa?"

It was clear that my sons, born and brought up in Mexico, had realized that there was something seriously wrong
with Mima. I wasn't like the other Mexican mamas they
knew. I made the best explanation I could.

"I'm a gringa," I told them, "but a gringa with a rose in
her teeth. You tell that to anybody who wants to know."

They solemnly accepted my declaration, although one
day not much later when I had had to send them sternly to
bed early for some breach of childish discipline, the two little
boys, in sleeper-suits with feet attached, threw open the door
of the *sala* where I sat reading and hissed "Jap-on-esa!" Japanese, just then, was their epithet for anybody who was anath-
ema. Behind the defiant name-calling, I recognized the same
old suspicion . . . there was something not quite *correcto*
about their Mima.

Another time they protested my activities.

"Mima," they said, "why do you get up and get washed
and dressed and go to town to work? Why don't you stay home
in your wrapper like other mothers?"

"Because I haven't got a nice wrapper," I answered, and we got through that crisis.

Over the years, my sons have often had to explain and defend me. Yet from the beginning of my life in California I felt inclined toward Mexico. I have lived in Mexico now more than twenty-five years, and although I have never given up my American citizenship, I am in some ways more Mexican than the Mexicans. Yet there is a little undying core of gringa in me too. Mamacita, my beloved mother-in-law, knew this, and she took steps to make sure that it was preserved. Mamacita was profoundly Mexican in her spirit, and she loved tradition, yet she was curious and independent and avid for new experiences too, and I think she lived some innocent moments of vicarious excitement through the adventures of her gringa daughter-in-law. She loved me and I loved her, and, since my own mother was thousands of miles away, Mamacita became my confidante and my adviser. And no matter what happened, she always took my part.

One day Mamacita and I sat in my patio on Morelos Street in Monterrey, under the shade of a domestic forest of pinoñolas, jasmine, helecho ferns, and rose trees. I was mending my husband's socks. Policarpo, my yellow-striped tiger cat, rumbled sleepily in my lap. My two little sons, Guicho (nickname for Luis) and Wiki (for Enrique) played on a *petate* (straw mat) talking baby Spanish. Guicho was Mamacita's *güerito* (a little blond). He was a fair and frail-appearing child, thin and pale, with a shock of golden curls and mischievous green eyes. Little Wiki, a year and a half younger, was fat and brown, with the enormous velvety dark eyes of the Gómez, Mamacita's family.

Mamacita comfortably filled the garden armchair, but her little feet did not quite touch the ground; her beautiful curly black hair was combed high and she was, as always, charmingly dressed in the latest fashion. She held a bit of crocheting in her small plump hands, and she needed no glasses. Those big black eyes of hers saw everything, from fancy work, to motives many members of her family considered well hidden. She stopped her work and looked speculatively at her small grandsons.

"Where will you educate them?" she asked, flashing a glance at the children, and then fixing her big eyes on me.

I was startled. Both the little boys were still in the rompers I had made for them out of the backs of my husband's old shirts, and school seemed awfully far in the distance.

"Probably your people will want them to go to college in their country," she mused, "and live with them."

"But there is no university in my home town," I protested.

"High school, then. To make sure they learn enough English. And then go to some college nearby, afterward."

I sat petrified. I knew that college educations have to be planned-on, built-toward, saved-for. College in the United States? Then my children would have to attend an American high school. A whole series of preparations would have to be worked out.

That evening over enchiladas and fried beans, raising my voice to make myself heard over a *serenata* which was being played next door to honor somebody's birthday, I opened an agitated discussion of higher education. My husband, with characteristic practicality, calmed me down.

"The first step, naturally, is kindergarten," he told me. "For Guicho. You could keep the little one at home a bit longer."

So on the morrow I dressed Guicho in his best white suit, piloted him toward the Circunvelación bus, and we lurched across Monterrey to where there was a "keender."

In a very large bare room, in a big old-fashioned house, about thirty small chairs were ranged in a circle. On these chairs sat thirty clean, washed, and starched young persons, none over four, or at the most five, years of age. In the center of the room a very pretty young Mexican girl in a flounced pink dress swooped about with outspread arms.

"I am a butterfly!" she caroled joyously. "Who wants to be a butterfly and follow me?"

One by one various little butterflies arose and got into line, and began dipping and fluttering in imitation of the teacher, while in the corner, another young woman played appropriate music on an old upright piano. When the butterfly dance was over and the children scrambled for chairs, an extra one was found for Guicho. He sat down sedately. But when the next activity began and he was invited to join the others and be a choo-choo, he refused to budge. The train got under way, chuffing under tunnels and puffing over bridges, but Guicho remained glued to his little chair. When the teacher took his hand and tried to persuade him to be the caboose at the end of the train, he first resisted, and then ran to me, wailing. I took him home.

We went again the next day, but this time he would not even sit down, but moaned and wrung his hands and cried steadily.

I tried leaving him and sneaking away on the third day, but when I returned at the end of an hour, I found him, not a part of the fun as I had hoped, but a sobbing small heap behind the piano.

I talked this over with Mamacita.

"Perhaps if Wiki went with him?"

"The maestra won't accept children under three."

"Well, try once more. Children have no sense of time, and they always think you are leaving forever."

A fourth time I arrayed my child in his shining white and we flagged down the hurtling Circunvelación. I delivered him to the teacher. This time he went straight to his little chair and sat on it, but he wept.

The music for the butterflies began. A little girl in blue organdy went up to Guicho and took his hand, whispering, "Ven conmigo" ("Come with me"). Sobbing, he went with her, and weeping and hiccuping, he spread his wings and became a butterfly at last. He swooped disconsolately, tears streaming down his little face.

The maestra shot me a glance of triumph, and I stumbled home exhausted and did a little weeping myself. Guicho's education had begun. And it has been painful all the way.

I had come to Mexico six years before, as a reporter, and the very first Mexican I met was young Luis Treviño Gómez. The Monterrey Chamber of Commerce had sent him to escort the visiting woman journalist across the border; he was to serve as her public relations manager and interpreter during her stay. The most Mexican of his family, the most traditional, the most conservative and the least impetuous, he was the last one they might have expected to get mixed up with a self-supporting, opinionated, independent American girl. But shortly after we met, something snapped, and he began to make love to me with old songs, romantic gestures, many special glances from his fine dark eyes and archings of his eloquent black eyebrows. The American girl reporter had made no plans to immure herself behind high walls and barred windows and devote herself to doing tatting and raising babies in a country as devotedly Victorian in its mores as Mexico. But something snapped in my head and heart too, and before I returned to my native country with a sheaf of articles on prominent Mexicans, I was an engaged woman. A year later we were married and I came with my husband to live in Monterrey and to begin a painful course in how to change a hard-headed career girl into a gentle, soft, and clinging Mexican señora.

In Monterrey I had no civic duties and no rights, but I was a beloved daughter (*hijita*) in a warmly affectionate, tightly knit, quarrelsome, noisy, and fascinating Mexican provincial family, whose heart and center was the rotund, indomitable, gay, and wise figure of "Mamacita." Mamacita was no calm mother figure, dispensing justice and comfort; she was flirtatious and changeable and she flew into rages, but abso-

lutely nothing could be done without her and no problem was
ever resolved before her comment had been heard. She maneuvered all barks into sunlit waters, outwitted all the men in
her family constantly, and had everybody eating out of her
little plump hands.

It was my great good fortune that Mamacita admired
Americans and had hoped to inveigle one into the family. She
became my passionate advocate. Her Eleesabet might make
mistakes (and often did) but Mamacita fought for her like a
tiger. Under her expert tutelage, I began to learn how to live
the life of a Mexican wife and mother, and it has dawned on
me these many years later, that I discovered more about the
meaning of Mexico from her than from anyone else. She
taught me, just by being herself, what dozens of meetings and
interviews with politicians and great and brilliant artists never
could. For Mamacita was Mexico—Mexican in her pride and
gaiety and sensibility; Mexican in her fierce loyalty to the
Catholic faith she lived by and which had set the pattern and
customs of social life in her land; Mexican in her appraisals of
human values, and in her management of her home and
family.

Mother she was, of ten children. She raised nine of them,
my Luis being her fifth, of whom she often said, "No *hay
quinto malo.*" (This is an old saying, meaning that there are
no counterfeit nickels, but a nickel is also a quinto or a fifth,
so fifth children love the refrain.) She brought up her children
loving and petting them, quarreling with them, inciting them
to ambition and achievement, ridiculing them, and spoiling
them. All adored her.

Wife she was, to a distinguished engineer, mathematician
and astronomer, subjects about which she knew nothing, but
he talked over his work with her and he made no judgments
without knowing how she felt. When the Revolution of 1910
drove the family north to take refuge in the United States, so
that the children could be fed and educated, Mamacita had a
frightened time before Papacito was called into a firm of San

Antonio engineers, when she, who had always had four or five servants to wait on her, had to learn to wash and iron and cook and sweep.

Though she was angry at the violence that had uprooted them, it was not in her nature to wail. She cooked, washed, and swept in a furious temper every morning, and spent her afternoons singing Mexican songs in her rich contralto for women's clubs and groups of friends. She developed a devotion, during those San Antonio years, for American men and women, for movies, for beeskits, ho-ca-kes with ma-play syrup, and stores like her darling Woolywort and Peely Weely. I held a certain place in her heart because in me she had at last achieved an American to belong to her, and she greeted my first-born son with a touching accolade: "My little gringo."

I was happy in Monterrey leading the life of a sheltered Mexican woman. Hortensia warbled "Rancho Alegre" in the kitchen while she baked and boiled and ground up and otherwise concocted the multitudinous Mexican delicacies we ate along with our *arroz* and *frijoles*. Blanca endlessly sang "Farolito" as she mopped and dusted and made the beds and fought the cockroaches. And Candelaria, peerless washwoman, intoned "Las Gaviotas" in the back patio as she thumped away and sloshed and rinsed my husband's shirts and my cotton dresses and Guicho's rompers and the baby Wiki's diapers.

Policarpo kept me company in my small office as I wrote columns of news for the Laredo *Times*, children's stories and copious letters, and he purred on my lap in the afternoons when I did my embroidery or read a book.

It was lovely to be looked after and coddled and told kindly but firmly what to do, after so many years of banging about looking after myself. There were, of course, some drawbacks. I had always handled my own money, having earned it for more than half a dozen years; it was a bit of a come-down to be doled out small amounts for the housekeeping, after the Monterrey custom. I fought this war of the *gasto*, or housekeeping money, to a finish, on a number of battlefields, and at last, with the serpentine wisdom of Mamacita behind my campaigns, I achieved a small regular allowance.

Mamacita taught me everything I learned of any real consequence, and I relied on her absolutely. It was she who incited us to move to Mexico City.

We had been living in Monterrey six years when a number of things happened that changed our life completely.

Our dear Papacito died suddenly, slumped over his desk, where he was writing a letter to one of his mathematician friends. "*And as a final point* . . ." he had written, and at that moment death had taken him, in full sail as it were, doing what he loved best.

But at his death Mamacita had changed. She lost her own joyous hold on life and she wandered about, from Monterrey to Mexico and back, distracted. The years became for her a time of waiting to rejoin her beloved *viejito* and she was impatient to go to him.

Then serious difficulties developed in Luis's business. We needed more room too, and we had offered to buy the little house we were renting, so that we might plan on enlarging it. But the owner refused to sell it to us, and so we were faced with the prospect of moving.

Lightning struck. Luis was offered an excellent position as manager of an import-export firm in Mexico City, to be opened by an American. Everything seemed to indicate that we ought to take the offer and move. Then a visit from Mamacita clinched the matter.

"Of course you must go," she instructed Luis. "Your best opportunities are there. The climate in Mexico City is wonderful and Eleesabet will love the concerts, the ballet, the opera, the museums . . . all the things she has done without, here in this rancho."

Mamacita always called Monterrey a rancho when she was annoyed with it, or engaged in any conversation about her beautiful Mexico City, where she had studied singing as a girl.

"But I have been happy here, Mamacita."

"You will be happier there, for soon the boys will be in school all day and then what will you do? Sit and watch the beans boil? Not for this did your Papa send you to college and let you learn the violin. And I don't see any more babies on the way," she added darkly, with a glance at my waistline.

We blew hot and we blew cold. I rang up Mamacita and told her I couldn't manage without her near me, and asked if she would come and live with me in Mexico City.

"No, *hijita*," she told me, thanking me. "But I will visit you. Short visits. '*El pescado y la visita, al tercer dia apestan,*'" she reminded me, but I carried on and cried, and she promised to visit me often.

We had dear friends in Monterrey, but the export-import firm was pressing Luis for an answer, and at last he made up his mind. He would take the position and we would move to Mexico City. It was a hard decision for him to make, for Monterrey is his home town and he is a man who likes friends to hail him on the street corners and ask him how many children he has now and what he paid for his necktie. The decision was so tough that he had one of his make-up-your-mind migraines. While he groaned on the couch, I went to a series of farewell parties given by my friends.

I was by now, both scared and intrigued at the thought of moving, but I didn't think it called for a migraine. There were trains, buses, and highways from Mexico City, and I was sure I would return. As a young girl when I had gone to Boston from my native California, I had not sung "Goodbye forever." I got at my packing.

Luis arose from his bed of pain and followed behind me, nervously repacking everything in a different place and in different boxes, until I became confused and angry, and I began to be sorry I had ever agreed to move. Luis was now regretting his decision with all his heart but he was too proud to wire saying that he had changed his mind. He was short with me, and I stamped my foot. He shouted and I wept. He went off glumly to attend farewell banquets, and to sing sad songs with his friends, and I went to bed in tears.

Guicho and Wiki played about during the upheaval. On the fatal day when the movers came and loaded their truck with our boxes and furniture, Luis and I were calm again, but sorrowful. The rooms which had been a world for us, full of children and friends and familiar things, were now only spaces inside walls that needed painting, unexpectedly small and shabby. As we drove away (after a desperate leave-taking of my darling Policarpo, who was to be sent on by freight after I had found a place to stay), what had been "home" was just another little house with a sign SE RENTA on it. I cried all the way to Montemorelos.

"Well, business was bad in Monterrey anyway," I reminded Luis, sniffing into my handkerchief.

"Yes, and it is murderously hot in summer. Pants never keep a press," he added morosely.

"You did perfectly right to accept this job." Gulp.

"Well, it's done now, anyhow."

We drove on in miserable silence.

We ate a dreary lunch in a roadside restaurant and continued driving resolutely. The sky was darkening; I looked around and saw heavy black clouds converging on us. As night drew on we were overtaken by a furious tropical rainstorm. Lightning streaked around us like lavender thunderbolts, the reverberations were deafening, and the rain fell in torrents.

"We'll have to press on," muttered Luis, "because if this keeps up some of the bridges will go out and we'll be marooned."

Soon he couldn't see at all, and I had to lean out of the front side window—being instantly soaked to the waist—and while dashing rain out of my eyes constantly with one hand, I told him to bear right or bear left, or keep straight ahead, according as I could make out the white painted line which runs down the center of the highway. It was absorbing work, driving in that downpour, and dangerous, for such a rain can start landslides that bury a car. But we kept at it, managing about five miles an hour, and at last Luis got us to a town where we could turn in at a modest inn and go to bed. I learned on arriving that while I had leaned out of the front window giving driving instructions to my husband, each of my little boys had leaned out of the back windows, in enthusiastic imitation, and they were wet as goldfish.

I was bone weary and *triste*. I dried off the children and put them to bed, and Luis and I dropped into bed ourselves, too tired to eat. In a short while I heard (I might have known it!) the barking sound of a croupy cough. *Two* croupy coughs. I got up. Both little boys were gasping and choking. I had no medicine with me but a large bottle of Sloan's Liniment, always carried in the car to rub on Luis's aching shoulders after a long day's drive. I slapped it on each little chest and smeared it up under their chins so that the fumes entered the small noses, and Mr. Sloan may have a signed testimonial from me any time. It worked like a charm. I then rubbed Luis's shoulders, and bravely deciding not to drink the rest of the liniment myself and achieve permanent rest, I lay down again. So we got through that night. In the morning, when I opened my eyes, I looked directly out of the window into the red patient eyes of two large black *zopilotes* (vultures) which had alighted on the fence posts just outside the motel, and were staring at me fixedly. I struggled to my feet.

I shook Luis and he groaned.

"Wake up," I commanded. "They have come for me, and if we don't get out of here soon, they will be justified in flying away with me."

We pulled ourselves together, ate some thick ho-ca-kes drenched in piloncillo syrup, and took to the road once more.

We had been driving through palm forests and rolling country the day before, and had come into the foothills during the storm. Now the whole towering range of the Sierras remained to be crossed. In those days the highway to Mexico

City was still new and I had no idea of what was coming. I am frightened of heights, and I get carsick on curves, but I thought I could stand it. After all, I said to myself, there'll only be about fifteen minutes of it, or a half hour. There were five and a half hours.

It is the most breath-taking, the most majestic, the most beautiful scenery in the world, but I felt like a girl scout who has climbed what she thought was a small mountain near home, and then suddenly finds herself on top of the Matterhorn. I could only clutch the edge of the seat and whisper, "Oh be careful! Oh please go slowly. Oh Jesus, Joseph, and Mary!"

Luis had begun to be lightheaded and lighthearted.

"I could stop and let you down to walk," he said, "but it's eighty miles. Hang on now. We are coming to the place they call 'The Curve of the Dead Gringa.'"

Luis had been over this extraordinary mountain road when it was being carved and blasted from the living rock, in the company of his beloved friend, Bill Furlong of San Antonio, who had watched the road's construction with passionate devotion and who had logged every inch of it.

"They call it 'The Curve of the Dead Gringa'," went on Luis, while I cowered and whimpered and hung on with both hands, "because some American girl took the curve a mite too fast and drove right out into space. Nobody ever even went to look for her; she'd have been *miles* down. . . ."

He went on, recalling some of the experiences of the first construction crew that had gone into this untouched wild mountain country to build the road.

"The Indians here couldn't speak English, of course, but they couldn't speak Spanish either. They were just like forest deer; they used to shy away from the machines and cars like startled fawns. But they had a sense of commerce. It is born in them."

I was riding with closed eyes, feeling the car veer around curve after curve.

"They came down to the construction camp selling their homemade cigars made from their own home-grown tobacco. Bill Furlong teased them by showing them his fine Havana cigars wrapped in cellophane. The Indians said nothing and went away. But when he came back along the road they were waiting for him. They had their cigars carefully wrapped in corn husks and tied with colored wool. He was so touched he bought their entire supply."

When I opened my eyes for a second, to make sure the little boys hadn't rolled down the window glass in back, I saw that both were asleep, lulled by the curves. I had one terrified glimpse of a deep chasm where fog whirled, far below. I shut my eyes again.

Luis droned on.

"There was an American genius who followed the construction gangs and set up a profitable business. He had an ice-cream machine, and he sold cones. The Indians of the Huasteca went mad about ice cream and would go to any lengths to achieve it. They traded fantastic amounts of corn, weavings, and tobacco for a cone of strawberry and vanilla. Talk about firewater! *Ice-cream cones* ruined the Indians of the Huasteca."

Luis continued to regale me with stories of the dreadful mountain road, while I continued to feel like the man we see yearly in the newsreels, the one who walks a tightrope stretched across Niagara Falls.

All this had one good effect on me. Once we got over that road and into Mexico City, I was there for keeps. Like Hannibal, after he got his elephants over the Alps, I felt that anything on the other side must be a cinch.

We dropped down onto the plain of the Valley of Mexico at last, and drove into the broad avenues of Mexico City. Suddenly I felt a little frightened. For this Mexico City, always called simply Mexico by the people, was an enormous, cosmopolitan metropolis. Traffic swirled around us, buses overshadowed us, streetcars clanged, and thousands of pedestrians thronged the streets, hurrying about their affairs. Brown-uniformed traffic police at intersections tried to make order out of chaos and were partially successful. The city, even at first glance, was a far cry from the leisurely tranquillity of the Monterrey we had left.

We followed Insurgentes Avenue, which bisects the city from north to south, and passed through the colonias or sections of the city called Villa de Guadalupe, Peralvillo, Cuauhtemoc, and Roma. We crossed beautiful Avenida de la Reforma, which extends from Chapultepec Palace on the hill to the splendid equestrian statue of Charles V, and which was laid out following the design of the lovely Champs Elysées in Paris. We drove on and into the Colonia Hipódromo. There, near the green lawns of Parque España, with its tall trees and leaping fountains, we came to the address we were seeking.

Mamacita had made a reservation for us at an apartment hotel, and she was there, waiting for us, full of affectionate welcome and wonderful plans. After we had recovered from the two-day drive, we settled into the business of wining and dining with all our far-flung Mexico City relations.

Jorge Treviño lived in Mexico, with his wife Maria Luisa and his three little girls. Carlos, another brother, had a home on Tokio Street, two sons and a daughter named Lourdes (called Yuyú). And then there were the Morelos-Zaragoza cousins, three of them, and Tia Juanita Albaiterro, who loved to laugh and play cards and tell jokes, and all her children and their families. We loved Alicia, who was a gifted *raconteuse*, and beautiful Carmelita, who looked like her daughter's sister.

While we had a gala dinner with a different relative every evening, we spent daytimes cruising around the city looking for a house. In our wanderings about Mexico, we came to realize that the city had grown in layers, like a coral island, and still retained characteristics of each age. Upon the original structure of the Aztec capital, with its many stone monuments, and its streets which had been waterways, the conquistadors had built a Spanish city, with broad, low, thick-walled palaces, many of which are still standing. The French style of architecture had crept in during the nineteenth century, the heyday of much cultural attachment for France in Mexico, and had left châteaux and chalets in the residential sections near the heart of the city. And now modernism, buildings as functional and clean-lined as anyone could wish, was changing the face of Mexico.

The city of Mexico is rather like an orange, too, made up of sections, with a hard, indigestible, unchanging aromatic outer peel. Except that each section is different. You must imagine an orange in which one segment is flavored with garlic, one with soy sauce, one with light beer, one with Stilton cheese, one with brown gravy, and one with red wine, and the aromatic peel, holding it all together, is thick with Mexican chile.

Here and there the foreign colonies have defiantly announced their original allegiance in the very type of residence they build. You may see a cluster of German-peaked and -beamed homes; behind velvety rolled lawns, English red-brick houses of Georgian design; high on a hill, Swedish and Finnish residences, with glass to catch every beam of sunshine. The Lomas is inhabited by Americans, and has an American stamp. Here are homes such as you would see in many American cities, comfortable, wealthy, within wide gardens open to view from the street.

But the colonias are more than a matter of individual houses and districts within the city. They have lives of their own, their own schools and churches, their own clubs and festivities, and they speak their own language.

I was startled one day to hear an Englishwoman sternly reproach her son for greeting me with a happy "Hello." She told him he must never say this, but only Good Morning or Good Afternoon. I innocently supposed that the child was being taken to task for using slang, but I was wrong. It was the Americanism of the Hello that was objectionable. For the boy was allowed (no, encouraged) to say Right-o, Jolly Good, and Bad Show. Learning this, I instructed my sons always to greet her with a merry "Hi," this being even more American than Hello, for I believe, with the Spanish, that "for him who hates soup, give him a plate and a half."

The largest foreign colony is, naturally enough, the Spanish, though they do not all cluster together. They have spread out all over the city, and are working diligently everywhere. The Mexicans who regretted the flood of Spanish refugees during the Civil War in Spain, did not object to their politics so much, for Mexico is traditionally open to political refugees, but they have come to deplore them for the same reason the gentle Indians deplored the men of Cortes. The Spaniards are workers, and they make everybody else work. They are drivers, tremendously energetic. It was a Spaniard who was convulsed with laughter one day when we stopped to stare at a Mexican statue to "The Worker." What was this Worker doing, in his workman's trousers and stub-toed working boots? He was resting. Not only resting, but, with head thrown back in a gesture of fatigue, he was laying his right hand against his brow in an attitude of utter weariness.

"If that's the Mexican idea of a 'worker'," laughed the hearty Spaniard, "no wonder they hate us Gachupines." (Gachupin is a word that means Spaniard, the origin of which nobody seems to know.)

Indeed the Spaniards are up at first light, they work all day and they reluctantly shut up shop and factory, and go home at eleven or twelve at night. While the Mexican is notoriously late to work, long about his lunch, devoted to a lengthy and peaceful siesta afterward (though Mexico City no longer closes shops and offices for siestas, as it used to do), and is ready to stay home at any provocation, from the death of a cousin of an aunt's sister-in-law, to having taken a measure of purge the night before. Naturally before long it appears that the Spaniards (devil take them) own all the bakeries, grocery stores, mattress factories, and most of the steel business.

The Spaniards cement their hold upon the industries they invade with nepotism, and here the Mexicans have a well-founded complaint. Let some poverty-stricken Spaniard arrive in Mexico with the clothes he stands in, let him work like a dog twenty hours a day for ten years, and build up a business, and when he has room for an employee, what happens? He sends to Spain for another impecunious relative.

But the Spaniards soon blend into the scenery in Mexico. After all, the Mexican race is Indian and Spanish, the social pattern is Spanish, the language is Spanish, and the faith was brought from Spain. Intermarriage has always gone on between Spaniard and Mexican.

The position of the Americans, in their colony, is different. They do not often intermarry, because of the difference in religious belief. More, because most of them are Protestant, they tend to keep themselves separate, and to form many clubs and groups of their own. American ladies, and even many American businessmen, I am sorry to say, do not often bother to learn Spanish, and few indeed study anything of Mexican history and literature.

The Germans perform a kind of double-take. They learn Spanish and Mexican ways, and they mix and intermarry. But somehow, they remain German. Just how, I cannot explain. Mexicans admire them, for they represent a disciplined race; and this I cannot explain either, for Mexicans hate discipline themselves. Still, it is nice for other people.

Then there are the Chinese and the Japanese, the French, the Arabs and Syrians, and many others, with their own schools and churches. And a large section of Mexico is known as Jerusalem the Golden. There I went to buy matzos when I wanted to make one of the delectable Jewish dishes I love.

There never was a city of such contrasts, Aztec, European, and American, Colonial Spanish and modern, and yet definitely itself, and wholly Mexican.

In my wanderings in search of a home, I came to know a good deal about the various colonias, and the over-all panorama of this lovely city so high in the clouds—at more than 7500 feet above the sea,—with its eternally snow-covered sentinels, Popocatepetl (Smoking Mountain) and Ixtacihuatl (White Lady).

I fell completely in love with Mexico City, and have never changed my mind about its being one of the most beautiful cities in the world.

Then the blow fell.

The company which had employed Luis to manage the Mexico City office branch had suddenly changed hands. The new management decided to close out a number of offices, among them the one in Mexico City. So there we were, with no home and no job. Luis developed the worst migraine of his career and went to bed blind. I left the children with Maria Luisa and Mamacita and got myself a small job. It was only morning work, but it brought in enough money (while Luis recovered and went to look for something) to keep the wolf from getting too familiar.

A few days after, Luis got up, shook himself and went out and got himself another position, better than the one we had left Monterrey to take. We bought him some snappy Mexico City clothes, and we found ourselves a little house in the suburbs, in an enchanting old-fashioned town called San Angel.

II ᢟ

A LITTLE HOUSE ON THE DESERT OF THE LIONS

Aquí somos Católicos. Viva Cristo Rey!
—SIGN AFFIXED TO THE DOORS OF MANY MEXICAN HOMES

Looking for a house in Mexico with my husband, I had laid down three rules. First, we must not even glance at anything beyond what we could pay, no matter what the real estate agent said. Second, the house must have a patio, or at least a garden where the children could play. Third, it must have a fireplace.

Our price possibilities caused the agencies to send us out with their weariest salesmen, their oldest cars. On the fifth day, reluctantly convinced that we could not afford an old Mexican Colonial house (though I long for one to this day), I consented to see a cottage in San Angel. I observed with pleasure that it had a patch of lawn in front, and a great *pirul*, or pepper tree. I went up three steps and entered a very small sala, which had a well-blackened fireplace, proving that it worked. My hopes began to rise. The cottage was country-style in design, with tiled floors in dining room and kitchen, and the walls were white, with great heavy dark beams across the ceilings. The windows were barred, something I demand, for I am timorous of robbers and I like to feel that my home is a fortress. If I could manage, I would also have a moat and a portcullis.

Encouraged thus, I strode into bedrooms and threw open closets. It seemed to me that they were too few and too small, and I wrenched open the last door in irritation, because it seemed to stick. But I had not expected to find the owner of the house cowering inside in her nightgown. This sudden encounter unnerved us both, for she had felt herself safe in her closet, and I had not expected to find a large quivering lady in flannel and curl papers inside. We did a lot of mutual apologizing and then became chummy. The upshot was that Luis and I made our first down payment on the house, and moved in.

The address was Calzada Desierto de los Leones. Despite its resounding name, our street is only one block long. A parked section runs down the center, dividing it, and tall pepper trees are covered with tiny yellow blossoms in the spring and with heavy bunches of red berries in the fall. Boys come to gather them to sell for bird food. The name of the street comes from the fact that it debouches into the highway that leads to the Desert of the Lions, an ancient convent high up in the hills beyond San Angel. The convent, in the midst of a wild forest, was a "desert" because of the Spanish fondness for calling any convent meant for meditation and penitence a desert, after the "desert" into which our Lord Jesus Christ went for forty days of prayer and fasting. And the "lion" comes from the fact that there were cougar in the forest.

Then my troubles began. First we had to cut down all our Monterrey curtains and double under our Monterrey rugs, for the cottage was small in comparison with the spacious, airy old-fashioned home we had enjoyed in *la provincia*. Then we had to rip out the charcoal stove in the kitchen, with its cargo of cockroaches and their friends, and fumigate, and we had to install a gas stove and a refrigerator. My husband would never eat anything which had been kept on ice, or in the house, overnight, but he was fond of refrigerators, and thought them handsome. He kept bottles of water in ours.

We had to buy all our fixtures, from chandeliers to faucets, for in those days vacating householders always carried these thriftily away, including plumbing fixtures, if the contrary was not stipulated in the contract, and they *always* removed their telephone, transporting it to their new home. I grew to sympathize with the latter procedure, for the telephone companies, with oily politeness, continued for months to deny giving us any service "because we have no more apparatuses, señora." More than one señora, on hearing this cliché, there and then opened her bag and extracted an apparatus, and that seemed to be the only way to make sure of getting a telephone installed.

I dickered with a friend who had two apparatuses, and then I girded up my loins in a powerful two-way stretch and went to do battle with the telephone companies. In that time, there were two, deadly rivals, and the miserable public had to take whatever company happened to have a cable near their house. In the end, one came out of the fray with an Ericsson telephone or a Mexicana telephone. Neither one communicated with the other. If one perforce became a Mexicana phone holder, the only thing to do was cultivate a circle of friends who were also on Mexicana, for with the Ericsson phone holders there could be no converse. One had to use the mail, or telegraph.

Of course we worked out dodges, as the long-suffering middle class always does. Nearly all of us inquired around until we found out the name of some plutocrat who had *both* telephones, and then we assiduously made friends with him or her, and courted the two-telephone household with hypocritical flattery. Then this friend could, if not tormented too often, take messages from friends on Ericsson, and have her maid relay them to us on the Mexicana. One inspired gentleman, who was greatly bedeviled by the two-phone system, used to call his sister in New York, via his Mexicana, and ask her to call back to Mexico to his mother on Ericsson and relay certain vital messages. There was even a time when one of Luis's friends, a man with some mechanical ingenuity, rigged up some kind of machine by which he could hitch the two lines together; then, advised in time, friends on the rival telephone lines could communicate by calling his number.

All this caused much excitement and confusion and made life full of interest and intrigue. Of course any illegal commu-

nication was fought most bitterly by the two telephone companies. I must say that the companies had some right on their
side, for Mexicans are clever and malicious people, and the
citizenry has been figuring out ways to get the better of authority for centuries. They are experts at it. One of these meth-
ods is to construct a *diablito*. I saw a *diablito* once in triumphant operation on a light meter. While the servant ironed
upstairs, the *diablito* reversed the meter by some magic in its
insides, and it registered less amperes consumed when the iron-
ing was done, than when it was begun. This little machine
sold widely for about twenty pesos, and was so popular (naturally) that it even appeared in a movie. The scene, which I
shall never forget, showed the big common patio of a *vecindad*
(tenement house), where, at some point in the story, all the
families in the tenement were having a fiesta together. Suddenly there was a peremptory knocking on the big *zaguán*,
or outer door. A spy sent to see who it was reported to the
assemblage that it was the light inspector, whereupon every
family sent a son to wrench the *diablito* off his light meter.

The telephone *diablito* therefore, was devised very early
to combat the tyranny of two telephone companies. It could
hook onto the line of any householder and provide service for
as many as six to eight succubi. What happened was that the
phone would ring in the proper phone-bill-paying household,
and someone would ask for Anna. "There is no Anna here,"
you would answer and hang up. But after you had hung up,
Anna (on her *diablito*) and her caller would enjoy their chat.
An inspector one time removed three *diablitos* from my line.
I had to pay him a very good tip for this, to constrain him
from reporting to the telephone company that I had hooked
my line onto an illegal cable in the back. But then, one has to
live, and in Mexico nobody despises you for making efforts
to better yourself. I had been told I would have to wait for
a cable on my street, but a friend had informed me of a cable
a block away, and lo! I found a mechanic who could connect
my telephone to it.

Just as in New England the motto used to be "Eat it up, wear it out, and make it do," the Mexicans have a saying, "*La lucha se hace*," which means, roughly, "One struggles."

Since those riotous days of the two telephone companies, the government has effected a combination of the two, and now phone owners can call anybody with a number. Theoretically. There was a great ceremony on the day the two phone lines were solemnly joined in holy matrimony, and all the radio and television companies had reporters on the scene. Smiling broadly the President of Mexico made the first call. He marked his number on the dial (for this innovation had come in too, heralding automatism in Mexico), his mother's number. There ensued a squawking and a sputtering, and then the annoyed voice of the "central operator" came on. "Wrong number!" she admonished the sheepish President, and all Mexico roared with joy at the sight.

So, by bribery and intrigue, I achieved my telephone, and then I began to think about a garden. Reflection made me realize that with a five-year-old and a three-year-old on the premises, flower beds and herb gardens would be quickly trampled into dust, while baseball, soccer, and basketball raged. I was right. Within a month my lawn had disappeared and I had a baseball diamond.

Trying to be very practical, therefore, I decided in favor of eggs. We had a strip of land behind the house where the washtubs and clotheslines disputed the right of way with a fig tree. I fenced this in and bought a hen and a rooster. It soon became apparent, even to me, who am not too observant about Old Mother Nature, that the hard-worked hen should have a helper, or two. Meanwhile my original hen had become broody (a condition I think we ought to be more quick to recognize in its human counterpart) and had sat down on a nest of eight eggs. Seeing that she was completely *hors de combat*, I bought my rooster a collection of wives to share his enthusiasms. Then transpired something which I understood perfectly, but I hadn't known that hens did. My broody hen, watching her husband sport with young and frisky wives while she sat on her eggs, first sulked, then grew despondent, and at last arose and danced on her eggs in a fury, and broke them all.

While I fretted over my brokenhearted hen, Nature swooped down and carried away all my chickens with the roup, the loop, the croup, or whatever it is that chickens get, and I was left with one unemployed rooster. After I had wistfully read a few recipes for *coq au vin*, I looked into his sad eyes, and lost my appetite. I pardoned him and gave him to a friend who had thousands of hens milling around in a field. I cannot bear to kill anything, and the idea of eating something which has shared my home and garden offends all my deepest feelings of hospitality.

But I resolved that I must do something to make my home more than a mere shelter. Flowers and herbs were out. Eggs were out. I took up knitting again. As a girl I had learned to knit, quickly earning the name of No-rip Borton because I wouldn't pull out my work and take up dropped stitches, but sneakily sewed them firm in back where nobody could see (I thought). The only person who would ever wear anything I knitted was my father, a very tender man, who never gave a hoot what anybody thought of his raiment.

So I began to knit a carriage robe for some expected Treviño baby back in Monterrey. Five years later when I finished it, and was about to send it to the third subsequent baby, my friend Malenita sent out cards to a tea reading as follows: "*Tea. To meet Mrs. Treviño, who has finished knitting a carriage robe.*" The thing, out of shape and very grubby by then, was on display in the hall, and caused a certain amount of comment.

But while I made my first laborious rows on this woolen monstrosity, my husband came home with a project for me.

"Mamacita is coming for a visit, and I think it would be a good time to bless the house," he told me.

We hadn't blessed the house in Monterrey, because it

was not ours. But now we had our own house, and, Luis said, "If I live the full twenty years and don't miss a payment, it will be ours, so we might as well have the ceremony."

"All right. What do I do?"

"You just prepare a big supper and leave everything to me," he ordered.

Mamacita arrived, and the blessing was set for the following Saturday at six o'clock. Afterward we would invite our guests to sit down to Mamacita's wonderful specialties. There would be a dish of chiles toasted, peeled and marinated in vinegar, oil and herbs for three days, then filled with *guacamole* (mashed avocado), and laid on a bed of lettuce and sprinkled with ruby pomegranate seeds. And there would be white rice fragrant with garlic, and spicy enchiladas made of shredded chicken, cheese, and tortillas. I had a cake too, a towering affair covered with white icing. All was in readiness.

Mamacita, who was staying with Jorge and Maria Luisa, arrived in a hat with feathers, showing that she gave this event the status of a wedding or a christening. (In Mexico hats are almost never worn by women except at weddings, where they tend to take fantastic shapes and to be decorated with all manner of tulle, feathers, sequins, and flowers.) Other relatives arrived, also in hats bearing fauna and flora, and many friends. There was a loud buzz of happy conversation, while we waited for Luis to arrive with the priest. He was late.

But at last he came in, very pale, and I saw that he had not brought our gentle smiling little Carmelite from the church two blocks away, but a tall, spare, austere Spanish monsignor, who bent a severe eye on all the feathers and on the table, now being loaded with good food.

Having quelled us all with a glance, the monsignor read a prayer in Latin. Murmuring the ritual, he then visited every room in the house, sprinkling holy water over its contents, and urging everything in it to have nothing to do with any sort of sin that might get cooked up on the premises. The climax came when he threw open the door of the kitchen, and stood there, filling the door in his imposing robes, and cast holy water on the occupants, who happened to be Maria, my cook, and Pancha, the new housemaid. Maria was pleased and paused respectfully in her work of decorating a platter of enchiladas, but Pancha staggered as the holy water bedewed her, gave a hoarse cry, and fell over in a dead faint among the carrot peelings and lettuce leaves on the kitchen floor.

The monsignor instantly knelt, revived Pancha with a smart slap, and told her in a strong bass voice that he would hear her confession at once. She instantly fainted again, but he waved us all out of the kitchen.

After a while he emerged, blessed our feast but would partake of nothing, and ordered Luis to convey him back to the church in Coyoacan. Maria meanwhile had assisted Pancha to her bedroom where, newly shriven, she lay in some kind of a stupor until evening of the next day.

Mamacita rang up to inquire about her.

"She must have been up to something," mused Mamacita. "The monsignor knew it, of course. I think you had better get him back, to exorcise her."

"Good Heavens, Mamacita, do they still do that?"

"Why certainly," she answered tartly, "and it's a good thing to know about. I can think of lots of people who would be improved by a good exorcism. You never know when you might need one."

But Pancha pulled herself together and was very quiet, diligent, and good before she departed some months later, obviously pregnant. She needed a different sort of exorcism from that which the stern monsignor could have provided.

The "Blessing of the House" was only one of many such ceremonies I attended in Mexico City. New homes and apartments always arrange for this ritual, among Catholics, and a great many factories and places of business are also blessed by high prelates. When this is the case, of course, a special robing room must be provided for the priest who is to do the blessing, for Mexico still has laws forbidding priests to wear their churchly garments in public places, or on the street.

Sometimes Mexican magnates live to regret having asked a priest to bless their places of business. Eagle-eyed men of God can make some perfectly reasonable demands. There was, for example, the time the Archbishop of Mexico was invited to bless the brand-new and gorgeous Hotel del Prado in the heart of Mexico City.

Newsreel cameramen, reporters, a select gathering of businessmen, politicians, and Mexican society, as well as the general public, were present. The archbishop, the late beloved Monsignor Luis Martinez, arrived in his plain black street suit, and was shown to a robing room, whence he emerged in soutane, magenta sash, and zucchetto, and fine pectoral cross. A privileged few, including the owners and managers of the hotel, escorted him personally to the place where the ceremony would begin. Meanwhile, he had spotted a fine, large mural by Diego Rivera on the wall of the dining room and he went to look at it. It is, indeed, a splendid work, beautiful in drawing, composition and color, titled "Sunday Afternoon in the Alameda." Diego, according to his custom, had filled it with his own personal view of Mexican history and of historical personages, and also with portraits of many of his friends, acquaintances, and public figures. Monsignor Martinez's eye discerned, near the painted portrait of Ignacio Ramirez "El Nigromante," a revolutionary and atheistic writer, a placard with a short quotation from his works, as follows: There is no God.

It is just possible that the archbishop had been advised to look for this detail, so tiny in the whole impressive mural. In any case, he turned to his hosts and told them gently that while this was no doubt historically true, in that the Nigromante had indeed written those words, he did not feel he could bless a hotel which displayed publicly such a sentiment. He returned to his robing rooms, and reassuming his black suit and hat, he went quietly home. Meanwhile, to coin a phrase, all Hell broke loose.

Diego, of course, was delighted with the turn of events, for he was never known to underrate the value of publicity. He trumpeted to the press that he would not change one line of his mural, and that if anyone dared to do so without his consent, he would sue. Groups of Catholic students formed a mob and entered the hotel bent on painting out the offensive words. Groups of antireligious students were on hand, and armed, ready to oppose them. Newspapers gave the whole affair front-page position, and wire services sent out long stories. The archbishop, having stated his position, remained aloof.

Things gathered momentum. Hordes of people swirled through the hotel to look at the mural, but nobody stayed to dine. In the end, the whole mural was boarded over, and only recently has it been brought out and set up again. With, I may remark, one small detail altered. Diego, in his grave, thunders no denunciations.

But the mural is still a storm center. The Mexican Institute of Bellas Artes asked the painter-architect Juan O'Gorman, a devoted friend and admirer of Diego Rivera, to report to them on whether or not he believed the mural by the dead master was now properly displayed.

O'Gorman, as colorful in prose as in his own paintings, and with all the wit of his Irish ancestors, answered in an excoriating letter which was published in all Mexican newspapers. In a word, he objected to the placing of the mural.

But Diego's "Sunday Afternoon in the Alameda" still glows on the walls of the hotel which commissioned it, and across the street in the Alameda itself, the same delicious light green shadows on the grass, the fountains and the tree trunks, the balloon and candy vendors recall the scene Diego remembered, even though he added, in his painting, peoples and thoughts which had impinged on his own life. And two great churches cast shadows over the Alameda he loved, and they are always filled with the faithful he tried to caricature. And perhaps partly on Diego's account, many Mexican homes are decorated with rosaries made of crepe paper and silver ribbon, in the months of May and October (months of Mary and of the Most Holy Rosary), or with the colors of the Carmelites (brown and gold) during July, and many *zaguáns*, in homes rich and poor, display the sign of the sacred heart, or a drawing of the Christian fish symbol, or the defiant announcement *"Catholics live here! Long live Christ the King!"*

III 𝄞

A TOWN IN THE CITY

Cualquier tiempo pasado fue major . . .
—FROM A POEM BY JORGE MANRIQUE

San Angel came into being early in the sixteenth century with
the founding of rival convents not more than a stone's throw
from each other. The Discalced Carmelites founded the Convent and Church of Our Lady of Carmen, and the Dominicans
built the Convent and Church of San Jacinto (Saint Hya-
cinth). To this day the life of the town revolves around the two
plazas which were formerly the church gardens—the Plaza del
Carmen and the Plaza de San Jacinto. The Church of San
Jacinto is now the seat of the parish, and the Convent of Our
Lady of Carmen houses a colonial museum. The parish priest
(*el señor cura*) lives and has offices in San Jacinto, but the
main fiesta of San Angel takes place on the sixteenth of July,
the day of Our Lady of Carmen, and centers around the Carmen church. There is a dispensary for the poor and a dining
room for the indigent in the San Jacinto church, and there are
free movies for children, an open-air art show once a year, and
free English and music lessons at the Carmen church. Most
of us in San Angel go regularly to both churches, feel loyalty
toward both, and take part in the fiestas and activities of both.

For years San Angel was a quaint colonial town, far
enough away from Mexico City to be a good morning's ride
in a horse-drawn carriage, and so it became a sort of summer
home or country seat for many wealthy and titled families of
the capital. At last a streetcar reached out from Mexico City
to San Angel and the aristocrats who had homes there began
to realize with dismay that soon common people might come

streaming into the town and perhaps (oh horrors) buy small lots and build dreadful little houses on them.

Not for nothing are the old aristocratic Mexican families known popularly as "*rancios*," which means, literally, the "rancids."

Quickly Mexico City grew out and around San Angel, encapsulating it. The wealthy people stayed on in their summer *quintas* or garden-orchards, many of them less and less rich as time went by, and they shut themselves up in their wonderful old colonial houses, behind twenty-foot-high walls over which tumble red and lavender bougainvillea, purple passion flowers, and blue plumbago. Beyond the walls, inside the old gardens, you may see the swaying tops of tall cypress trees, jacarandas, elms, apple, and pear trees. And you can smell the fragrance of honeysuckle and roses by day, and *huele de noche* (night-blooming jasmine) at night.

Many of the streets in San Angel are narrow, irregular, and winding, paved with cobblestones, just as they were centuries ago. Occasionally when an enormous *zaguán* or great door is swung open to admit a gardener or a servant, you can catch glimpses of tiled benches that flash in the sun, peacocks strutting across velvet lawns, a stone cross or a saint in a niche, and you can see the crystalline patterns of a fountain. The great blossom-laden walls enclose the peace and beauty of a time gone by, when family life was circled about with infinite physical and moral protection, and when the ladies, in order to dream of far-away places or of a lover, had to repair to their towers, or *miradors*.

Along the street of the Santissimo I walk today, pausing at the open-air shrine to Guadalupe where the street gives into Aureliano Rivera. The shrine was painted long ago by Juan O'Gorman, when he was a boy, living on this very street. I stroll down Aureliano Rivera, past the ancient Bishop's house, to the copper-colored Church of San Jacinto, and go and stand amidst its cypress garden. Then perhaps I walk up Hidalgo Street toward the Plaza de los Licenciados (named for a little

clutch of lawyers who lived there once in the past), passing on
the way a watering trough for horses and wayside fountain let
into the wall of the historic old Montes de Oca house, and
surmounted by a great fluted shell, indicating that some member of the original family who owned the house had been
across the seas to the Holy Land. Down the cobblestoned
street I may see the dignified gentlemen of San Angel riding
out on their Arab horses and wearing their traditional charro
dress, the tight trousers of homespun tweed, short bolero of
velvet or leather, and sweeping wide-brimmed sombrero of
heavy felt trimmed with silver. They make a merry jingling as
they pace along.

The riding customs of the past and the charro (gentleman
rider) dress are preserved with affection by the old families of
San Angel, some of whom keep their grandfather's carriages,
out of respect, beside their Cadillacs or Mercedes-Benz, in the
converted stables. And not one man who can afford a horse
does without, even though he has time to ride only on Sunday,
after Mass.

There is a Charro Association to which many gentlemen
riders belong; it is quite exclusive, and socially reminiscent of
a country club, although, with one or two special exceptions,
only men belong to the Charros. They meet and hold *rodeos*
and *jaripeos* (very often for charity), practicing all the old
arts of riding, roping, branding, and horsemanship which were
part of the life of the haciendas, now largely consigned to tender memory. The word "charro" is of uncertain origin, but
the costume is that of an Andalusian gentleman rider, although the Mexican sombrero has grown larger and wider-
winged than its Spanish counterpart, with a great flared brim
rolling up from the crown. The charros wear homespun trousers and leather jackets for the "work" of roping and bulldog-
ging and branding, but they have a "dress" outfit, which is
usually velvet, embroidered with silver threads. To my mind,
no costume has ever been designed which so flatters a manly

figure, as a black velvet charro suit, worn with a silver-decorated pearl-gray sombrero.

One of the loveliest of weddings was performed in San Jacinto Church not long ago. The bridegroom wore formal charro dress, of black velvet buttoned with silver, and the bride an exact copy of her first communion gown, all fine tucks in delicate white lawn, with a pendant pocket for her missal and her rosary. Over her hair she wore the white lace mantilla from Spain which had been her grandmother's.

Whenever I felt lonely for Monterrey and the peaceful provinces, I need only ramble in San Angel's old streets, and I would be transported back in time to the Mexico of the last century, the Mexico I dearly love for its tradition and poetry.

San Angel people cherish the past and are willing to battle against the future. Once a boulevard ate its way through the old plazas and gardens right up to the Municipal Palace of San Angel, with its old-fashioned archways and terraces, and bulldozers came to knock down everything that stood in the path of a great speedway, planned to blast straight through San Angel to a great stadium near the university, where football is purveyed to the public. Progressive city planners, who are all in love with automobiles, thought everything should give way so that cars could swoop out and away from the stadium as soon as each game was over. And they wanted great parking lots near the stadium too, for it seemed to them unthinkable that people should be put to the trouble of walking two whole blocks. San Angel would simply have to be taken apart and redistributed.

But the ladies of San Angel got wind of this plan and they laid aside their tapestry needlepoint, suspended their catechism classes, and rose in their wrath, united. They forced their husbands to get *amparos* (legal stays of action) and they stopped the tractors and bulldozers in their tracks. Touch but a stone of the next San Angel building and there will be guerrilla war! The ladies came down like furies on the city planners and made them put back the cobblestones they had uprooted and rebuild the walls. And a triumphant new Municipal Palace went up—in colonial style. Automobiles were arrogantly ordered to retire, and once again little flop-eared burros picked their way along the narrow cobblestoned streets, as they had always done.

Football stadiums indeed, the ladies sniffed—these ladies with faces pale as moonlight and hair black as *azabache*, descendants many of them of the crusading Knights of Calatrava and Guardians of the Holy Sepulchre. Automobiles indeed, upstart machines! San Angel is not to be destroyed for them or their like. Bypass us, we don't care. Leave us to our tranquil afternoons in the cypress shade, to our retreats in hidden convents, to gentle tea parties, to our walks along the twisting streets in the candlelit dusk, to Rosary service in an old church. Let somebody else be progressive.

Like the Spanish poet Jorge Manrique, who is so often quoted in Mexico, the ladies of San Angel believe that "any time in the past was better than now."

San Angel, I learned to my joy, shortly after I became acquainted with a few ladies and had begun to make friends, has her saint, too. When I first heard about Doña Concha Cabrera, she had not been dead more than twelve or fifteen years, and yet she was a legend "on the flower of the lip" of all San Angel people. Now indeed, her cause has been entered, and the first steps are being taken toward her beatification and eventual sanctification in the eyes of the Church. In San Angel it has been known for years that she was a saint.

Doña Margarita told me about Doña Concha, who had been a close friend of her own mother.

"She came from San Luis Potosí, a pious married lady and devoted mother, to make her home here," Margarita told me. "My mother was active in all sorts of church work and charity, and so was Doña Concha, from the very beginning.

"Once in a while my mother would meet her looking very pale and wan and with bruises on her arms and shoulders. 'I have been wrestling and fighting with the Evil One,' she used to say, and curiously enough, nobody ever thought her peculiar or hysterical. They simply thought it must be so, for she had the most candid, the most beautifully pure and innocent gray eyes you ever saw."

The Evil One tempted and pursued and hurt her with frustrated fury, but her written meditations, after she had won over him, are said to be, by those who have read them, as profound and important in the realm of spiritual literature, as the works of Santa Teresa of Avila. Doña Concha wrote fluently in several languages she had never studied and in which she could not converse.

Before her death she founded an order of nuns dedicated to penitence and to contemplation, and she herself took innocent joy in being photographed in their habit. But neither her mystical writings nor her founding of the order are the things remembered by the simple people of San Angel who knew her. They remember her absolute faith, her loving charity, and her visions. And they remember when she was seen in elevation, and by many. My friend Margarita herself saw this strange thing happen.

She had gone to the Church of Our Lady of Carmen on some errand, and as she entered, she saw that Doña Concha was kneeling before an image of the Crucified. Having finished her devotions, Margarita was leaving the church, and it occurred to her to go and greet Doña Concha, her mother's friend. But as she drew near she saw that Doña Concha, still kneeling in the attitude of prayer, had been elevated to about three feet from the ground. Her hands were locked together, and her face was very white, intense, and withdrawn.

"A curious thing is," Margarita told me, "that I felt nothing odd about this at all at the moment, but only a shy respect, and I hurried away as I would if I had intruded on someone reading a letter, or enclosed in some powerful private emotion. However, once outside, in the golden afternoon, I suddenly felt scared and cold. I began to tremble. But then Doña Concha came out, plump and a bit bustling as she always was, and she laid her little hand kindly on my arm.

" 'My dear,' she said, 'there is nothing to be afraid of because all that God does is beautiful and perfect beyond imagination, no matter how it may seem here on earth.' She stooped then and picked a little flower that was growing up between the stones of the walk in the church close. 'Look at this,' she said, touching its petals tenderly. 'Could anything be more mysterious, the way it comes to life from the rotting seed, and grows up to blossom, knowing which shape and color to take, knowing all God's law within itself? Could anything be more rare and wonderful?' And then she reached up, for she was short, and kissed me on the cheek, and then she trotted away."

While San Angel, the town where I was to live, was dominated by the families who wear the tradition and the past around them like a protective mantle, it was also, I found, touched by other influences. The tragedy and disillusion of the countless European refugees who found their way here after the last war, is sometimes almost palpable, but at the same time, the refugees brought in a restlessly intellectual note, a despairing wish to understand the currents of world thought. They still live, many of them, in refined poverty, and they are great collectors of Indian artifacts; I have often wondered whether the grotesqueries of the little pre-Spanish images did not in some way appeal to their conviction that the world has gone mad. These refugees have fitted themselves into activities by which they can earn their bread, but when they see their children absorbing the life and look and color of Mexico, they feel a sharper exile.

Then too, because of San Angel's beauty, its trees and gardens and its old colonial architecture, it has become a favorite residence for artists of every nationality, especially painters of the Mexican vanguard. For years Diego Rivera lived in an aggressively modern studio, across the street from the old Hacienda Goicochea, with its atmosphere of the paternal-

istic past that Diego despised. Around Diego gathered a collection of painters, writers, and sycophants, who hung to him
like a hive of bees, all buzzing with admiration of the Communism he professed. Many of these artists have since changed
their minds; the wind of public opinion in patient old Mexico
had changed, and they were caught frozen in attitudes they
might now prefer to disavow. Some continue, with ire, well
rewarded by handouts from the Soviet Embassy in Mexico
(which has over 300 employees to Mexico's three in Moscow),
to denounce the Roman Catholic Church, imperialistic gringo
capitalists, and the perfidy of all Mexicans who do not at once
take up the hammer and sickle and liberate everybody in sight.

So San Angel was populated by people who lived spiritually in the old Catholic Mexico of colonial days and people
who lived spiritually in the Soviet Union, and by a sprinkling
of foreigners who had just happened to land here . . . Americans from the Middle West and from California, English from
London, Scots from Glasgow, Italians from Genoa and Padua,
Swiss from Berne and Zurich and Lausanne, French from Paris
and Finisterre, Irish from County Clare, Czechs, Hungarians,
Yugoslavs, and South Americans. All rub shoulders, and
sometimes noses, in San Angel.

In short, San Angel, when I arrived from the sleepy provinces, was fascinating. It was like a wonderful fruitcake, full of
exotic spices and flavors, and with plenty of nuts.

I was told of a dinner party given by an old San Angel
family, who were slowly starving to death behind their great
walls, all of the family being unwilling to work, and all against
selling the ancestral home and treasures. Guests were received
with exquisite courtesy and dinner was served by an ancient
butler on fine China and silver. The wines were excellent (the
cellar was still well stocked), and the dinner consisted of rice
for the first course, beans for the second, and a banana each
for dessert. I was told that the Château Yquem was excellent
with the rice.

One scion of such an old family worked out a unique

way of achieving a little pocket money. He had an ancient motorcycle which chugged about noisily with an air of importance. If he drove up beside a motorist, wearing goggles and a leather jacket, and blew sharply on a whistle, chances were good that he might be passed a driving license, with a ten-peso note discreetly attached. (Or maybe even a "blue-eyed gringa," the nickname for a fifty-peso note, which is blue.) He would take the note quietly, return the license, kick his motor, and resume his travels. Not a word would be said, and if people in their stupidity assumed him to be a traffic officer, well, whose fault was that? Fools and their money are soon parted.

Strange legends cling around old San Angel still, around the ancient houses and decaying families, and many of them have taken on a patina over the years, not always of the most wholesome sort. Other families seem to this day to live surrounded by a mysterious enchantment which passes beauty from member to member, down through the years. Still others carry legends which might be the sort of stories woven into old tapestries.

One of the tales told over San Angel teacups casts a spell of tragic poetry still, though it happened many years ago. In the last century, when some of the old families still rejoiced in enormous wealth, it was the custom to send boys to England to be educated, and the girls to convents in France. One of the oldest of the twenty children of this family who, during his high school and college years abroad had used only one of his many family names, took passage on a ship to return to Mexico. This ship touched at Le Havre to take aboard more passengers, among them one of his little sisters, aged fourteen, who was returning home from convent school. Eluding her chaperone, and giving a false name for her protection, this pretty and precocious child initiated a flirtation with the handsome young Mexican-Englishman, who never dreamed that she was his own sister. By the time they arrived in Vera-cruz, they were madly in love. When apprised of their true relationship on arrival at home, they ran away together to some country in South America. They vowed to marry and they believed they could secure Pontifical permission. Whether they did, or whether they merely announced that they had done so, they returned to Mexico as man and wife. The scandal was shattering, but these two took their love "with death upon the tread," like shadowy figures in a medieval tapestry who embrace while the couchant lion threatens behind them, ready to pounce with unsheathed claws.

This then was the town I had chosen for my home, and where my little boys would grow to manhood. This town was to be my town, with its society as flamboyant and varied as the society of Monterrey had been simple and candid.

In San Angel I found a kindergarten to which I trundled my two little boys. Not long after, they confronted me with their question as to my racial allegiance, and I realized that here in San Angel, with its multitudinous Continental European, old Spanish, and colonial Mexican strains, I would have to fight to keep my influence over my children. I was going to have to choose sides, and keep my ammunition dry.

IV ❧

GUICHO AND WIKI

> *Juventud, divino tesoro,*
> *Ya te vas, por no volver . . .*
> —FROM A POEM BY RUBEN DARIO

I had word from the kindergarten that my little boys should attend class in white shirts and white or dark woolen short trousers, according to the season. Strong admirers of Superman, my two demanded red capes like his, so that they could fly when the occasion arose. So I bought red flannel and Maria and I made them. These capes they laid aside during classes, but they set a style, and a good many little Mexican boys trudged to school, in ensuing weeks, also enveloped in *capas de Super-Hombre*.

I taught both my children to read, in order to save myself the labor of reading the "funnies" to them for hours at a time. I used the old-fashioned, sound-it-out system, by which I had learned as a child, and in no time at all they were reading their comic books with bated breath, while I had leisure for other activities. Frankly the idea of their getting to high school before they could read, as friends had written to me of their children in the advanced schools of my native country, seemed to me a bit long to wait.

There were occasional problems, though, as when they came to me with their Mickey Mouse books in English, to ask me to explain which hurt the most—biff, boom, or bam, and when they wanted to know just what was meant by ker-plop. These onomatopoeic words are not the same in every language. In Spanish one says *trac* or *prácate* meaning biff or bam, and *zas* instead of ker-plop. But having got them started, the old enchantment of an evening with a book kept them busy with Peter Rabbit and Black Beauty and later with Julio Ver-nay, and then with Oliverio Tweest and Da-veed Co-per-fee-eld. There is no magic like a book to keep children quiet and parents in their right minds.

About the time my sons arrived at the first grade they ceased to be babies, and became little personalities. Every day they provided me with some new shock. But I never became shockproof. I am still constantly bopped over the head by the manifestation in one child or the other, of some gene contributed by a long-forgotten Moor, Romany, or Basque, or Spaniard, Jew, or Aztec in Luis's line, or some ancient Dane, Hollander, Irishman, Scot, Frenchman, or American Indian in mine.

Luis, my older son, known to us as Guicho, and as "Looie" in the states, is fine-boned and nervous, with a thatch of curly light hair and sharp little green eyes, under brows which are inverted V's. He has an aquiline nose, and a sudden smile that makes him look older than he is. He is proud, vain, passionate, belligerent, fierce in his loyalties, hard-headed, and incapable of feigning, or even of the mildest social acting for the sake of peace or appearances. He doesn't really care for peace, and as for appearances, he couldn't care less. He looks almost exactly like his paternal grandfather, who was half-Basque, but also hauntingly like my maternal grandfather, who was a mysterious and mercurial Dane.

Guicho loves drawing. He drew before he spoke. He made a caricature of me when he was five, and it actually looks very like me. When I received this drawing as a gift I pretended to object to the likeness and I coyly asked him if my mouth was really that big. He assured me that it was. "Yes Mima," he told me firmly. "When you are still, your mouth is very big, and when you laugh it takes up your whole face."

At six he brought me a drawing which he explained, patiently. "I made you very small here, where you are going down the street. That's to show that you are far away. Haven't

you noticed that when things are far away, they get smaller?"
He had discovered the principle of perspective, and thus, it
seems to me, he was one jump ahead of a good many other
painters around nowadays.

He has never wanted to do anything but draw and paint,
and when I tearfully deplored low marks on his report card,
he would answer, "But you know I am going to be a painter,
and they don't have to know anything!" He has since learned
better, but his passion to dedicate himself to art has never
faltered.

Enrique (Wiki), my younger son, is called Hank in the
States. He has the look of the Gómez family—their olive skin,
large velvety dark eyes, and dark brown hair with coppery
lights. But he has the Borton lawyer's jaw and my short nose.
He is philosophical, playful, merry, and a tease. I discover
more than a little of Mamacita in him.

Mamacita was always restless as a gypsy. When she could
not move to another town she would move to another house.
Somehow, she achieved new surroundings every year. Perhaps
this was partly to relieve the tedium of life in the provinces.
She had many recipes for keeping life exciting. For instance,
she might start a big family row, which would end in a general
discharge of emotion, like fireworks. Or she might plan a
picnic, a *día de campo*—one of those Mexican expeditions to
the countryside for lunch which took a month to organize,
a week to cook for, and a year to recover from.

When all else failed and monotony seemed about to set
in, she would move. These movings are remembered by my
husband, who was a child of many tender attachments, as
times of utter horror. After an initial period of uneasiness (he
told me), during which she would try to work up some jealousy somewhere, or at least a good shouting quarrel, she would
call out the horse and carriage and go house-hunting. As she
had a new baby every second year there was always some obvious justification for requiring more room. The family lived on
Hidalgo Street, on Ocampo, on Padre Mier, on Calle Washing-

ton, on the Purissima Plaza, on Pino Suarez, on Madero . . . Luis has lost count. After a new house had been found, there would ensue a great tearing about, packing and boxing, at which Mamacita would superintend all the maids and *mozos*. Then the moving carts would come, and Mamacita would stand out on the narrow sidewalk looking terribly pretty, with her black eyes sparkling and her curly hair tumbling out of its combs, and she would direct everything and give many orders, feeling a heady surge of executive power. At last, from the now frighteningly empty house, where the children would have been left with their *nanas*, a carriage would come to fetch them to their new home. But the children couldn't share in Mamacita's pleasure in arranging the new home, in hanging new curtains and experimenting with new groupings of chairs and sofas. They saw only a strange place, disordered, and piled high with furniture, boxes, and carpets. By candlelight they would creep into improvised beds and there they would lie, feeling lonely for the nooks they knew, the familiar shadows, the creakings and tappings they were accustomed to, and they were terrorized by the new rattlings and whisperings in the walls and along the beams of the strange house.

Wiki is like Mamacita. He loves change. His eyes shine at the thought of a journey. His plan is to go first around the world, and then to the moon.

Guicho constantly produced drawings for me, which I have saved, as I hope to cash in on them some day when he is famous. Whenever he was naughty and I felt obliged to administer a warning or a smack, he would run and get his latest drawing, tear it into bits before my eyes, and dance on the wreckage. Having believed every word of my fulsome praise of each drawing, he was sure that destroying it would cause me pain. Wiki always laughed indulgently as he observed these tantrums.

"Isn't Guicho silly," remarked my practical child, "to tear up his own drawing, when it was *he* who was bad."

The two little boys were not compatible, but they were

brothers, so they had to get used to it. They shared a room and they shared confidences. They did not share tastes and enthusiasms, although they once (hold onto your seats!) wrote a medical textbook together. I still possess this historic document, and at times I pore over it with morbid fascination. It was a true collaboration, arising out of their decisions on what to be when they grew up. At that time Wiki was sure he wanted to be a doctor, while Guicho, of course, was going to be a painter.

The first chapter in their medical book took up the disease of measles. Wiki, who could not yet write fluently, dictated the text to Guicho, who wrote it out beautifully in different colors of ink, numbering the paragraphs and interpolating many decorative little drawings of rabbits, automobiles, horses, and flowers. Wiki's texts began with a description of symptoms, described the progress of the disease, and gave what he could remember of treatment. Guicho then prepared a drawing showing the disease raging in the victim, and these plates are what attract my eye to this day.

"Measles," wrote Wiki, "begins with your nose running and fever and then you get the spots. They come out all over you, even down there. They hurt a lot and itch, but after a while they go away and you get better. Your mother pulls the curtains down so the light won't hurt your eyes and makes you lots of lemonade. The doctor gives you injections and then you are through with the measles."

Guicho's illustration, done in red and blue inks, carefully portrayed a boy with virulent measles all over, even down there.

The next chapter in their book took up the subject of mumps. From this they went on to chicken pox (where Guicho portrayed the sufferer modestly from the rear) and so on, through their whole repertory. At about this time they wearied of it, or perhaps that was when they became embroiled in the Bat Club.

Their collaboration on the medical textbook foreshadowed their character development, for Wiki took to detached study, while Guicho was always attempting some passionate transformation of reality. But their joint enterprises fell apart when Guicho began to exhibit some of his more American characteristics, while Wiki steadily grew more Latin. Guicho loved to organize. Wiki's Latin blood was sturdily against organization or cooperation of any kind, and group activity seemed to him to be something you indulged in on occasion to celebrate a festivity, like ice cream. A thoroughgoing individualist, he resisted membership in anything.

Guicho, though, got all the boys of the neighborhood together for the Murcielago Club, of sorrowful memory. Murcielago means Bat.

Even the Castillos were invited to join the Bat Club. Here I must digress and interpolate a few remarks about the Castillos. These brothers (there were two) rose and fell with the regularity of wet and dry years. Or perhaps there was a materialistic leitmotiv in the curious friendship between the brothers Treviño and the brothers Castillo. When the Treviños had a volleyball, the friendship waxed warm. Then there was a fight, and a great silence. When one day it appeared that the Castillos had a bicycle, relations were re-established and both Treviños learned to ride on the Castillo bicycle. All was well until a Treviño knocked down and broke a Puebla vase on the Castillo terrace while riding the Castillo bicycle, and Señora Castillo quite understandably thought this a bit thick. The iron curtain came down with a bang.

Time marched on. Then the Treviños became proprietors of a football, and behold, once more the Castillos appeared, offering friendship. This lasted a few months until there was some misunderstanding about a certain football helmet. The allies then found that their ideologies were, after all, quite opposed, and all peace treaties were torn up. Recently the presence of a motorcycle in the Castillo home seems to have permitted a reopening of negotiations and agreements have been signed permitting trade and communication.

At the time of the Bat Club, Guicho was about eight

and a half, Wiki just past seven, and the Castillos around the same ages.

I should have had premonitions when I heard the name of the new club. I learned later, to my distress, that the whole thing had been organized around my pampered mimosa tree. Guicho wrote out a constitution and bylaws for the Bat Club, in which it was stated that the meeting place of the club was to be in my mimosa tree, and it was set forth that each and every member of the Murcielagos had the right to construct for himself a lookout in the tree.

I had paid little attention to the tearing up of old packing cases and fruit boxes and the hammering that had been going on in the back patio for some days, since I am the kind of mother who never rises from her chair or puts down her who-done-it until she hears a roar of pain, quite close. I thus enjoyed my murder in innocent ignorance while the Bats built seven tree houses and attached them to the seven delicate branches of my darling flowering mimosa. Then there was a great rending and a crashing, and seven assorted bleats, squeaks, and howls of dismay. Both my Bats were covered with gore, and Guicho had lost a front tooth. I gave first aid to the wounded, and shooed home all uninjured Bats. When the whole story came out and I was allowed to see the constitution, which had been lettered in fancy type and adorned with many mystic symbols, several of the bylaws caught my eye. "No Bat can talk back to his parents without just cause and permission from the Head Bat." This was interesting to learn. Guicho, of course, was Head Bat. The constitution also stated that all Bats must be practicing Catholics, and they were enjoined to say their Rosary in their Bat nest daily. Despite these fine precepts, I felt obliged to dissolve the Bats by parental edict, from which there is no appeal.

This wasn't the end, though. Guicho wanted a club. Some kind of a club. Any kind of a club. He wanted to be in a club, and preferably president. Correct me if this is not an American characteristic.

"I don't want to be in any club, Mima," protested Wiki. "But if I won't be, Guicho beats me up."

"Hit him back."

"What's the use of that?" cried the philosophical Wiki. "Then he just hits me again, and it goes on and on. I'd rather there was no fight. The only way to stop Guicho from beating me up is to give in. He will make me be in all his clubs. He says I have to be the treasurer and handle the money because he doesn't trust the Castillos."

"How do the others like it when one Treviño is president and the other one is treasurer?"

"They don't like it, but if they say anything, Guicho beats them up too."

"Well, it looks as if there were a strong tendency to conform among you. At least until some boy stronger than Guicho gets in one of his clubs."

"I guess so," agreed Wiki sadly.

A number of other clubs were invented, organized, and eventually abandoned. Guicho did get some pleasure out of a football club which actually met and played a few games until wiped out by mumps. His thirst for organization continued, and so, alas, did his belligerency. But it had its uses, after all.

There came a week when Wiki began getting noticeably restless and nervous at lunchtime, usually one of his favorite times of day. Also he started begging me daily, for a few centavos with which to buy sweets. Usually I gave him a little money, but my suspicions were aroused when one day I found I had no coins, and Wiki burst into tears and refused to go to school. Under cross-examination by the crown, the witness admitted that he was under severe pressure to provide sweets for some boys on Bus 4, who had advised the extremely peaceable Wiki that when there was no candy for them, he would be taken apart. Guicho listened to the whole story, but made no comment. He merely went with his little brother to school and awaited the arrival of the extortioners on Bus 4.

I heard the results later. When the bus drove up and the

boys clambered down, Guicho, holding both hands clenched
behind his back, shouted, "Which of you is expecting a present
from my little brother?" Two grafters stepped forward to collect and Guicho hit them each a mighty clout, felling one. The
other ran roaring for the principal of the school, who simply
ordered all hands into line and marched them to their classes.
The principal directed the belligerents to take their private
quarrel to the *prado* (meadow) after school. No fighting on
the school grounds.

This *prado* was where many differences of opinion were
brought into alignment. The school principal believed firmly
in the salutary doctrine of a *prado*, where there was no adult
supervision, and where might made right. Perhaps, on the
whole, his attitude was a good one. Guicho came home with a
torn shirt and a black eye, but definitely the victor, and there
were no more shakedowns for protection on Bus 4.

Wiki was very proud of his older brother and came to me
to brag about him.

"It was a wonderful fight, Mima," he recounted. "They
knocked down and grunted and got up and the other boy
hollered bad names. One of those Bus 4 boys has to get a new
tooth, and the other one's nose ran *mole* for an hour." (*Mole*
is a rich red Mexican chile sauce, and it is the name small
fry give to blood.) "But of course I knew Guicho would win.
He has been to the *prado* lots of times."

"Dear me. Has he?"

"Yes, and he always licks everybody. Even boys that are
bigger than he is, because he gets so terribly mad. I have
observed," said my small philosopher who prefers at all times to
be an attentive bystander, "that if you get mad enough, people
get afraid. And it is a good thing, because Guicho isn't big.
But he gets madder than anybody."

So the two began to develop, despite any twig-bending
I attempted, each in his own way—Wiki in the character of a
fair-minded reporter, a born middle-of-the-roader, and Guicho
passionately ready to do or die. Left or right, however his

temper listed, he went in with both arms swinging. A born one-hundred-percenter, a Mexican revolutionist. I remembered the name my parents had called him before his birth, and because his birthday fell on November 20, Revolution Day. They always referred to him as "The Little General."

I began to get faint, uneasy stirrings of worry. The boys were not going to be easy to sort out. The genes were all mixed up. Guicho was the organizer and the club man. He had the American love of comradeship, an Irish glory in a good fight, and a revolutionary ardor straight out of Mexico. Wiki was both philosopher and individualist, but likely to fall victim to terrorist gangs. Was this Mexican?

I wanted to become acquainted with other mothers of San Angel who had children the same ages as mine, preferably, as an English friend put it, "little mongrels" like mine. I use the word advisedly. As every dog lover knows, mongrels are animals in which you recognize the oddly assorted characteristics of many noble breeds.

V ❧

LOVE AND THE OFICINISTAS

Ay amor, ya no me quieras tanto,
Ay amor, no sufras mas por mi . . .
—MEXICAN SONG

Long before I had made friends with other mothers in San Angel, I had become a sort of older sister to the young women who worked in the office where I was employed mornings. My little boys were in kindergarten and then in primary school during the morning hours only, and I hung onto the little job I had rounded up when first we had seemed to be faced with starvation on arrival in Mexico City, though Luis had long since reassumed his favorite role of the Good Provider.

I wrote publicity releases in English for a group of private persons and companies who dedicated themselves to promoting travel to Mexico. This was long before the organization of a government tourist department, and the whole travel business was in its infancy in Mexico. Publicity releases about the beauties of Mexico were really a sort of pioneering. The gentlemen who hired me realized that it was necessary not so much to write purple prose about scenery and quaint customs, as to try to overcome a formidable list of mistaken ideas about Mexico—a far harder task.

My plan for the releases, based on my experience as a reporter, was to write up bits of news that would not normally be used over any wire service or by a regular staff newsman stationed in Mexico. I combed my sources for information which tended to throw a true light on Mexico and Mexican ways, hoping that the bulk of my reports might in time help to tip the scales toward a more correct appreciation of Mexico's many mysteries. And I convinced my employers that my news releases must be very short, never running over half a page, and preferably only "one stick" in length. If short, they had a good chance of being picked up for column fillers.

One of the hardest things we worked to overcome was the bad effect of certain date lines. The date line is the name of the city and the date which precedes news stories, generally, such as Mexico City, February 4, or Monterrey, Mexico, June 5, and so on. Wire services customarily date their releases from the city where the news is "filed" or sent out by telegraph. This can be very misleading, as the reader generally assumes that the event chronicled took place at the city in the date line. Such is not always the case. For example, when there was an obscure uprising in the hills of the state of San Luis Potosí, many miles from highway or railroad, news dispatches on the revolt were date-lined San Luis Potosí, the capital of the state, where there was telegraph service. This caused many Americans to rush to their maps, where they learned to their horror that San Luis Potosí is an important city on the main railway line into Mexico, and they canceled tours to Mexico City by the hundreds.

And then, Mexico suffered, and still does in some degree and in some localities, from the following misconceptions:

1. You can't eat anything raw in Mexico because you will catch dysentery and infectious hepatitis.
2. You can't drink the water and you should even wash your teeth in Coca-Cola or Delaware Punch or whiskey.
3. Mexico is in the tropics and therefore it is boiling hot everywhere.
4. It is a primitive country full of dear little artistic Indians who have been cruelly treated for centuries. (This is a line much favored by Communists and fellow travelers and people who think the only Indians are the ones they see working in the fields.)

5. There are no good hotels or restaurants except in the capital or Acapulco.

6. Everything is frightfully cheap because the money is no good.

7. You must always bargain and beat the vendors down on their prices (while loudly expatiating on "the awful poverty").

8. Mexico is full of rabid Communists and the United States ought to move in with troops and clean up the place, or

9. Mexico is a fine free democracy moving toward perfect social uplift.

> Note: Neither 8 nor 9 is really based on all the facts, and these two ideas cause a great deal of trouble in Mexico to this day.

10. Mexicans hate all Americans (wrong).

11. Mexicans adore all Americans (wrong).

I collected many small items of news that could be expressed in a few lines and began sending them out to editors. Because of their brevity, they were given consideration. (I well remembered when I was a reporter, being passed quantities of "publicity releases" with the order, "Cut these down to a stick each.") So our releases began to be picked up and used with some regularity. I developed a fine incandescent missionary feeling, for I wanted Mexico to be known and loved for what she really is, and not for qualities alien to her integrity.

The head of the association I worked for, and my boss, or *jefe*, was a learned and dignified scholar, Don Lucas de Palacio. He will always typify for me that admirable creation, the Mexican gentleman. It is a type as rounded and complete and individual as is Don Quijote de la Mancha. It is a type neither European nor American, but rather a homogeneous blend of Spanish pride and individuality, Mexican tenderness, reserve, and stubbornness, and inborn hospitality and courtesy.

A thoroughly well-organized and methodical man, Don

Lucas used to have an attack of nerves whenever he was obliged to search for anything in my files. Once when he had been forced to go through my desk in my absence, in search of a letter, the shock brought on a chill and pneumonia. I am, unfortunately, the kind of worker who cannot think when surrounded by order and neatness. I function in disorder and neglect, like a fungus. Later, organizing his archives, Don Lucas wrote out a neat label and pasted it on my desk drawer: OLLA PODRIDA. (This is a Mexican-Spanish stew which contains anything that can be thrown into it, like a French *pot-au-feu*.)

When he hired me, Don Lucas set forth his requirements. He then courteously asked me mine. I said there was only one: I had to be allowed to go out and get a cup of coffee at eleven. (This was years before the coffee break became as sacred as marriage.) This request of mine he granted, and whenever anyone inquired for me around eleven o'clock, Don Lucas would say calmly, "Señora Treviño is not here. She has gone to get her gasoline."

Don Lucas was fine-boned and delicate, with the unmistakable look of the aristocrat. He had a slightly disconcerting habit of stepping back from the person addressing him, for he was farsighted. But this habit at first, along with his dignity, gave the impression that he wished you to keep your distance. He smoked fragrant cigars constantly, wore a gold signet ring on his little finger with his family coat of arms engraved upon it, and he dedicated some time every day to studies of genealogy, a subject on which he was expert. His interest in ancestors dated from a trip to Spain he had made in his youth, in which he amused himself by tracing his family back through old records of the Knights of Calatrava until he found the tomb of one of them in Seville, where that worthy had fallen in the wars against the Moors. Don Lucas was a lay Franciscan, and kept a plain wooden coffin, in which he proposed to be buried, under his bed, to remind him that all is vanity. Once in a while, he would get into his coffin and lie there and meditate, or so I was told.

Don Lucas's inner office, where he wrote his learned articles on history and genealogy, and where he carried out his administrative work for the tourist association, was a veritable library. There he felt at peace and at home. I was startled in my early days at the office to hear him announce solemnly that he intended to die at the stroke of eleven that morning. He then lighted a new cigar, went into his inner sanctum and shut the door. I nervously asked one of the Spanish secretaries for information. "He can't be intending to commit suicide?" I gibbered.

"Don Lucas? Never. That would be a sin," she answered, and went on typing.

"But . . . but . . ." I stammered.

"Oh, that? That just means he won't receive anybody today after eleven. He dies frequently," she assured me. "He has to. Tourists come in and ask him such foolish questions and drive him crazy. He has to rest his nerves, sometimes."

Occasionally, when we were not very busy, Don Lucas would call me into his office and tell me wonderful stories of the Revolution, such as the one about his honeymoon. The revolutionists at that time were keeping their hands in by blowing up trains with some regularity, and usually the engineers would stop to fraternize with the rebels along the way. Don Lucas did not want this to happen on his wedding journey from Guadalajara to Mexico City, so after boarding the train, he locked his bride in their compartment and went forward to the engineer's cabin. There he placed a pistol at the engineer's back and said, "Keep going. No stops until we get to Mexico City, no matter what happens." Thus encouraged, the engineer complied.

He recounted to me also many fascinating tales of the haciendas. He had grown up on one and was often nostalgic for that leisurely plantation life. Once a relative of his had made a bet with a friend that he could beat him in a *diligencia* race. (The *diligencias* were the old stagecoaches, pulled by seven, nine, or eleven horses, and it was a delicate and special skill to manipulate the reins and drive them.) The word was sent round to several contiguous haciendas, arranging that a road about two hundred kilometers in length, through the haciendas, should be kept free of animals and foot traffic at the time of the race. The drivers were to be allowed a few changes of horses along the way. Excitement ran high, and so did the betting. To make a long story short, Don Lucas's relative won the bet, but when he stepped down from his *diligencia*, it was found that he had torn all the flesh off the fingers of his two hands. Ever after, he had to wear special gloves, and the matter was never mentioned, except after his death of course, when the story became public domain.

Many other tales Don Lucas told me, revealing to me a Mexico chivalrous, exaggerated, romantic, and macabre, a fairy-tale country of heroes and sacrifice and beauty, with an undercurrent of strange, harsh humor under a delicate surface of poetry and mysticism.

Don Lucas himself, in his impeccable integrity, was the reason why six young women from decent Mexican families, could work in his office. Each one (and even our Spanish Rocío) was the daughter or niece of a friend or relative of Don Lucas, and his own honor and reputation preserved them from the onus of working just "anywhere." For young ladies in Mexico are not career-minded, even today, when industrialization is bringing its inevitable changes so swiftly. They work mostly, because they actually need money, but guardians choose the offices where the young ladies are to work with the greatest of care, and, if one cannot arrange that the señoritas work where there is a relative or a trusted compadre to protect her, she must at least be where there are many other young women, for there is safety in numbers.

When I first moved to Mexico City, many girls were still escorted to their offices and called for at the end of the work day by strong brothers or uncles or papas, and even now a parent nearly always checks the office and working conditions, really "casing the joint," before allowing a girl to take employment. Mexican young ladies nearly always go home for lunch and live at home. The separate apartment for young women is almost unknown, except in the case of mad foreign women, such as Americans. Indeed, Mexican working girls, living at home, are not even given latchkeys. I know, for I have never been given one. I ring the bell at my gate when I get home from work and when my husband arrives, he asks the maid what time I got in. This is perfectly acceptable, for it means that one is being watched over, even if the times are such that sometimes the little woman, or a daughter of the family, must add to the total family income.

My little job became a sort of morning course in education, for which I was being paid. Even after Luis had begun to earn far more than we needed, and we were quite prosperous, I could not have given it up.

Besides, I had a swelled head because of the treatment accorded me by the young girls in the office. They regarded me as an authority on all subjects, especially that most important subject of all . . . men. I was thought to have much to teach them, since I had actually got one of the shy creatures to the altar. They brought me little presents of flowers and cookies, and of handmade handkerchiefs, and shared their luncheon *tortas* with me. They wanted to learn my Secret. I had married a Mexican, and I was still married to him, so they thought that I, a blunt American, might actually tell them things their mothers or sisters wouldn't reveal. How did I get him to propose? How could one tell when the young man really loved one? How could he be made to declare himself, to sign on the dotted line? They thought of nothing else from morning until night except how to get a husband, by fair means or foul. I gave advice lavishly, and it must have been effective, for all are married now except the quiet little one who always wanted to be a nun anyway, and she is now Sister Elena, in a convent far to the north.

The Mexican señorita, in the cosmopolitan capital, is not the haughty maiden of the provinces, who makes the boy go through many tests of persistence and valor before he may think of her as his intended bride. In the provinces the señorita has much to strengthen her position and give her the advantage. There is no social life to speak of for men over thirty in the provinces, if they haven't married. The enviable lot of the "single man" in the United States, or Mexico City, has no counterpart in the tightly organized social life of the provinces. If a man can't get himself a wife by the time he is thirty, he is considered a bad hat and a bad job, and little time is wasted on him by progressive hostesses.

In Mexico City, though, the lonely male can have a very good time indeed, and the wiles of the female have to be much more cunning, in order to bring him to his knees. The girls in the office wanted to know which was better, to deceive the men and make them think you were popular and fire their jealousy, or cling to them and wound them to the core, with your innocence and dependence.

If I gave sage advice, it was mostly based on hindsight, for the señoritas and their adventures (conducted in large part through the office telephone, to Don Lucas's infinite annoyance) taught me a great deal about how to *lose* a beau. In fact the more I listened, and the more often my shoulder was drenched with the tears of the defeated, the more surprised I became that I had ever landed Luis at all, and I became a better and a kinder woman at home.

Catalina, the office beauty, had enormous gray eyes, thick golden hair, and a seductive figure. She laid waste the youth of the capital in buses and elevators on her way to work. She was chaste as sleet and entirely without guile, and never knew why men followed her and winked at her and sometimes managed to pinch her. She was blindly in love with a young man who soon achieved first position on my list of blights, jerks, and all-around no-good-niks. Often he would ring up and invite Catalina to meet him on a certain street corner after work, with the proposal that he would then accompany her home and ask her mother's permission to take her to the movies. Thrilled, about an hour before closing time, Catalina would go to the ladies' room and do her nails, dress her hair, and for all I know, take a bath. She would arrive at the trysting place all resplendent beauty and youthful anticipation, only to find that her swain had amused himself by also inviting, to the same corner, and with the same bait, another girl, as well. The rivals would at first pretend they were delighted to see each other, they would chat and try to outwait each other. But at last, since the young sadist would prudently stay away altogether, they would be united in grief and disillusion, and go home together. This louse, by the way, was eventually married to a strong-minded American girl who leads him a dog's life, I am glad to say.

It took poor candid Catalina a long time, and many pep talks from me, to cease trusting the perfidious male and to treat them all with disdain. As soon as she did, she caught a very nice husband, who didn't want to be disdained, and now they have three lovely children.

We had another beauty besides Catalina. Her father, a devotee of opera—and particularly of Puccini, I presume—had named her Tosca. She was dark and sultry, with cascading black hair, black eyes edged with thick sooty lashes, and a fruity mouth which she outlined in raspberry lipstick. Tosca's trouble was that her people were from Monterrey and she had fixed ideas about what qualities she should look for in a husband. The main one was money.

"The Meesus' husband is from Monterrey, and she is happy," she would announce, stopping any argument. She was determined to get a Monterrey husband, if possible.

I, the Meesus, would murmur that my husband was very nice, but he certainly didn't have much money, but to this

Tosca would always reply, "He will have. He is from Monterrey."

Thrift was her second requirement. Since her husband-to-be must have money, it followed that he must know how to hang onto it. She was very thrifty herself. The other maidens used to chide her for wearing out all her aunts' and cousins' old clothes, and they would suggest that she go and purchase a striking new outfit for herself next payday. But Tosca always replied, "No, *que horror!*" She was saving her money. Thus, beaux who tried to impress her with lavish expenditures were never given a second chance, and yet she couldn't work up any interest in the poor young men who only wanted to walk around the block and hold hands.

Then we had Socorro who, when she starved, had admirers to burn, but who when driven to food, got instantly very fat and lost them all.

"Why do they mind, Meesus," she sobbed on my shoulder, "if a girl is fat before marriage? Because all the girls get fat right away afterward." I could not answer this question, logical as it was, for a great many Mexican girls do indeed get fat after marriage, and stay that way, so all I could advise was that when she found a prospective husband she liked, she must simply refuse nourishment entirely until she got his name on the license and the holy water sprinkled on them both.

"Look at it this way," I told the dear thing, when I saw tears standing in her eyes as she watched the skinny little girls eat peanuts and chocolate drops while they typed. "Just look at it this way. You are going to eat the biggest wedding breakfast a bride ever ate. Just manage to hold off until then."

Maria Teresa was one of the skinny ones. She had no curves at all, and this can be a worry. But she had worked out one of the strongest weapons known in the unremitting war of the sexes. She had developed a deep, throaty, purring, Dietrich-like voice for answering the telephone, a voice that suggested all the curves anyone would want.

"*Buenoooooo*" she would croon, taking the phone up from its cradle, and with that single word she implied an invitation to come and see her sometime. Many gentlemen hastily took the alluring bait and rushed right over and upstairs to see what was on the other end of the line. To their complete befuddlement, on arrival they would encounter a fifteen-year-old innocent, her brown hair in two little pigtails, bobby socks on her thin little shanks, pimples on her forehead, and horn-rim glasses hiding her really lovely intelligent brown eyes. She hopefully bought large brassières and filled them out with cotton, and put castor oil on her eyelashes, to make them grow, and drank lemon tea to clear her skin, and asked me for ballet exercises to do in secret to fill out her calves. But though she got beaux in droves when she spoke, she lost them by the dozen when they set eyes on her.

That voice of luscious charm was certainly potent, though. She once gave me a very bad quarter of an hour when, after talking softly into the mouthpiece and seemingly having a delicious flirtation with an unknown, she turned to me, passed me the receiver, and said, "Meesus, it is your husband."

Then into our midst, like a queen into the tiring room where her maids are busy, came Rocío. She was of the blood of Spanish grandees and never for one moment, did she forget it. Her people were early Spanish refugees, who came to Mexico even before Franco's time. They were royalists. Rocío had to work to eat, but she harbored no socialistic nonsense about being a brave part of the great laboring classes. She loathed the laboring classes, and felt and lived miles above us. But she was kind as only royalty can be kind, exquisitely courteous as only Spaniards can be, and she was proud as only the Spanish are proud, no matter what their position.

Pursuing my study of how girls in Mexico City met the transcendent problem of how to fascinate the boys, I asked Rocío how she thought suitors should be treated. She turned on me a look all Spanish hauteur, and hissed through clenched teeth, "*Para los hombres, castigo, castigo, y mas castigo!*" and then sailed back to her filing cabinets like a galleon coming home treasure-laden. Translator's note: "For the men, punishment, punishment, and more punishment!"

The willowy, beautiful, and scornful Rocío had the Indian sign on all her suitors. She dispensed punishment with a lavish hand and all male creatures within running distance of her came hastening to eat out of it. Not for nothing is a fascinating female called *muy castigadora* in Mexico.

Rocío was the wise one, for before any of the others, she had married a rich, handsome, and eligible son of a resplendent family.

VI ൠ

LA FAMILIA DESCENDS ON ACAPULCO

Sobre las olas . . .
—OLD MEXICAN WALTZ

Luis's brother Jorge, who was living in Mexico City with his wife and two little girls and tiny baby, was, Mamacita told me, her favorite. She said this with all the frankness of a mother of ten, who just can't help having one or two favorite children.

"But why?" I asked her, feeling that my dependable, always-on-time, dignified Luis should not thus be lightly tossed aside.

"Why? Because Jorge is *alegre*," she answered. "He makes me laugh, and besides, he sings."

They were good reasons. Jorge was always surrounded by laughter . . . shrill children's laughter, guffaws from the men, titters and giggles from the girls and women. He was a born entertainer and a marvelous mimic, and he never forgot anything ridiculous or amusing that anyone ever said or did. It instantly became part of his repertoire. He was, therefore, always the center of a little laughing, half-hysterical group, which egged him on. We have a picture of Jorge at some meeting of the Treviño tribe, surrounded by Luis, Roberto, Ricardo, and Porfirio, his brothers; he is smiling, having just told some anecdote, but each of the brothers is in some position of exquisite torture from having laughed to the point of pain.

He kept his children in an uproar of comedy, teaching them to be straight men and feed him lines, or to play certain necessary roles whenever he gave the cue. For example, when the baby Chiquis was bad, he would snatch her up and an-

nounce "I'll have to operate," and putting her down on a sofa
he would go into his act. Nena and Chacha, the older girls,
would be instantly transformed into surgical nurses, and would
pretend to slap surgical instruments into his outstretched hand
as he called for them: "Hammer! Saw! Potato masher! Egg
beater! Chocolate whip! Scissors!" and so on, until everyone,
including the little nurses, was dissolved in mirth.

Maria Luisa, his wife, was of French origin, with all the
practical, artistic, and homemaking gifts of that race. Jorge,
who loved the United States, preferred to be called George,
and he called his wife Mary. (Though he sometimes addressed
her as McClure, when he wanted to put on an act in which
she had to be the butler.) While George presided over his
admirers and gales of laughter surrounded him, Mary was usually busy whipping up the North Mexican dishes he loved,
or the French *plats* of her childhood. They ate Mexican
machacado (jerky) in chile sauce with wheat tortillas (a poor
man's dish but delicious), or *coq-au-vin*, according to the state
of the exchequer.

Jorge and Luis looked very much alike, though Luis was
thin, and Jorge weighed well over two hundred pounds.
Maria Luisa (Mary) used to call them Before and After. (Before and After taking cod-liver oil.)

We fell into the habit, when our children were small, of
meeting on Sundays at our house, for just as Jorge was Mamacita's favorite, he was also Luis's favorite brother, and for the
same reasons.

George and his family would tumble out of a cab in front
of our house, George tightly encased in a baseball suit and
with a small baseball cap perched on his shock of thick black
curls; he would be carrying four or five baseball gloves. We
provided the bat and ball, a pitcher (Luis) and a couple of
fielders (Guicho and Wiki). Uncle George made do with that
sort of team.

Mary, Nena, Chacha, and Chiquis would tumble after.
Mary was usually carrying a sack from which protruded about

a yard of dead fish, and the little girls would have their arms full of fruits. Nena and Chacha would run for my apron drawer and pull out aprons to tie around their small waists; Mary would start laboring over her fish in the kitchen. Out in the garden George and his satellites would smack balls through windows, thunder around the bases tearing up grass, and generally create havoc. George was umpire, first baseman, catcher and anything else needed, as well as snatcher-out-of-danger of the baby, Chiquis, and all to a running commentary of instructions and imitations, while the other Treviños whirled around him, trying to keep up, to stop laughing, and to follow instructions properly, or at least realize what they were supposed to be doing.

Nena, plump and dark and the picture of her father, played baseball whenever she could get into the act, and made excuses to pass the candy dish inside the house as often as possible. Chacha, who was slim and blue-eyed like her mother, was also like her in activity and in the practical arts. Little Chacha was my beater of eggs and my peeler of apples and my shucker of peas; she set the table and fetched and carried. From these three little girls I learned much of the life of schoolgirls in Mexico City.

As we were a big family, and my dining-room table is one piece, with no "leaves" to set in, we used to organize a first and a second table. First table was for the grown-ups, and second-table, inside the breakfast alcove, was for the small fry. We were all greatly embarrassed—we "mature" people—when, one day, our conversation about the rising price of eggs had fallen to a sudden silence and we heard the little piping voices from the second table.

"No, I prefer Beethoven's Ninth," said one, and another countered with, "My favorite is the Tchaikovsky Piano Concerto."

The education of Nena and Chacha had been as swift as my little boys' with regard to reading and writing. Both read before they went to school and wrote legibly by the end of second grade. (It is still a sign of good breeding and good education to write a fine legible hand in Mexico, and only signatures with which gentlemen decorate their checks are absolute masterpieces of curlicues, scratches, and mystic abbreviations.) By the time they were eight, each little girl could sew an acceptable seam, knit such things as scarfs, and crochet doilies. They made quantities of doll's clothes, and many embroideries . . . that is, Chacha did. Nena became a teller of tales, the bedtime narrator for her little sisters, and she bribed them with wonderful adventure tales and fairy stories, to do her household tasks for her. Because, by the time they were ten, they were also supposed to be able to cook breakfast, and even prepare dishes for the *merienda* (supper).

The little girls seemed unaware of sex per se, and took their male cousins for granted, though Mary and I had talked over the Sunday family meetings with a view to letting the girls know that boys are only human and the boys ditto about girls, since both went to schools where the sexes are not mixed at all. Yet both these little girls had all the historic wiles of the female. They loved going through my perfume collection and my boxes of necklaces and earrings; they loved dressing up and "going to call"; they adored little boxes and purses and all sorts of ribbons and other frippery. They could be kept quiet for hours experimenting with lipstick and eyebrow pencil, yet the creatures for whom all these arts and coquetries were destined simply had not yet heaved into sight, at least not in their consciousness. Guicho and Wiki were merely cousins.

Uncle George was an actor by profession, a singing actor, who had started out in opera, with a fine robust tenor, but who had found that engagements in opera companies were few and far between, whereas a comic entertainer was always in demand. Mamacita learned of this in a rather shocking manner one year in Monterrey.

George had been away from home for years, studying voice in Mexico City. Like most sons, he was not a voluminous letter writer, and Mamacita fondly believed, when his telegram came saying that he was to have a professional appearance in Monterrey, that he would come out on the stage in black tails and white tie and launch into "Celeste Aida." Rather rashly, she got up a party for the opening, and she bullied everyone into appearing in evening dress and all his best real and imitation jewels. The fact that the engagement was announced for an outdoor dancing pavilion didn't really deter her, for after all, she had studied singing in Mexico City in her youth, and had heard the great Caruso when he gave a concert in the bullring.

Nevertheless, she was unprepared for what she saw when the MC called out "Treviño, Carr, and Esperon." Uncle George and his two cronies rushed out into the spotlight arrayed in tramp's costumes—broken shoes, patched shirts, and baggy trousers. They wore false noses and funny mustaches, and worst of all, Uncle George had some patent arrangement in his baggy pants so that when he heaved them up, and let go, his belly seemed to bounce down on the floor and then snap up into place. It was done with a weighted elastic globe inside, and as it hit the floor, there was a fine "*Boom!*" from the drummer in the orchestra. Poor Mamacita was completely mortified when this happened, and burst into tears. But she controlled herself, drew herself up to her scant five feet and began to sweep out, in high disdain. But she made the mistake of looking back. Jorge, her darling Jorge, her favorite, had begun to tell a joke, in his inimitable way. She laughed. She laughed so hard that she had to hang onto Papacito's arm, and in the end, the whole party went back to their table. Thereafter she attended Jorge's act every night of the engagement.

He continued to sing, and very beautifully, but mostly privately at parties and at home, when people would let him off from telling jokes and doing imitations. In time, Mamacita was almost reconciled, though never entirely. She dreamed of seeing him as the dashing Duke in Rigoletto, or dying in lyric beauty as Cavaradossi in Tosca.

One day Uncle George arrived at our house with a wonderful proposition. We had a car, but he had a friend who had a house in Acapulco. This friend had offered it to Jorge for a week, and as it had four bedrooms, we could all go . . . in our car. In those days Acapulco was a long, tiring drive of some twelve to fourteen hours, all curves, but the vision of a sparkling sea at the end of the journey, and best of all a furnished house free was tremendously enticing. Mary and I got together and made our plans. I would roast a leg of lamb and a big chunk of beef; cold meats would be wonderful at the shore, and we wouldn't have to cook. Mary sent her maid down to Acapulco on the bus (which took all night), and early in the dark of a summer morning, we started out.

Luis drove. Uncle George, Wiki, and Chacha occupied the front seat with him. Mary, the baby, Nena, Guicho, and I, in addition to the baggage, brought up the rear. Singing joyously, we started out. But trouble started in with the first curves. Mary's three little girls had queasy stomachs. First they groaned and wanted to stop the car. Then it was too late.

"Might as well keep on going," urged Uncle George glumly. "It's only another ten hours, and I don't think they could possibly fill up the whole car by then."

We were in no state to exhibit ourselves to the scrubbed and clean tourists happily thronging the quaint streets of Taxco, so we kept steadily on past that enchanting town, sitting atop its silver mines.

We labored on until we got to a stretch of fairly level road. There we decamped and tried to clean up the children and the car with river water. Uncle George, on whom had fallen most of the two little girls' breakfast, simply tore off his shirt and threw it away, and continued forward in undershirt.

Somewhat calmed, we climbed into the car again and braced ourselves for five hours more. The curves began again, and once more we heard the preliminary groans. "I forbid you to vomit!" shouted Mary, at the end of her wits, and she was promptly disobeyed.

Worse was to come. Two wasps got into the car through the open window. One bit the baby, who had been quiet, and the other stung Wiki. Accompanied by groans and retching, by howls and shrieks, we finally achieved Acapulco, and made it to the loaned cottage by the sea, where we dreamed of showers with lots of soap and long cool splashings in the bathtub.

But while the cottage was ours, and properly furnished with a big terrace and a divine view, plenty of beds, and four showers . . . there was no water. It was by then dark night, far too late to go to the water company and sign papers asking to have it turned on. And there was no light, either; we would have to go to the electric light company also. But we didn't mind that so much. We found a few bits of candle.

Luis and George, provided with buckets, went down to the ocean and brought back tepid water from the bay. We stripped our children and sponged them off, fed them sandwiches, and put them to bed. Finally nothing was heard but the soft swishing of the Pacific, George's exhausted stentorian snores, dreamy whimpers from the children, and Luis's steady moan with a migraine, "Ay yi yi yi yi, ay yi yi yi yi."

In the morning Mary and I, with the newly arrived and exhausted maid, went to market and bought eggs, cornflakes, buns, and coffee, and fixed breakfast. The Pacific shone like a sapphire, and the air was soft. We all went swimming. The water and light were switched on at the cottage. Life began to be worth living again. But the roasts I had planned to get us through the week were gone by the end of the second day and we faced the prospect of cooking for our herd, whose appetites seemed to increase by the hour.

The town of Acapulco clings to the shore around a perfect curve of bay. Points extend out into the ocean like arms, enclosing the safe waters of the harbor; on an island just outside is a lighthouse, which sends silvery beams sweeping over the town at intervals all through the night. Acapulco was for centuries a sleepy tropical port, visited romantically each year until about 1815 by the Manila galleons during the time that

Spain held the Philippines, and occasionally by coastal freighters. About thirty years ago it was "discovered" to be one of the most beautiful settings for a resort in the Americas, with better beaches and bluer water than the Riviera, and now it has been given over to many luxury hotels, summer villas, yachts, and ski clubs. But when we visited it, Acapulco was still far from its present elegance, and retained much of the charm of a provincial port.

On the third day, while diving through a great comber at Hornos Beach, Uncle George dived right through his trunks too, and these, after a tantalizing moment in view, were sucked under and away and we never saw them again. When he learned the awful truth, we saw Uncle George's large white form putting out for the open sea in a desperate crawl. Far out, he yodeled for help, and Luis then began a tour of all the shops trying to find some bathing trunks size 42, and finally came by a pair in red cotton, printed with large yellow pineapples. Buckety-buckety he hurried back to the beach, got into his own trunks again, and began the swim out to where Uncle George was paddling about in growing anxiety. At last they met. There was a furious shower of spray as Uncle George maneuvered himself into the rescue trunks, and then the two began their swim back to shore. Meanwhile Mary had left her watch by her towel, and as she ran back down to the shore to welcome back the long floating husband, the watch "became smoke" as the Mexicans say. It was stolen. Small wonder that after supper at the cottage, Luis and George went out to buy themselves a comforting beer together somewhere in the town.

"They won't be back until morning," Mary told me darkly, after we had bedded the children and given the maid the evening off to stroll on the beach. "George will find cronies . . . he always does . . . and he will be telling about his adventure over more and more beer. Well, thinking of that possibility, I sent Maruca out to buy you and me a bottle of gin."

So, through the lovely, long tropical night, we sat on the terrace and drank Tom Collinses, our children mercifully slept, the great beam of the lighthouse silver-plated us every five minutes, and we remained in our deck chairs a long time. Sometime during the night our husbands came home. We don't know just when; we woke up, on the terrace, in morning light.

The next day my little Guicho began to cry with an earache. The throbbing ear felt eased only when it rested on Mima's shoulder; that left Mary and Maruca to wrestle with the cooking for ten people. Being an energetic and practical French housewife, Mary took a long look at the heap of dirty clothes in the hall, and having cooked, she washed. She washed everything . . . shirts and dresses and little pants and towels and sheets. Everything. Maruca rinsed and hung out, and attended the cooking pots. The next morning when we awoke, there was a new smell and a new sound. It was raining. It rained all day, steadily. While the clothes flapped wetly on the line, the Treviño family sat around in bathing suits. These had to be taken off once in a while and then we had only one set of underwear each.

So Uncle George passed a law. The law was that everybody was invisible until he spoke, and when not speaking, he became invisible again. Moreover, just to take care of everything, when one spoke, one became visible only from the neck up. This was a wonderful law and set everybody at ease. Mary cooked in pants and bras, I nursed Guicho in my bikini, and everybody went around in small clothes. The baby went here and there (she was learning to walk) in a knotted handkerchief.

But poor little Guicho was visible all the time, his sick ear on Mima's invisible shoulder, and we could find no comfort for him. At last we were able to dry clothes enough for me to go in search of a doctor for him. The doctor gave penicillin shots (which were rather new then), and ear drops, and prescribed hot packs, but the child's misery was unabated. Actually his earache lasted until, at the end of our glorious ten days in glamorous Acapulco (as the ads say), we drove groaning and vomiting around the curves again, and got home. Just as we drew up to our own red *zaguán* in San Angel, and Mary conducted the little girls into my house to sponge them off once more, the penicillin took hold, and Guicho lifted his ear from my shoulder and smiled.

We often speak of our vacation in Acapulco. Uncle George did imitations of everything that happened, from the curves and the wasp through the loss of his trunks, to the invisibility program and the earache. He even recalled a political speech he had made one morning from our terrace, with all the most patriotic clichés and all the same old promises and the usual denunciations of the party in power, to a flock of vultures, who were nesting in a tree nearby. The vultures paid courteous attention until George ran out of words, and then they all rose and flapped away into the distance.

We remember everything that happened and we laugh ourselves into insensibility.

"A week in Acapulco, in glorious Technicolor!" trumpets George, and we all scream with mirth.

Forgotten are our miseries en route and in the cottage, the wasps, the earache, the stolen watch, and Uncle George's Gargantuan sufferings, trunkless, in the briny deep. We remember only that we were all together, that there was love and laughter, and that we reveled in the blue waters of the Pacific.

"Wasn't it wonderful?" we ask one another. "Wasn't it fun? Didn't we have a marvelous time?"

VII ஃ

THE WAR OF THE GARDEN WALLS

A quien no le gusta el caldo, taza y media.

While I labored in the mornings, and worried over my little mongrels in the afternoons, I became involved in a kind of personal row which took up all my attention for a time. Perhaps my readers can dredge in their memories and find an analogy. The fact is, I had a fight with my next-door neighbor.

Doña Fela was a widow and childless. She was young; blonde, quite pretty, with deep tragic eyes, an elegant figure. One might think she would have remarried, but this does not often happen in Mexico, perhaps because there is always a new crop of beauteous young creatures of seventeen coming on the marriage market, and Mexicans traditionally prefer youth to experience. She lived quietly alone. It seemed that she had two intense dislikes—children and animals. She called on me when I first moved into my house in San Angel and told me that she was very pleased to see that I didn't have any children or any dogs.

"My children are coming with the next busload of furniture," I told her, "and I have promised them a dog."

She looked as if she had swallowed a bad oyster, and left.

My garden was divided from hers by a hedge of shrubs called *truenos*. It seemed quite thick and secure, so I bought my sons a little dachshund whom they named Tipo, which means "fellow" or "guy" in Mexican slang. Tipo was a darling, affectionate and good, and a fine watchdog. But he was sociable and he liked to exchange calls with a dog friend a few houses up the block. When he went to visit this friend, he passed across the well-manicured lawn of Doña Fela. Being a really thoughtful dog, he used to leave a small mound on Doña Fela's lawn, in transit, rather than on mine, as is good dog custom. I have had dogs all my life and this sort of exchange is part of dog mores; they won't dirty their own lawns, unless locked in, but other people's dogs think the same way, and they come and leave their mounds on your lawn. It all evens up, and dog owners take this for granted.

Looking back in the "had-I-but-known" school of memoirs, I realize that nothing of what eventually transpired would have come to pass if we had been able to acquire a real Mexican house, with its safe, tall, enclosing walls, its patios, and its absolute control over all the life within. It must be said for the record that we searched high and low for such a house, but were unable to afford any that we found. They were either very large and luxurious and expensive or large and in need of thousands of pesos' worth of modernizing. In such a house, I would have cleaned up after my own dog and all would have been peace and mutual admiration.

I suppose Doña Fela had never had any real dealings with dogs. Maybe she had a trauma. Anyway, she built up a terrific tension over Tipo and canine customs in general, and one evening she called on me with a package. She was trembling, and in a state of nerves which Mexicans call "altered." She gave me the package and asked me to open it. I did so. It contained Tipo's mounds, which she had gathered up and saved.

I passed back the package.

"Since you have gone to the trouble of collecting and preserving these," I told her, "instead of simply turning the hose on them and washing them away, I presume they must have some sentimental value for you. You are quite welcome to keep them."

She shook visibly then and told me that she had merely brought the mounds to prove the dog's perfidy, and to tell me that she wanted him destroyed. At once.

I wouldn't agree to destroy Tipo, but I said I would put

up a fence. I therefore had a double-wire fence strung up among the *truenos*, and bought Tipo a friend, a little animated floor mop we called Raggie, to keep him company and keep him home.

But though my dogs ceased to torment Doña Fela, my sons began to "alter" her nerves in new and dreadful ways. For one thing, they played. Since I had found that I couldn't afford a house with a big, spacious, inner patio, I had turned the boys loose on the lawn in the front yard. Now soccer, volleyball, basketball, and baseball all have one element in common. They involve a ball. It was inevitable that sooner or later a ball should go sailing over the *truenos* to hit and break one of Doña Fela's windows. I hastened over to pay for damage and to promise that it wouldn't happen again, but I was met with a look of such chill distaste that I half-expected her to ask me to have my children destroyed. At once!

I prohibited baseball and passed a law that only volleyball and soccer could be played in the front garden. But one dreadful day an extra heave on the volleyball resulted in its landing on Doña Fela's now utterly pure and sacrosanct lawn. Wiki went to ring her bell and ask for his ball, but the servant who came to the gate advised him that Doña Fela considered that whatever fell on her front lawn was legally her property, and that she didn't like Wiki well enough to make him a gift of anything.

I talked this over with my husband, who said, "Now don't let that lawyer blood that runs in your family get you into any rows down here, because I am too busy earning a living to stop everything and bail you out of jail. Let the ball go; I'll buy them another one. And tell them to play only on the far side of the garden."

I agreed.

However, life is a repetitive business, tending to follow a pattern, and it was bound to transpire that yet another ball should one day sail over the *truenos* and come to rest on Doña Fela's lawn.

This time Wiki did not ring the bell. With admirable practicality he decided that the thing to do was climb the fence, pick up the ball, climb back, and bother nobody. He scaled the fence and went to get his ball, intending to scuttle home fast. But a hand fell on his shoulder. Doña Fela bore the screaming and struggling child inside her house, locked him in a dark closet and called, not me, but the police. In due course the police turned him over to me, hysterically crying and frightened almost to death. He wasn't quite five.

Despite Luis's wise injunctions, my lawyer's blood all rose to my head and I marched over to the house of Doña Fela and demanded to see her. When she appeared, tight-lipped, in answer to my summons, I lashed out at her.

The plaintiff did there and then declare, allege, and shriek, as follows: "You harpy! How dare you frighten a little child in this way? I loathe the sight of you! I repeal the Good Neighbor policy! The curse of ten lawyers and fifty gypsies on you!"

"You shouldn't have said that about the gypsy curse," worried Luis later, when I had recounted the events of the day. "Now she will be afraid of you."

"I hope she is," I muttered, feeling considerably altered in my nerves, too. "Maybe she will behave more like a human being if she thinks a witch is living next door."

Then my cook, who had been away for a weekend visit to her *tierra* or home country, arrived back with a present for me. A live chicken. She proposed to fatten the chicken and kill and roast it for my saint's day. She therefore tied it by one leg to a tree in our tiny back yard. But chickens are contrary creatures, and it was my fate, it was written in the stars ten thousand years ago, that this chicken should get loose and should make for the front lawn of Doña Fela as fast as its silly legs would carry it. From a window, paralyzed with horror, I watched Doña Fela swoop out, gather up my chicken and disappear with it into her house. Later she came out with stakes and built a small stockade. Inside this she put my chick with a measure of corn, and lest I should not understand her plan, she sent her maid over to inform me that she intended to fatten and eat my chicken herself, on *her* saint's day.

Generations of lawyers in my past rose up and whispered to me that this was not equity. I went to the local *delegación* or police station, chose a policeman from among the many who were standing around picking their teeth, and demanded that he retrieve my chicken for me. But when he appeared, in his dark blue uniform, at Doña Fela's gate, he was told that she was not in, though I, who accompanied him, saw a curtain twitch. He then advised me to "raise an act" as they say in Spanish, a legal procedure which might involve telling my true age, so I hesitated. Finally I decided just to give up. I never had any luck with chickens anyhow. I would just write the whole thing off as profit and loss, mostly loss. I would buy a large fat dead chicken and have my cook roast it for my saint's day. Less wear and tear all around.

But a few days later, on arrival home from my labors in the tourist office, I found a formal notice that I must appear before the judge at the *delegación* and show cause why I should not receive from the hand of Citizeness Fela one chicken.

I was startled at the turn events had taken. It hardly seemed equity that I should be called into court to state why I should not receive my personal chicken that had been wrongfully reduced to possession on the front lawn of my enemy. But as Luis wasn't home to advise me, and some dire trouble might result from my not answering the summons, I put on a dignified dark dress and a pale make-up for court, and proceeded to the *delegación* at the hour specified.

A small harried judge was having difficulty in convincing an inebriated gentleman that he had disturbed the peace, and finally simply banged his gavel and sentenced the offender to spend the night in the Carmen jail. Doña Fela and I were then called to the bar of justice. She stood to one side, breathing hard, holding in her left hand my chicken with its feet tied together. The judge consulted his calendar. Then he spoke to Doña Fela.

"What is the trouble?" he asked her, kindly.

"Well," she began cautiously. "This is *her* chicken," she said with a nod in my direction.

"It's no misdemeanor to own a chicken," commented the judge.

"But it got into my garden. I hate animals in my yard. This woman is simply boiling with horrible animals and horrible children and they all get in my yard!"

The judge turned to me, and struck his desk with his gavel.

"Keep your children and your animals out of her garden."

"Yes, your honor. I try."

"And besides, she's a *foreigner!*" hissed Doña Fela.

I thought, By golly, that isn't equity either, so I stepped forward.

"May I speak?" I asked the judge.

"Certainly," said the judge, and he walloped his desk. "Speak."

I drew a deep breath, and remembering the rich organ tones of home and family to which all Mexicans vibrate, I began.

"Yes, your honor. I am a foreigner. I admit it. I came to this country because I married a Mexican, and we have purchased a home here and are raising our two sons here. Mexican boys they are, born here. Mexican citizens. Doña Fela lives alone and has only her own personal preoccupations. Perhaps she doesn't realize that children have to have room to play and shout and animals to love and take care of. What's the matter with my being a foreigner, anyway? The Constitution of Mexico itself says that the wife of a Mexican citizen, making his home for him in Mexico and raising his children here, is entitled to all the rights and protections of the State!"

The judge was getting very emotional and patriotic with my speech, when Doña Fela broke in with a sob.

"But this foreign woman says she hates me!"

Now the judge turned to me, aghast.

"Is this true? Did you say you hate her?"

"I certainly did!" I stamped my foot. "She took my little boy and shoved him in a dark closet and sent for the police to come and get him. She frightened him almost to death and I hate her!"

Furious, the judge turned back to Doña Fela.

"Did you lock up her child, as she says?"

"But he had climbed over my gate and was walking on my lawn!" screamed Doña Fela.

"If I have to say that I love, or even like, this mean señora," I shouted, now quite beside myself, "lock me up! Put me in jail! Shoot me!"

The judge gave up. He whacked his desk and roared, "Give this woman her chicken, and throw the two of them out of here! Next case."

It was pouring rain when we left the court and there was only one cab, so Doña Fela and I frugally shared it home. We rode with averted faces, however, and we did not converse.

When, at dinner, I recounted the events of the afternoon to Luis, he struck his forehead with the palm of his hand in a gesture of intense despair.

"You should never have answered that summons," he groaned. "Now we'll have real trouble. She'll call you to court for every little thing, for slamming doors too hard, for parking too near her gate, for everything!"

But Doña Fela having brooded all night about me and my children and my animals, had got up early in the morning and brought home masons and a truckload of bricks. They set to building a tall wall between her garden and mine. When he came home and saw the progress of the wall, Luis, who had been cold with me, now turned back with the lovelight shining.

"Darling! That's wonderful!" he exulted. "You got her so mad that she is building a wall! Why it would have cost us five thousand pesos to build even a small one! I wish you would have a fight with the people in back. It would be nice to have a wall there too."

In due time, Guicho and Wiki hurled a rock from the top of the servant's staircase, which fell on the head of one of the children of the house in back, removing hide and hair. The irate parents drove off, returning with masons and a truckload of bricks, and began their wall.

We already had a wall on the right-hand side, so at last we were enclosed. Happily isolated, I sat in my garden, with chickens and dogs and shouting boys on every hand. At peace. And in time, I think, before she moved away, Doña Fela forgave me.

VIII

I TRY TO BECOME A PROPER MEXICAN MAMACITA

> *Cada cabeza un mundo.*
> —OLD MEXICAN SAYING

But my war with Doña Fela had unnerved me, and I was very much ashamed when my father wrote me, in mild reproof. "Honey, I never thought you would become a battleax." I decided to call on some gentle-mannered Mexican families and consider their ways. Also, I thought, I had better look up a few friends who are also bringing up children with only one Mexican parent, and see how they manage.

First I went to visit Pilar. Pilar is of Spanish origin, but born and brought up in Mexico, and her husband is a Mexican of the old school. She had children older than mine. I was pleasantly impressed when Chela came in to ask her mother if she might go to the movies with her girl friend from school, and Pilar answered calmly, "Only if your father gives permission. And you may not phone him at the office until after five." Chela was fifteen years old at the time. So the upshot was, she didn't go to the movies.

I had lingered a little while in Pilar's house, as Luis was to call for me and take me home. So I saw Don Ramón arrive home, and I saw how his children greeted him. Each one took his hand and kissed it, then kissed his cheek. It was all formal and correct and dignified, and the children, though they seemed to have few privileges, were respectful and affectionate.

I brought up the subject that night, after supper, when it was time for my little boys to go to bed.

"I think you must kiss your father's hand for good night," I told my sons.

Guicho flatly refused.

"It's sissy," he said.

"I will," volunteered Wiki, "if Wees will tell me the story about Tijerina!" This was a long, continued adventure story about Tijerina, or Mr. Scissors, who walked across the country in great strides, rescuing good little boys from dragons and pursuing bad little boys to where the dragon's cave lay, belching smoke and sulphur fumes. This story had gone on for years, and Luis was getting a little tired of it.

"All right," agreed Luis, and extended his hand, but Wiki gave it a Tipo-type kiss, very wet, and there was instant pandemonium.

I gave up on the hand kissing.

I returned to my American mores about many things but Mamacita, herself, threw me off center once at a meal, when she refused her vegetables. "*Para caballo viejo, poco verde*" ("For the old horse, little green grass"), she pronounced, and then, to make it stick, she intoned an old Spanish proverb, "*De lo que come el grillo, poquillo, poquillo!*" ("Of what the grasshopper eats, very little, very little!"). I managed to sneak carrots and beets into the menu sometimes, but it was a long time before anyone would eat lettuce or coleslaw again.

I complained about this to Malenita, who had become one of my closest friends. Her ancestry takes a line or two of explanation. She is Mexican, and descended on her mother's side from a long line of titled Spaniards and patriotic Mexicans, one of whom is still depicted on a common Mexican coin. But Malenita means Mary Ellen, and even among her mother's people, there were many Irish. Her father was pure Irish. He had come out to Mexico to make his fortune, and had been told to look up some distant cousins of the same name. He did so and his eye fell on the gentle and pious face of a sixteen-year-old daughter of the house. He gave nobody any peace until he married her and Malenita was their only daughter.

"Mamacita won't eat vegetables," I told Malenita, "and now my children will eat nothing but rice and meat and beans. I'm distracted."

"It won't matter much, either way, I think," answered Malenita, in whose voice there is still something of the Irish melody she heard on her father's lips. "My grandmother once took me aside," she confided, "and said to me, 'Never eat any vegetables my dear; they are very indigestible.' And I've always had perfect health."

"But of course, you eat them!" I cried, aghast.

"Never touch them," said Malenita, "except a potato, once in a while."

In my many visits to Malenita's, to have tea with her, we always had great talks about painting and literature and the state of the world. We were never bothered by noisy or whining children. Malenita had strong-minded ideas about the young and felt they should not be allowed to roam about at will, like a herd of young elephants. Even at her table there was pleasant conversation, on an adult level, with an occasional child passing the butter and saying softly, "Might I have another piece of cake, please?"

Malenita proclaimed that there were three things she wanted from her children: obedience, respect, and quiet. But she said if she could only have one, she would plump for quiet.

One day we got to talking about education.

"I suppose," she pried gently, "you will send your children to the American school?"

"In the first place, I can't afford it," I told her. "And in the second place, my sons were born here. I think they should learn Mexican history and geography first. We aren't at all sure we will be able to send them to school in the States. If we were both Americans, there would be no question; we would, of course, want our children to be abreast of the American school curriculum. But I am the one who chose to marry a

Mexican and live here; I think it would be wrong to try to bring up my children as if they were little aliens in their native land."

Malenita poured another cup of tea.

"You'll be criticized," she warned me.

But I did not regret my decision.

My children went to a Mexican Catholic school, where religion is taught under another title. But discipline also is taught, and the school progress in such basic subjects as mathematics, reading and writing, history and geography is swift, because the schools do not occupy themselves with entertaining the children in any way. It is assumed that they can do that for themselves very well when classes are over, and no time is lost "integrating" them either. The children integrate with a vengeance as soon as class is dismissed. The Mexican view is that school is where you learn. Mexican schools are old-fashioned and strong on homework, and the teachers have never gone over to the idea that learning should be a form of play. My children came home wearing gold stars on their foreheads when they were good, and gold medals at the end of the year. And when they didn't know their lessons, they were put down in a chair in a quiet place and made to stay there until they did learn.

The teaching brothers had several good dodges for a warm and sleepy study hour, too. Wiki told me that the brother in charge of study hall set an alarm clock on his desk, where it rang shrilly every ten minutes.

"We will say a Hail Mary, now," he would announce, and all would pronounce the words of the prayer. This was pious and good training; it also woke up the student body at regular intervals.

My husband and I sent our boys to private schools, where they were taught their religion, for two reasons.

First, no responsible Mexican citizen will send his children to a public school, taking the place some poor child should have, if he can possibly pay for a private school. Mexico is struggling to achieve enough schools, and though many

groups of private citizens, in clubs, or in separate foreign
colonies, have given schools, there is still a scarcity of buildings
and of teachers. Second, Luis and I were agreed that the time
to teach a child his religion and integrate it with his life—make
it part of his thoughts, motives, and actions—is when he is
young, in the school years. We wanted our children brought
up in our faith every day and not just on Sundays and holidays.

Sometimes, I admit, I felt lonely for the old ways of my
childhood.

In my zeal to be a completely Mexican mother I paid
attention to the admonitions of the *frailes* in the school, and
I did not have a Christmas tree.

"The Christmas tree is a pagan custom which has become
identified almost exclusively with one or two foreign countries," they told the children at school.

So, we had a Nacimiento, or a Crêche. I bought the moss,
the little figurines of animals, the small stable, and the images
representing Mary, Joseph, and the Holy Child. We set aside
a corner of our sala and built some little hills with boxes and
bits of carpet. Then we set up our stable, hung the star of
Bethlehem above, and placed the Holy Family within (but
without the Infant Jesus, until Christmas Eve). Then, there
is in Mexican homes, a tender ceremony. A little before midnight the image of the Child Jesus is laid in His mother's
arms and all the gentle animals are placed around the cradle,
watching with wondering eyes. The shepherds stand in awe on
their little moss-covered hills, and far away, the Three Wise
Men come nearer.

Before the child is laid in Mary's arms, the mother of the
household rocks Him in her Mass veil, and sings a lullaby to
Him, then all the family kneel and kiss the image of the Holy
Child, and give Him to His mother. Still kneeling, all repeat
the Rosary. Then the whole family attends midnight Mass.

After my first disappointment in not having the shining
Christmas tree and tinsel and Santa Claus and the reindeer
and the other beautiful rites of my childhood, I came to love

the religious devotion and tenderness of the Nacimiento. Little by little, I, too, began to speak of El Niño Jesus, instead of Kris Kringle.

After the Mass, we would come home to chocolate and buns, and the next day we often went to Uncle George's house to eat the traditional Spanish *bacalao*, or dried codfish cooked in oil, tomatoes, and many spices—a kingly dish. But often too, we would all meet at our house in San Angel, and I would bake the Christmas stuffed turkey with that strange accompaniment which my cook called "the señora's gray-bee," onions in cream sauce (also a queer thing to eat, my servants thought), and what came to be Uncle George's favorite "pudding boiled in a rag." This last was our family Christmas pudding, a recipe of my great-grandmother's.

As the twelve days after Christmas go by, the figures of the Wise Men are moved nearer and nearer to the stable in Bethlehem, where the Holy Child lies. On January 6, they arrive, with their presents of jewels, perfumes, and incense. This is the Day of the Magi, or the Three Kings, and it is on this day, in imitation of the Three Kings who came to worship, that presents are exchanged.

We gave our presents on the Day of the Kings (Twelfthnight), and cut our Rosca de Reyes, a big circular coffee cake, to see who would find in his portion, the tiny china image of the Holy Child. He who found it was expected to give a party on Candlemas Day, which in Mexico is observed on the first of February.

But, in deference to my memories, we also gave presents on Christmas Day. So our children profited doubly by their mixed inheritance. They received clothes and books and candy and fruits on December 25, and toys on the Day of the Kings.

While my children sometimes came out ahead, because of their gringa Mima, sometimes she got them into trouble, too. My husband often, when worried beyond endurance, accused me of wanting too much independence, and truth to tell, I wanted a certain measure of it for my sons as well. For this reason, perhaps wrongly, I did not tell him of one of their activities.

My little boys, aged eight and ten, came to me one vacation time, and suggested a plan which I thought a good one. They wished to ride a different bus or streetcar every day, over its whole route, and thus learn all about Mexico City. I approved, provided the necessary cash, and required only that they never get off the bus or trolley, until it had made its entire round-trip and they were back at their starting point, or transfer point, to the home-coming vehicle. They were busy and interested every day, and they could recite to me the streets crossed and districts visited on every means of municipal transport in Mexico, D.F.

Now it transpired that we were invited to Uncle George's apartment for a great gathering of the clans on a certain evening during school vacations. Here I must explain that in Mexico City schools close around mid-November and take up again toward the middle of February. I had errands to do, and I knew that I would not have time to get all the way to San Angel before I was due at the apartment. So I telephoned home, told Maria to see that the little boys were washed and in clean shirts, and told her to put them aboard the streetcar that passed one block from the apartment George always called "Treviño Manor."

By bad luck, my husband arrived at the apartment shortly after I did, and raised his black brows at me.

"Where are the children?"

"They are coming in by trolley."

"With Maria?"

"No, alone."

At this news, he literally had a fit. Every muscle jerked, and he turned first white and then dark red.

"It's impossible! It's terrible!" he sputtered. "Those two little children *alone* on a streetcar! And it's *dark!*" He rushed to the telephone to tell Maria to keep the boys at home, that he would come for them in the car. Or she could bring them in a taxi.

Maria reported that they already were on their way. Luis raved. He was ready to call the police. He ran out to wait on the corner, then he ran back into the apartment to scold me further for my dreadful, independent, gringa ideas. In the midst of a second tirade, the little boys strolled in, calm and happy, without a mark on them.

"Don't feel so bad, Wees," comforted Guicho. "We've been going on everything and we know every stop on every bus and streetcar in Mexico. Mima let us go."

I got another desperate black look.

"But what if people spoke to them, asked them to get off and have an ice cream . . . or anything?" cried Luis.

"Well naturally, I briefed them about speaking to strangers, and they were told never to answer, either," I defended.

"That was easy," explained Wiki. "When anybody spoke to us, we always said, 'Spik Inglis plis. No onnerstan Spanis.' And everybody would say, 'Crazy American children. Their parents let them out alone.'"

This was fuel to Luis's fury. When we were home and the children safely in bed, I was ordered never again, under any circumstances, to allow them to voyage around the city unaccompanied. I humbly gave my promise; they had learned their way around and need never be frightened of being lost now, anyhow.

Luis was angry with me for several days, and was reduced to cooking his morning egg for himself. Somehow, when I cook it, it always tastes better, or so he had led me to believe. But now, I was not to be allowed to perform this wifely office. Maria was ordered to cook his egg and she never did it right. Her nerves were finally "altered" by the incessant criticism, and came a morning when she refused to have anything else to do with Luis's egg. I then heard him giving her a lesson in the kitchen.

"First, you chop up half an onion, very fine." Sound of

chopping. "Then a chile serrano, very fine." Chop, chop.
"Then you peel, seed, and chop a tomato." Demonstration.
"Then you put into the frying pan, this much oil. Then you
put in the onion, and say one Pater Noster." Both repeated the
Our Father in Spanish. "Then the chile, and the tomato.
Another Padre Nuestro." Again the devotional murmur.
"Then, at the last, in goes the egg, well-beaten, and you say
three Hail Marys." The prayers were said, and Luis bore his
breakfast, absolutely perfect, to the table, where he consumed
it in silence.

Perhaps the prayers softened his heart. Anyhow, he forgave me, and life went on.

I had to agree with Luis, not about the gaining of independence at an early age, but about conformity to important
customs in my country of adoption, when I considered the
case of my English friend, Phyllis. She was married to a Mexican and had born her daughter in Mexico, where they lived and
had their house. But only England was ever referred to as
"home." In a way, this was hard on her husband, but one
must honor the fierce and touching loyalty of English ways.
It is the sort of thing that makes them dress for dinner in the
jungle and swelter through soup, fish, joint, and savory, when
lesser breeds would give up and just lie in a hammock sipping
coconut milk.

Yet my friend Malenita and I used to wonder, sometimes,
what would happen if Phyllis's daughter might one day remember that she was only half-English and actually take to
Mexican ways. What if she did not really carry in her blood
and bones her mother's Anglo-Saxon memories?

We had a glimpse of the result. Came a day when
Phyllis packed her daughter off to finishing school in England.
What was her bewilderment and despair when she received a
letter from the girl moaning that she was homesick.

"But I can't understand it," confided poor Phyllis bleakly.
"How can she be homesick when she's *home?*"

Luis and I fought over a few more yards of terrain, in the

battle of our children; sometimes he made a touchdown; sometimes he was penalized for being off side. Sometimes I performed a dropkick that sailed right between the goalposts. I thought the boys should have an allowance and that they should earn it by cutting the lawn. Luis said they should do no such thing—taking work from a good man who needed it—but that they could wash the car. The allowance he would not agree to. Instead they got their *domingo*, Mexican style. Domingo means Sunday, and it is Mexican family custom to give each child some money on Sunday, with which to go to the movies, buy ice cream, or otherwise indulge in riotous living. I tried to get a *domingo* too, but here I was shouted down.

So we rocked along, sometimes the Mexican team was ahead, and sometimes the Visiting Opponents had the high score.

Generally we both tried to keep our voices lowered and spare the children the vision of their parents in altercation, but as every parent knows, such a schizophrenic life can't go on forever.

One day Guicho came and stood before us and said, with an air of discovery, "You and Wees are fighting."

"We are not," contradicted Luis fiercely, and kissed me, to prove it.

"It's this way," he explained to his son. "She's my cross, and I'm hers."

This explanation suited the boys, and it had to suit me, too.

About this time there was a great scandal in the newspapers about an escaped convict—a dangerous murderer—who had somehow hidden himself in the caves of the Pedregal (or lava flow) near San Angel. The case was exciting and there was much hue and cry. The criminal soon received the press nickname of "The Tiger of San Angel."

One morning, after Luis and I had disagreed severely about long trousers versus short trousers for our eight-year-

old and ten-year-old, he slammed off to his office without saying goodbye to me. I was left to wonder about whether it was
ever worth while to try to have opinions, though married.

The telephone rang about an hour later, and Luis's voice
said, "Hello, Tiger."

I realized that this was both apology and a reassurance
of his affection, so I answered, "Hello."

And from then on, whenever we had a row over anything,
Tiger was the magic word that indicated "All is forgiven,
come home at once." I became the Tiger of San Angel—the
Gringa Leopard who can't change every single one of her spots,
only some of them.

IX &

GUICHO ON WHEELS

> *Carácter y figura, hasta sepultura.*
> —SPANISH PROVERB

I have never been automobile-minded. From the day my
father led away old Frank, whose satiny flanks and velvet
lips I can feel to this day, (though I was only two when
we were friends) and brought home a nasty little Maxwell,
I have never really liked the contraptions. The fact that
Daddy's Maxwell was one of the first cars in Bakersfield,
California, never gave me pride. I only remember the dreadful
Sundays we spent sitting on fences in the country while Daddy
whanged at the Maxwell from underneath it and addressed
himself to the Deity. There were other fearful Sundays, later,
when, after getting up steam in the Stanley Steamer in the
garage, he would drive around to the front door in a great
sibilantly hissing machine which sounded like a teakettle at
the boil. He loved this Stanley Steamer with all his heart but
eventually progressed from it to an Overland, then to a Buick
and to a Cadillac, and at last to a monstrous Pierce-Arrow. I
never felt really en rapport with any of these death dealers,
and to this day I tend to whimper if the speedometer registers
more than forty miles an hour.

I was therefore not prepared to rejoice when I found that
my father's passion for cars had been inherited, in most of its
frenzy, by my oldest son.

When Guicho was five, he spent all his time drawing
automobiles with great care and in much detail. He differen-
tiated among all the makes and could tell their names and
characteristics a mile away, but he had his own names for

them, according to the people he knew who owned that par-
ticular model. Thus one was a Rivera, another a Deek (for
Uncle Dick), one a Sanchez. He spent so much time drawing
automobiles that I was advised by his first-grade teacher in
the Marmua school that I had better warn him that this was
extra-curricular activity. In the end, the school seemed willing to accept him complete, with all his idiosyncrasies, for
when they cast the school play, they wrote in a part of "Little
Artist" for Guicho and ordered me to provide him with a
smock and an oversized beret. "He won't have to learn any
lines," the teacher told me. "All he has to do is sit there on the
stage and draw. Automobiles, of course." He was provided
with an easel, which was in full view of the audience, and he
performed his role perfectly, putting the finishing touches on a
resplendent Deek as the curtain closed.

From the time he was allowed to ride around the city on
buses, he spent every spare minute in automobile display
rooms. By the time he was nine, he was absolutely obsessed
with cars and determined to be a race car driver.

Because he was, and is, temperamentally, a one-hundred
percenter, he thought and talked of nothing but driving until
his father took him to the country and, along a few quiet
roads, taught him to drive. Thereafter, his passion seemed to
subside. But it had been boiling gently within him all the
while, as I learned on a vacation trip home to my parents in
California.

One day a friend of my mother's, Mrs. Derby, came to
tea. She drove up in a new Studebaker, and for the first time,
upon the arrival of a mature visitor, Guicho did not immediately duck out the back door. He remained, quiet and
courteous. He sat at Mrs. Derby's feet and looked at her
soulfully. I finally lured him away with promises of chocolate
in the kitchen, and my mother and Mrs. Derby drank their
tea.

That night, ready for bed in his sleeper suit, Guicho consulted me.

"Has Mrs. Derby got a husband?"

"No. She's a widow."

"Well, then I'll marry her," he told me.

They say mothers always tend to oppose the marriages of their sons, and I fell right into line. I felt the proverbial flash of jealousy, which I rationalized by telling myself that the gap between their ages was too much. Ten and pushing seventy. I pulled myself together enough to advise Mrs. Derby that she had a suitor. She replied that she was frightfully flattered, and that she had had no idea that her charm, for which she had been famous as a young woman at the turn of the century, was still high voltage.

"I suppose we'll have to postpone the marriage a few years," she mused, "until my bridegroom grows up. But I always did love being engaged!"

Meanwhile, I was reminded of the general perfidy of male creatures, something I almost forget at times. It seemed that Guicho's was not, after all, a pure love. I overheard him talking to his little brother in Spanish. "And as soon as I marry her," he told Wiki, "the car will be mine"—he reasoned as has many a man before him—"and then you and I can drive all over the country!"

I felt it my bounden duty to advise Mrs. Derby of this development, for, after all, it would not be right to allow my mother's good friend to walk into this marriage blind.

"Well, it is a bitter disappointment to me," she commented thoughtfully, "but I don't think I'll break the engagement. I have my pride, you know. And then, besides, why not be practical? I *am* charming just as long as I have my Studebaker, so I might as well be philosophical about the whole thing. You can't have everything, and at my age a bona fide proposal of marriage is something of a triumph. I'd be glad if he could put it in writing. Can he sign his name yet?"

The engagement was a long one, naturally, and just seemed to come quietly unstuck in time. Mrs. Derby always referred to Guicho as her fiancé, and sent him cards at Christmas and on his birthday . . . cards with automobiles on them. She must have taken considerable trouble to find them.

He was faithful, after his fashion. That is to say, he remained crazy about cars.

When Guicho was about eleven, his father had to make a trip to Monterrey for a few days. I kissed him goodbye and he departed, in a taxi, for the airport. I was startled, upon answering the phone a little later, to hear my husband's voice.

"I don't know why," he said, "but I'm afraid Guicho might take the car out. You know how severe the police are about underage children without licenses who are caught driving. Better get the car keys and keep them in your purse, just in case. Goodbye now, just time to get aboard."

I looked for the keys, but I couldn't find them just then, and after a short distracted search, I went out, as I had an engagement. When I returned home, late in the afternoon, the car was gone, and there was no sign of Guicho anywhere. The servants had been washing in the back patio and hadn't noticed anything. Wiki was happily and dutifully occupied with his homework.

I realized that Luis had had some kind of revelation at the airport; it was a case of extra-sensory perception. I sat down to worry and to wait until they brought my child back home to me on a stretcher, or until they phoned me to come and identify his body at some emergency hospital. I had walked over miles of carpet and cried quarts of tears when, about two hours after dark, I heard the familiar purring of our car at the *zaguán*, and my husband's jaunty *beep-beep* signal on the horn, which instructed the maid to fly out and open the gate for him.

While I remained rooted to the sala carpet, I heard the *zaguán* swing open and then the gentle breathing of the car as it nudged softly up the driveway and into the carport. A door slammed. Within a couple of minutes my eleven-year-old (and small for his age) strolled in, looking happy and carefree.

At first I hugged and kissed him, in desperate relief. Then I reproached him.

"Where were you?"

"I just went out for a little drive."

"Where did you get the car key?"

"Where Wees always leaves it. In his bureau drawer under his socks."

"That was stealing!"

"Why? Isn't it our car?"

"Yes, but you know you are forbidden to drive it alone. And you haven't any license. You aren't old enough to have one. Anything might have happened."

"Oh no. I am a good driver. Much better than Wees."

"But you are not allowed to drive without him."

"He isn't here, so how could he go with me?"

My hands were beginning to itch, the first sign that a licking was coming on. But I tried to control myself. I tried to be reasonable and calm. I wanted the facts.

"Don't you realize that you could have had an accident? And if you did, and were lucky enough not to be hurt, you could have had your father's license taken away from him and his car impounded? You are underage and have no license and you know it. We might have had to pay a big fine and damages! And besides, you could have been killed!"

"Well, I wasn't. Nothing happened."

"But if you had been stopped . . . and any policeman could tell, just looking at you, that you're underage!"

I stamped my foot. My control was hanging by a thread.

"Don't get so upset, Mima. Nothing happened, and only you and I know about it. And besides, I thought about that . . . that a policeman might notice that I wasn't eighteen. So I wore a disguise."

"A disguise? What, for Heaven's sake?"

"Wees' old hat, and Uncle George's mustache."

Uncle George often gave impersonations while wearing a mask that fastened over his ears in the form of heavy-rimmed spectacles, to which were attached a large red false nose and a big droopy hay-colored mustache.

My son went out and then returned, wearing his disguise. He was only a child, and he looked very odd, but perhaps, driving along through the dusk, he had simply seemed to be a rather peculiar little man.

"And," added Guicho, "I had a cigar too. A chocolate one. Only I ate it just now, before I came in."

X 🦢

FURRY AND FEATHERED FRIENDS IN MEXICO

Al loco, siempre dale la razón
—PROVERB

Doña Fela, having built her wall, the top of which she adorned with fragments of broken glass, surmounted by several strands of barbed wire—she was taking no chances with the Horrible Treviños—sold her house and moved away.

The very nice people who moved into the house had no sooner installed their furniture than they went out and bought a large galumphing Doberman pinscher pup, which they named Truman, in honor of a certain much-admired person in the "Unait Esteit." (President Truman had laid a wreath on the tomb of the Mexican Boy Heroes, who had fought to the death to defend Chapultepec from invading American soldiers in the somewhat odoriferous Mexican War, of a hundred years before, and this act had, in a few moments, torn down years of dislike and resentment of Americans. It was a master stroke.)

The youngest boy of our new neighbors was named Pepe, and he and Wiki soon became fast friends. He and Guicho and Wiki and Raggie and Truman all rolled and chewed and played happily together, first on our lawn, and then on theirs. We got Raggie through worms, and Truman through having his ears trimmed (he used to lay his head on my knee and tell me about what he suffered through this outrage), and the children through tonsillitis and mumps.

Encouraged, I provided myself with a Mama cat and also a parrot.

I came by the parrot in the following manner. One

Sunday, Luis had given me the *gasto* (the daily food allowance) and with it clutched in my fist, together with a list of purchases to be made, I started toward the market. I was to bring home a roast, two vegetables, tortillas, fruit, and salad greens. But on the way I passed a man who was selling baby parrots. I got no farther. There was one little parrot who sat huddled dejectedly in his sparse green feathers, who looked as if he needed a home and Tender Loving Care. I advanced and cautiously asked his price. The vendor and I began to bargain. About an hour later I went home, the *gasto* spent, with a small green object clinging desperately to my finger.

"Look what I bought!" I chirruped to Luis. He studied the little bird. "Very little meat on it," he observed. "It will never feed us all." He then got in his car and went to market himself, returning with Sunday dinner, while I installed Sinforoso in an appropriate cage and fed him what the man said he ate—bread soaked in coffee and ripe banana. It seemed a heavy diet for a baby, but he flourished.

Sinforoso and I became very thick. He bit other people, but he only pecked me softly and then rubbed the place with his beak, gently, indicating that he was very dangerous, but that he loved me.

Then one day he got sick. I found him cowering miserably in his still scant little green suit. "He has caught a cold," said Maria, the cook, "and now he will die. Because baby parrots never recover from colds."

But I am like the doctors in romantic novels; while there is a breath of life, I fight. I made Sinforoso a little coat of purple wool and pinned it around his shivering little shoulders. I rubbed Vicks VapoRub under his wings and on his beak and on the top of his head. I heated his coffee and mashed his banana, and put a little aspirin in his water. I sat up with him and told him not to worry, everything was going to be all right, and he would bury me some day. One awful day he spent the hours from dawn to dusk with his head under his wing. But he must have drawn in hearty whiffs of Vapo-

Rub, because by night he drew out his head and bit Maria. Came the day when I was able to unpin and remove his coat, and he danced up and down on his perch and fluffed his feathers.

I brought him up carefully and taught him to say "Hello, honey" to ladies, and "Where's your wife?" to men. Then one day, a passing child with a slingshot took aim as he sat on his perch in the garden. I buried Sinforoso with tears, and now I am looking for a big, tough parrot from Chiapas, a parrot with a strong beak, who can defend himself. A parrot a bit like the one who has learned to whistle like a traffic cop and ties up traffic on Juarez Street regularly. People who know this parrot tell me he does it from sheer meanness.

I believe deeply in the continuity of love, and when one pet is gone, I think one should immediately transfer all the affection one felt to some other little creature, and not bury capacity for devotion with memories.

When I lived in Monterrey I had a wonderful golden tiger cat named Policarpo. He was a cat of brains and charm and of extraordinary solemn wisdom. When we moved to Mexico City, we had to make a two-day automobile journey, and I did not know where I would eventually live. So I left Policarpo with Cosme, my husband's boy-of-all-work, and instructed him to build Poli a good stout cage and ship him to me by railway express as soon as I sent the word. I believe now that Policarpo understood the whole conversation. Anyway, he was too smart for Cosme and me. He "became vapor" as the wonderful Spanish saying goes. He disappeared.

When this news was conveyed to me in an apologetic letter from Cosme, I was undone. I sent out SOS calls to Monterrey. I wrote to Adela, my sister-in-law. I sent letters to various friends and neighbors on Morelos Street to ask them to keep an eye peeled for my golden Poli. I prayed to San Antonio, asking him not to get Poli back for me, but only to let me have news that he was all right. As usual San Antonio acted promptly and was disconcertingly literal.

I received a letter from my friend Camille, in Monterrey. Policarpo, she wrote, had appeared. He dropped in one day about five, stayed for tea, and passed the time of day chatting agreeably with her. "He is sleek and fat and is wearing a fine chased leather collar," she told me, "so I advise you to calm down and tell yourself that Policarpo is a very sensible cat, and that when he realized that you had abandoned him to Cosme, he simply stepped out and found himself another admirer. You know the old saying, 'There are just as good fish in the sea as ever were caught on Morelos Street.' So Poli is fine. You get yourself another furry friend."

I carried on for a few weeks. I alternated between a guilt complex and a sense of having been jilted. But at last I convinced myself that Camille was right, and that Poli had had more sense than I. I would also behave philosophically. And so on. Time heals all wounds, etc. I went out and brought home Gardenia.

Gardenia was a thin and restless lady cat, strong for self-expression and free love. She was white with dashing little patches of tiger stripes. She soon provided me with Rose, Violet, and Black Narcissus. We found other boardinghouses for Rose and Violet but I couldn't be parted from Black Narcissus. He was a handsome fellow, pure black, and he had been born with a little bump on his head between his velvet ears. This caused my sons to nickname him "Chipotitos" which means "bumps."

Chipo, as we all began to call him, was a strange wild jungle creature, full of subtlety and wiles. A mighty hunter, he caught countless lizards and moles, and the rats, which had formerly coursed happily around the garbage cans after dark, now took my house off their list of ports of call. Whenever Chipo and a rat engaged in mortal combat, the yowls and growls could be heard for blocks, and I used to hide my head under a pillow and cower. Always Chipo would stroll in later, lithe and swaggering as a gypsy, dusting off his paws in a dashing way, and would call for a small glass of manzanilla.

Eat a rat? Never. But he would accept a little diced chicken liver.

I was mad about Chipo, but who could expect to hold the love of a cat like that? A Supercat. I'm getting old now, I've lost my figure, and there is gray in my hair. The inevitable happened. He left me.

I sorrowed, but Gardenia saw her duty and she did it. She presented me with Daisy, Pansy, and Tiger Lily. Daisy and Pansy were accepted by a grocer and a butcher as apprentice mouse catchers. Tiger Lily grew up to sit on my lap in the evenings, and purr softly as I read my Whodunit. One winter evening, as we sat thus, with the firelight flickering over us, I suddenly heard a familiar voice. Chipo had been away for a year and hadn't so much as sent a postcard home, but I knew that rumbling bass.

There followed a scene much like one from *El Amor Brujo (Love the Sorcerer)*. I tumbled Tiger Lily out of my lap and ran pelting into the night, screaming "Chipo! Chipo darling!" I couldn't see him, for it was a moonless evening, but something large, strong, velvety, and invisible threw itself into my arms, almost knocking me flat. It was Chipo; I felt his bump. He was almost as big as a wildcat, and he had a pawspread of almost three inches. Oh, a wonderful cat! A Mr. Universe among cats. I poured cream. I cubed liver. I diced a chicken breast I had been saving for my husband's supper. I was beside myself.

Chipo stayed three days. He didn't even fight Tiger Lily, who hovered in the background looking pained. Chipo merely glanced at him in pity and disdain, twitching his five-inch whiskers. Then he left again on his mysterious travels.

Tiger Lily should have washed me right out of his hair, but he was a truly broadminded cat, full of loving forgiveness, and he crept back into my perfidious lap. When Gardenia produced Gin Blossom, Tiger Lily just moved over to make room for him.

So then we had three—Gardenia, Tiger Lily, and Gin Blossom.

But one day Wiki came upon a woman who was trying, without much success, to drown a little black female cat in a bucket of water. Knowing my weakness, Wiki stepped forward and saved the cat, and brought her home, trembling and terrified, to give her to me. We named her Jasmine.

Jasmine, quite naturally, took a dim view of anything in skirts. She would have nothing to do with me or Maria, and spent her days hidden in the garage until Luis came home at night. She soon learned the sound of his car and when he drove in through the *zaguan*, she would emerge from the shadows and wind herself around his ankles, as soon as he got out. Only he could touch her; only he could feed her. She was off women for life.

In the end, as it does to all women, love came to Jasmine. And, as so often happens, it completely changed her character. After the first mad rapture, she found herself abandoned to her fate; men were deceivers ever. As her hour drew near, Jasmine began to feel the need of a woman friend. A confidante. She began appearing around doors in the house, looking at me with a wary but hopeful eye. One afternoon, she threw caution to the winds, came over to me, sat down and told me the whole story. Shyly, putting out a paw, she asked if she could sit in my lap. Step by step, she advanced nearer, and at last climbed up and collapsed with a tired sigh, and set up a heavy drumming purr. When her hour came I was near to look after her.

I had studied the magazine articles about natural birth and had seen many pictures of ladies in the delivery room looking straight at the camera with big brave toothy smiles, and I told Jasmine that they had learned all this from the animals, and that the whole thing was going to be easy as pie. But she was recalcitrant. She wouldn't accept the truth about how painless parturition was. She screamed with each pain, and between them she whimpered and shoved her head under

my arm, begging for the petting that had been so comforting
up to then. At last two little black velvet scraps arrived in their
cellophane packages, and one of them had a distinct bump
on the top of his head.

In the meantime, Gardenia had settled down to her knitting once more, after a series of ear-splitting open-air concerts,
and I got her maternal box ready. We had Gardenia (expecting), Jasmine and her two babies, Tiger Lily, and Gin Blossom. The cat population was rapidly reaching a point at which
I would have to come out strongly for birth control.

Here I should point out that Mexicans in general do not
personalize their animals as I tend to do. I will always be
grateful to my husband for his patience with me about my
formidable army of pets, which I spoiled, kept in the house,
and made a fool of myself over. He was brought up to value
a good animal, such as a spirited horse, or a self-respecting
dog, or a handsome mouse-catching cat, but my feeling that
life is empty without something to purr to me or take walks
with me or sit on my shoulder and gently peck my ear, awakens
no answering note in his makeup. Gradually, because he lives
with me, he began to perceive that dogs and cats are really
people in disguise. My Mexican friends and servants always
just took my foolishness over animals as the something queer
about the señora, well knowing that everybody has something
queer about them, and the señora's madness was, on the
whole, harmless.

However, when our cats totaled six with prospects of
more, Luis's patience snapped.

About this time, Maria, my cook, appeared at the gate,
after her day off, wearing a white fur. Luis, who went to open
for her, saw that she was not really wearing a fur piece. She
was wearing a large white cat.

Luis struck an attitude of utter despair.

"If there is anything we don't need around here," he
groaned, "it is another cat."

"But he's such a nice cat," murmured Maria. "They

didn't want him, where I visited, so I brought him." The cat was huge, with a black nose and black goatee, and black stockings, and a neat black modesty patch under his tail.

"We have enough cats."

"I thought the señora loved cats."

"She does, but we can't be just overrun with them. I have to support my children and save something for my old age. I can't let every cent I earn go to support a whole tribe of useless cats. You'll have to get rid of this one."

"Get rid of him?"

"Yes. Take him back. Give him to somebody."

"But he's not a kitten. Nobody wants an old cat."

"Including me. I can't have him here."

"You are sure?"

"Absolutely certain."

Maria sighed.

"In that case, señor, I will have to eat him."

Overhearing these words, I charged into the garden, panting.

"What did you say, Maria? You'll what?"

"I will eat him," she explained patiently. "Cats are very good, señora. A little like chicken, a little like rabbit. Once I had a very nice fat cat, but the señora I was working for wouldn't let me keep him, and I had no one with whom to leave my cat, so I put chile and lemon on him and did him in the oven and ate him. He was very delicious, and then of course, I didn't have to worry about him any more."

Her words had logic, but I was swooning.

"Maria," I protested, "how could you do such a thing?"

"This one will be good," she told me. "Feel him, he's nice and fat. Tender."

"I will buy him from you for ten pesos," I interrupted. She looked startled.

"Fifteen, then." I am used to bargaining.

"Well . . ." Reluctantly she turned the large, gentle, tender white animal over to me. He instantly put his furry arms around my neck, and pressed his whiskers against my cheek. Maria put the fifteen pesos in her apron pocket and started toward the kitchen. "His name," she called over her shoulder, "is Mitchie Foo."

This sounds Oriental, and it is, but not Chinese. Mitchie Foo is the name many Spanish-speaking families call their cats. It is a tradition, stemming from the fact that one of the first cats brought into Spain was a Persian, and his name was Musa Fuf. Mitchie Foo is so common a cat name that by calling "Mitchie mitchie mitchie," almost without vocalizing, you can get the attention of a cat anywhere in Mexico—cats who will pay no mind at all if you call "Kitty kitty" or "Pussy pussy."

The words for calling and training animals, as they differ, always interest me, and for "whom it may concern," let me say that if you want a Mexican dog to take after any sort of enemy, you do not say "Sic 'em" or "Go get 'em," you grunt, "Ush!" and should you sneeze with an ush-like sound, in the presence of a Mexican dog, you may have to pay damages to somebody, for he will take off at any moving object with bared teeth.

Saved from the stewpots, Mitchie Foo became my devoted slave, or maybe it is the other way round. He spends hours stretched out on my coral corduroy bedspread, sound asleep, his head on my pillow.

I must say that he earns his keep, for he raises all Jasmine's and Gardenia's babies, bathes them, teaches them manners, and sings them to sleep, with his big white arms around them, until they are as big as he is. Never has he unsheathed a claw, and his only fault is that he steals asparagus, for which he has a passion.

Luis says that what really happened is that Maria saw a chance to pick up a few pesos from the softhearted and softheaded señora.

Yet she never repeated the trick. It must be said in her defense that she had often told me about when she "passed the hungers" as a child. I had heard of the terrible famines that used to rage in remote districts of Mexico, before the age of airplanes and airlifts, of many roads and thousands of automobiles. It used to be that when crops failed, in some faraway section, the people simply starved. Maria remembered one occasion when the hungers had come down on her village. Her father took his family into the woods and taught them to survive on anything they could catch . . . lizards, snakes, rats, monkeys. People who wouldn't eat those things, died.

I was fond of Maria and I trusted her, but ever after I always took a careful look at the meat she brought home from market. Just in case.

THE SAME CUSTOM

Algunos traen la música por dentro.
—OLD SAYING

Sooner or later, happy homes are confronted with the birds and the bees, and eventually with the $64 question. Even in Mexico, where children are never allowed to see their parents in aught except complete dress—Luis had a fit whenever I walked around the house in my slip and insisted that I cover up with a dressing gown at least—there comes a time when the eternal Why? is applied to natural processes.

I had paid little attention to impending problems of this sort, but when Guicho was getting on for eight, I began nervously telling myself that I would just answer questions naturally and calmly as they came up. It struck me later that, secrecy being the normal cloak of all such matters in Mexico, I might not get the chance to answer any questions at all. Guicho might just find out for himself, as so many Mexicans seemed to do. Mexican mothers told me, with a blush, that they never spoke about *aquello* or *that*.

This thought preyed on my mind because, while on the one hand it would be pleasant not to have to take up sex in executive session at all, on the other hand, I had been reading a lot of advanced thought about how one should be open and above-board with the young so that they would develop healthy thoughts with reference to *aquello*. (All the open and above-board dealing with *aquello* hasn't caused young people to get into any less trouble, it would seem from a perusal of American papers and magazines.)

While I was working myself up over all this, Mamacita

was away visiting in Monterrey, so I couldn't ask her anything. And of course, I couldn't write anything. If *aquello* is seldom talked about in Mexico, in the best circles, it is *never* referred to in the letters which begin, "Dearest Mamacita, All are well here, thanks be to God, and I hope this finds you in good health and spirits, and in God's grace."

Then I received a call from a Hungarian friend who had moved to Mexico recently with her ten-year-old son, Turi. She was a very wise and worldly lady, so I asked whether she and Turi had taken up any biological problems.

"Oh, I told Turi everything before we left Hungary," she told me. "But when we came to Mexico, I observed that customs were so very different, and that people were very much more reserved in such information with their children. As I wanted Turi to make friends easily and not alienate any Mexican mammas, I took him to one side and talked to him, this way. 'My son,' I said, 'I have told you about how the animals mate, and the way people marry and have families. But that was in Hungary. Now we are here, in a new country, and I do not want you to speak of any of these matters with your friends, because customs are different. These are different people and they have different points of view and different ways.' "

"I knew school would be difficult for him," she went on, "and he was having trouble enough with a new language. I didn't want him to do or say anything that might cause the families to look askance at his own."

"Very thoughtful of you," I commented admiringly.

My friend chuckled reminiscently.

"However," she went on, "one day Turi came home from school and took me to one side. 'Mommy,' he said, 'you needn't have worried about my telling how the people get babies in Hungary. Antonio told me today that they do it the very same way here! They have exactly the same custom!' "

This school talk caused me to take up the subject with my husband. "I think Guicho may want to know things soon," I said.

"What things?"

"Oh you know. About life. And everything."

My husband, a prudent man, a Mexican, and fanatically modest, gave me a look of horror and dismay.

"Well, don't tell him anything!" he shouted. "It's none of his business!"

I realized that I would have to measure my actions and my words against the ideals of ultraconservative Mexico and I did not want to offend, nor to plunge around breaking traditions about *aquello*, like a bull in a china shop. The old ways have a lot to be said for them. I decided to consult with friends whose problems and whose children were similar to mine in racial background and in general education.

I was spurred on to this by the sight of a seven-year-old Mexican guest, who was visiting me, taking a bath in her panties and I felt that while I am conservative by nature, this sort of training was not typical of the attitude toward the body which I wished to instill in my children. Too much modesty and self-consciousness can be a torment, just as too much swinging of the pendulum to the other side, can cause heartaches and disappointments, too.

Among my acquaintances was an American lady who didn't go quite so far as to believe in free love, but she did believe in a lot of free looks. She assured me that it was fine and healthy for parents and children to stride around unclothed, in their home, so that boys need never wonder what girls looked like, or vice versa. Quite in character, she explained in detail to her fascinated children all about mating and birth, and she was sure that she alone, among all her rabbity female friends, had the right approach to the mysteries. She was jolted out of her complacency when her children asked respectfully if they could watch the next time she and Daddy ordered a baby. That reduced her to the ranks of the rest of us, and she, also, took refuge in jittery double talk.

I kept silent a little longer, thinking over something Mamacita had said to me one time. She believed that it was best for girls to know practically nothing about men until marriage. I had disputed this with her, but her answer made me thoughtful.

"Marriage is a sacrament, in our belief, you know," she reminded me, "not just 'something natural,' like eating, or drinking. It is a coming together, but with the mystery of God in the act, for a new life may result from it, and only God can give the new life. That is why it is better that the girl should feel fear of the man, and much fear of the whole idea of giving herself, because fear, after all, is a sign of respect. Besides, most men are kindly and tender toward what they love, and there is nothing that makes a man more considerate, more gentle, than some evidence of fear. Mind my words, *hijita*, it is not intelligent to teach girls to be big and strong and brave like men. They will rue the day."

Then it occurred to me that Malenita might help me. She was half-Irish, but had been brought up in the austere and dignified Mexican tradition.

"Oh," she answered me, "I learned everything out of books. And I have simply let my children do the same."

"You mean," I asked hopefully, "that you have a special book that explains things?"

"Oh no," she answered airily. "I mean that my father turned me loose in his library and let me read anything I wanted to—in French, English, or Spanish, from Dickens to Maupassant, and from Boccaccio to the Bible, and Homer and a few other people in translation. His only injunction was that I was not to bother him with questions about what anything meant. And so, as I went, reading as much as I did, I sort of got the general idea."

"But surely you didn't understand. You must have got everything all mixed up."

"Oh yes indeed," she assured me, "but this protected me, and saved me from a lot of foolishness. Besides, in due time, my husband unmixed me, and I presume that is what will happen with my children."

This seemed to be a comfortable middle course, and I do have a rather extensive and reasonably catholic library. But that very night, Guicho came and fixed me with his glittering little green eyes and asked, "Mima, where did I come from?"

"From inside Mima," I answered bravely, feeling like John Gunther.

This pleased him very much, and he conveyed the information to the first visitor the next afternoon, patting me in the region of the waistline with great pride.

When I told him later that he musn't tell everybody that he came from inside me, he asked, "Why? Is it a secret?"

"No."

"Doesn't everybody come from inside his mother?"

"Yes."

"Why can't I talk about it, then?"

"Because they know it already," I snapped.

"Oh."

Silence. Then, "Mima, have you got another baby inside you?"

"No."

"How do you know?"

"I just know."

"Oh." Another silence.

"Why don't you get another one?"

"Go to bed!" I roared, as bad as any of the Victorians, and willing to sow complexes on all sides. Because the trouble with starting to answer questions is that you are never allowed to stop.

Guicho told Wiki the information as to his origin that night when they were stowed in their little beds, and Wiki came at once, in his sleeper suit, to accuse me.

"Guicho says I came from inside you!" he reported.

"Yes, you did. From in here."

"I did not!" he howled and would have none of it. He rejected the whole theory. And could I prove it? Not easily. So we went along for a while with Guicho sure that he came from inside Mima, and Wiki certain that the whole thing was another elaborate adult lie.

To anticipate any more questions, and scenes, I provided myself with a female dachshund and arranged that she should have puppies as soon as convenient, since Jasmine and Gardenia were temperamental, and would allow no males in the room at all, when we were having our kittens.

I told the children that puppies were growing inside Tipchen, and that when they were born, we would all watch and help her.

But Guicho was, by now, getting bored with the subject. "Why they just come out," he said. "There's nothing to it. She lays them, like the hens lay eggs. Only she won't cackle."

Sure enough, in due time, he came in from the garden to report that Tipchen had laid five puppies and that was that.

Time marched on, and the Treviños were happy and busy about their small concerns, when suddenly I was felled by the question that causes as much anguish as the loyalty oath.

"Mima," asked Guicho, "how did I get in there?"

I took him by the hand and we went to visit our family doctor. He was a friend, a kind and serious man, a fellow Catholic. I explained my dilemma and he undertook to instruct Guicho in the facts of life, with medical plates and scientific terms. He set aside two hours a week of his busy practice time, and I was to send Guicho for his lecture at that time.

Guicho took his classes very seriously. In the midst of baseball in the front garden, he would throw down his mitt and ball and announce, "Sorry, 'manos, I have to go to my class with the doctor now."

"What class?"

"About the babies," he would explain. "How they get started and when the fingernails start growing and everything. It's very interesting. I finish the course next week."

So well, dryly and scientifically, did our friend the doctor impart his instruction, that once when there was a shameless exhibition of canine amors near our front gate, and all the baseball team went to watch and titter, Guicho, the authority, called them back to their game.

"It's okay, fellows," he told them. "The big dogs won't hurt the little female. They're only helping her. She wants to have some puppies. It's perfectly all right. She will get her puppies now in nine weeks. Who's up to bat?"

Wiki was of a much less scientific turn of mind, but when I proposed that he go to the doctor and have lessons, too, he said impatiently, "Oh Mima, I don't have to. Guicho told me everything as fast as the doctor told him and drew me all the pictures. I know all about it."

I had been inept and scared and unorganized all along, but after all, the final results were not so bad.

One day I was taking my two sons and a friend of theirs to the movies, and we walked along the beautiful Alameda Park in the center of Mexico City. The park is adorned with statuary of nudes in various postures, and I noticed that our little party had paused in front of a work entitled "Malgré Tout." It is a statue of a naked woman, prostrate on the ground, in chains, but she is exerting tremendous effort, in an attempt to inch herself forward. The whole figure reveals tension and struggle and a kind of desperate hope.

Our guest, the same age as Guicho, giggled and blushed and was ashamed to look and yet looked.

Guicho looked and said to me, "Mima, how did the man who made the statue know how to chip away the whole thing from one block of stone, and just leave the woman?"

And little Wiki, the tenderhearted, stared at the statue with tears in his eyes and murmured, "*Ay pobrecita . . . pobrecita!*" ("Poor thing!").

XII ॐ

THE SECRET PLACE OF THE MOST HIGH

Si al cielo escupas, te caerá en la cara.
—PROVERB

One lovely springtime Mamacita arrived to visit us. She had come with a religious pilgrimage by train from Monterrey, because the fare was so economical, but two nights and a day on the slow coach in close confinement with so many fellow Christians had proved to be too much for fastidious Mamacita. She got off the train in a towering temper and demanded an immediate bath with lots of soap and "Eleesabet's baubles." My passion for bubble-bath had always amused her before; now she recognized it as a necessity.

It might be mentioned in passing that these "pilgrimages" to Mexico's patroness, the Blessed Virgin of Guadalupe, are an essential part of Mexican life. Every day some great pilgrimage arrives at the Basilica, by special train, by bus load, by automobile caravan, or on foot. They come from sections, such as the Pilgrimage from Monterrey, and they come by profession or interest, such as the Pilgrimage of the Journalists, or the Pilgrimage of the Aviation Employees. There is never one day that goes by, without the arrival of some pious group. And besides these pilgrimages, there are many others . . . to the Christ of Chalma, to Our Lady of Lagos, to the Christ of Cubilete, and countless more. The poorest Mexican can enlarge his life with a religious pilgrimage every two or three years, and the pilgrimages reward the pilgrims with stronger faith, with a look at the country, and a kind of glorious excitement, such as must have been experienced by the Crusaders centuries ago.

Clean, and with the smell of too much humanity dispelled, Mamacita said a Rosary as penance for her impatience at the rigors of the pilgrimage, and then questioned me briskly about when the children would make their First Communion. I told her we wanted to have them make it in December, preferably on her saint's day, December sixteenth.

"Very well. Then, since this is May, it would be nice if they took flowers to the Virgin."

It is the lovely custom in Mexico to observe May, the month of Mary, with a ceremony of touching poesy. During this month the image of the Blessed Virgin is moved to a position near the altar rail, and sometimes a special altar is set up for her. At the hour of the Rosary, in the afternoons, ladies of the parish preside over the offering of flowers by the little children. Usually a table for the blooms is provided, near the entrance of the church, and between recitation of decades of the Rosary, the little ones march, two by two, toward the altar, carrying their flowers which they leave at the feet of Our Lady. Then the children separate and each one returns to his place along a side aisle. Hymns are sung as the children's procession begins, and then another decade of the ancient and beloved prayers is chanted.

Very often I have been deeply touched at the sight of a humble family going toward church in the late afternoon of a day in May . . . the father, perhaps, in overalls and wide straw hat, the mother in flounced calico skirts and *reboso*, with two or three little children in shabby hand-me-downs. But all are leading their special treasure, usually a tiny girl of three or four, dressed in sparkling white, on her head a white veil held in place by a wreath of white flowers, white shoes on her little feet and minute white gloves on her hands. One can imagine the love and sacrifice that have gone to procure this costume, in order to provide the little one with her special moment of glory and importance. Usually someone in the family has an armload of flowers, and the little queen goes to church to act for them all, to offer prayers for the whole family, prayers made shining and precious by her innocence.

"Call up Maria Luisa!" ordered Mamacita. "We will take the two oldest girls, the Nena and Chacha, and you will bring Guicho and Wiki." Mamacita unlimbered her executive qualities and threw herself into planning the festivity which would conclude with a fine *merienda* to be eaten afterward by the two families. This, she decided, would consist of the basic tamales and chocolate, but also there would be tiny liver-paste sandwiches and "You, Eleesabet, will make one of your wonderful American cakes."

Mary was alerted and told to have ready the white dresses and the veils. I had white suits washed and starched for my little boys. I made the cake. Mamacita bought armloads of flowers.

Having arrived at the church we settled Mamacita into a pew, well forward so that she could have a good view of all the proceedings, and Mary and I delivered our progeny to the parish ladies at the rear of the church. Then we went to sit with Mamacita, who had got out her handkerchief, and was weeping with joyful emotion, for she loved beyond all things these devotions in which were brought together all the things most dear to her heart . . . little children, family, and the tradition and beautiful ritual of her faith.

We prayed our Rosary, and after the Gloria, the strains of a hymn were heard and everyone sang with the organ. Then the first two little children came walking uncertainly down the aisle, hand in hand, a little boy of three, and a tiny girl of a bit less. Their round black eyes were full of wonder and their free hands clutched their offerings of flowers while the little feet moved forward slowly. Other small couples, also pale with importance, followed after, carrying their blossoms. Then we heard the voice of Chacha, raised, at the back of the church.

"But where's *my* husband?" she demanded. "All the other girls have husbands!"

Mary rose to her feet in horror, but it seemed that Wiki was pressed into service at once, so that Chacha should not walk down the aisle without masculine accompaniment. There she came, the one we all called "little Frenchy," coquettish and chic, with her veil on one side of her head, and she began to throw kisses to everyone, and then to the image of the Virgin herself. I didn't regard this as reprehensible, but Maria Luisa (Mary) was mortified, having lectured her girls on how to behave the night before. She went to wait at the back of the church, snatched Chacha out of line, and administered a smack in a suitable place in the church garden.

Meanwhile Wiki came round again, this time partnering the sedate little Nena. Guicho appeared with his partner, a little girl from the school in San Angel. Somewhere Guicho had learned how to walk like a duck, a gyration he performed to make all his cronies laugh, and now, as he approached the altar, I saw with dismay that he had got it into his satanic little head to walk like a duck here.

Mamacita could hardly believe her eyes. At first she registered worry, then suspicion, then fury, as he bobbed stiffly past, his chin going forward and back, his back ramrod-stiff, his feet moving so as to cause him to waddle in a very strange way. The other children tittered nervously, and as he turned from the altar we saw that he had also made one of his silly faces, with goggling eyes and stretched mouth. This was too much for Mamacita. She got up at once and took her grandson by the ear, and later from the garden I could hear her angry whacks at his small rear. I waited for the ceremony to come to a close. Wiki and the Nena revolved beautifully in the next four processions, leaving their flowers at the feet of Our Lady, and returning to their places like little saints. Maria Luisa and Mamacita remained outside with the criminals.

When it was over, we marched glumly home.

I was a little disturbed at what Mamacita might tell Luis. He arrived home early for the festive *merienda*, and he wanted to know all about everything. Mary and I looked apprehensively at Mamacita. But she had a mother's sportsmanship about the misbehavior of small fry.

"The church was beautiful," she said, "and there were so many children and beautiful flowers. A lovely ceremony."

Tamales were eaten and chocolate was poured.

"I think we will take the children and go again next week," she concluded. Luis was satisfied.

However, she drew me and Mary aside later, when Luis was safely in the library with his newspaper, and whispered, "I will take the Nena and Wiki. But you had better take the other two to the circus. I am afraid they are not going to be religious types."

The persistence of these ceremonies of devotion, the countless pilgrimages, the fact that no marriage is considered really binding until it has been blessed by the priest in the sacrament of matrimony, all these things merely reflect the fact that Mexico is, by her own government statistics, 97 per cent Roman Catholic in faith.

Then why, my American friends ask me, is there such a rigid withdrawal from any religious expression in the Mexican government? I think it can only be explained by saying that government officials are able to develop a kind of conscious schizophrenia. In their role as government officers, they are non-religious (even anti-religious sometimes), and yet not one but wishes his daughter to marry in the Church, and many of them, proclaiming the strongest possible free-thinking in public orations, and insisting on strict separation of Church and State, especially in the schools, secretly pack their children off to convents in Canada.

Earnest foreigners who try to figure this whole thing out are generally completely baffled in the end, and others who tend to make studies and researches based on "official" figures, are thrown by the realization that underneath the government attitudes and reports, is a whole world of strong private thinking which is thoroughly Catholic in point of view.

The Constitution, which Mexicans all revere, has two or three articles that many of them resent and would like to see deleted, because, as long as they stand in the basic law, there is always danger that some fanatic may try to enforce them. One such law is the article which declares that no religion whatsoever may be taught in any school, and which defines the Mexican State as strictly non-religious.

Indeed, though the articles are written into the Constitution, Mexico is not only Catholic, but warmly and devotedly Catholic, more fervent in her faith than many other traditionally Catholic countries. Yet occasionally a zealot tries to outrage this deep devotion and carry out the provisos of the Constitution and subsequent legislation based on it, quite literally. One of these was President Plutarco Elías Calles. Resting on the authority of the Constitution and laws on the statute books of the land, he decreed that all temples of religious worship should be closed and all priests and nuns were ordered out of the country. With one swoop of the pen on a decree, he intended to rid Mexico forever of "the opium of the people." Thus worshipers were shot down or machine-gunned as they emerged from Mass, prices were set on the heads of priests, and anyone who maintained a private chapel in his home, or harbored a priest, was liable to arrest and to a prison sentence. People on both sides became more intense in their feelings and a full-fledged revolution broke out all over the Republic.

For some reason which is not clear to me, this was never fully reported in the foreign press; perhaps the government of Mexico itself imposed censorship. Though some knowledge of trouble did leak out, as witness the powerful novel of Graham Greene, *The Power and the Glory*, about a priest who chose, with all his frailties and faults, to remain and to die in the performance of his spiritual duties. In the north of Mexico, the people rose in a rebellion called the "Cristero Revolution," because of their banner and rallying cry of "Viva Cristo Rey!" ("Long live Christ the King!") In the south (the setting of Greene's novel), the people were greatly oppressed by a governor named Garrido Canaval. They called him "the Cannibal," which sounded much the same.

At last the Calles government, unwilling to give in, but ready to hand the people a sop, set up a "Mexican" church, and named a puppet archbishop. This man, known as the Patriarch Perez, had some opulent vestments tailored for himself and rather idiotically sat down to await the people, who were expected to flock in. With really astounding stupidity, the officials who established the "new church" were under the impression that Mexican Catholics were just people who liked the trappings of a religion, and that any old religion would do.

Despite Patriarch Perez's resplendent robes and high hopes, nobody came to be ministered unto, and it appeared that the Mexican church was likely to expire for want of a communicant. Then one bright day, two giggling young persons arrived and asked to be married. The Patriarch Perez was delighted, and made ready for the ceremony, though it seemed an odd pair—both very young, and the bride so rawboned and gauche. They were attended by several young men and women, and all seemed to be in order. The wedding service hadn't proceeded very far before pandemonium broke loose. The wedding party had consisted of college students, who quickly got out of hand. The bride and groom were in disguise; the bride, actually, was young Juan O'Gorman, Mexico's now famous artist, muralist, and architect.

Ridicule is an arm of horrifying effectiveness in Mexico; to be laughed at is a fate worse than death. The Patriarch Perez packed up his vestments and vanished into the night.

There are many wonderful stories about the time of the troubles in Mexico, when the present archbishop and Mexico's first cardinal had a price on their heads. The former was kept a prisoner in a damp cave and the present cardinal, José Cardinal Garibi y Rivera, wrapped in a voluminous white apron, fried *tacos* on the street corners in Guadalajara, while administering the sacraments to the faithful in secret.

Many families in Mexico still have the "hidey holes" where they concealed their priests, as the Catholics in England did under Queen Elizabeth, and my friend Licha has told me that when she was a child it used to be a matter of much wonder to her how many "uncles" her mother produced, during the trouble, each of whom seemed able to say Mass in the family chapel.

My husband has told me what happened in Monterrey when the edicts expelling all priests, and ordering the closing of all churches, reached that city of hardheaded businessmen. The Regiomontanos (as they call themselves) argued that a citizen cannot hold his own, with a rifle or a pistol, against a soldier any more, as in the dear dead days gone by, but they knew from experience that governments, like people, can be severely wounded in the pocketbook. So the whole city, co-operating to a man and to a family, went on a buying strike. Nobody did anything illegal, but they simply didn't buy anything except the barest necessities . . . beans, rice, a few vegetables. People exchanged eggs for fruit, over their garden walls, and made do with almost nothing. No shoes were bought, no furniture, no dress material, no stockings, nothing. Nobody went to the movies, nobody rode the buses, nobody paid his bills, nobody worked. No taxes were forthcoming. Shops and businesses closed. Monterrey, one of the richest sources of income for the federal government, had demoted herself to a cipher.

Mexico City blustered, but you can't make people buy if they won't.

Not a shot was fired, not a priest nor a soldier died in Monterrey. But churches were mysteriously and quietly opened up again. Monterrey rolled up its sleeves and went back to work, money started flowing toward Mexico City once more, and the sigh of relief from the capital could be heard for six hundred miles.

Mamacita could, like many of the Mexican ladies I knew, eat extraordinary amounts of rich tamales, drink thick chocolate, and put away pounds of egg-and-cream-rich desserts; also, she could fast absolutely, when she had made a vow. She explained the non-aggression, no-tax rebellion to me in simple terms.

"Tyrants are like tapeworms," she told me, out of her long experience of curing dogs, horses, and children on the ranchos. "Starve them awhile, and they get weak. Then you can clean them out quickly."

I don't suppose this procedure will work against a really brutal adversary, such as Nazi Germany or present-day Communists bent on conquest, but there is a grain of truth here that ought to be chewed on. Governments today, so ponderous and heavy with bureaucrats, are immediately sensitive to a pain in the coffer. Citizens still have an arm, and a powerful one; it is their purchasing power. While there is a vestige of freedom in a country and people can buy what they please, they can raise Cain if they get together and stop buying. Reduced consumption of goods can quickly bring the most relentless adversary to the conference table.

My husband, who was working on the west coast of Mexico during the first desperate years of the Cristero rebellion, took part in a strange wedding in those days, not as a counterfeit bride, I hasten to add, nor yet as a legitimate husband. He was merely a guest.

One of his *padrinos*, or godfathers, was Don Ernesto Madero, and Luis was often invited to the country estates of the Madero family near Parras, Coahuila. There they had vast tracts of land in grapes, and they had started a wine and brandy business which has now become a major industry in Mexico.

In the worst months of the persecution of the Church, Luis received an invitation to attend a wedding at Parras. The invitation came by word of mouth, and yet, despite the care and secrecy this evidenced, he supposed that the wedding would only be *por lo civil* (a civil wedding). The Maderos would never dare bring down troops of *rurales* (Federal soldiers) on the innocent participants in a religious wedding. Of course, Luis said to himself, as he packed his suitcase and made ready to go to Parras, the bride and groom would probably go on a wedding journey to the United States, and there be properly married in the church.

When he arrived in Parras, he learned that the Maderos, who had been prominent in the Revolution of 1910, were in no mood to duck out and escape the Cristero Revolution. The wedding would be performed by a priest, but just how or where, the guests were not told. They were all asked to wear fancy dress, or charro clothes and Indian costumes, to a great evening dance, and a pavilion was set up and country musicians were hired. When the music began, horses were hitched to posts all around the pavilion, which was covered over by a canvas like a circus tent, and there were little *puestos* or booths on every hand, providing crisp fried *tacos*, hot enchiladas, or drinks made from crushed fruits and seeds, cooled with ice. Also there was *barbacoa*, with its spicy sauce, and tequila to wash it down. The guests began to arrive, nearly all the men in the tight trousers of homespun and short jackets of the charro, and many girls in flounced cotton *enaguas* (big skirts) and *rebosos*, though there were a few Harlequins, dominoes, bakers, and Spanish dandies among the masked dancers. Provincial Mexicans adore dressing up in fancy costumes, or *fachas*.

As the dancing got under way, there were a few enthusiastic shots into the air, and a lot of shouting, as is the custom at country hoe-downs. All was merry as the traditional marriage bell. After a couple of hours a mild little Indian guiding a donkey came quietly through the Madero lands, bringing *aguamiel* (fresh cane juice) in two great jars on his beast.

"Aguamieeeeee-e-e-l!" he called. That cry brought out all the guests; *aguamiel* is a favorite country drink. While they dipped their clay mugs into the cane juice in one cask, the other was unloaded and taken inside the pavilion. Shortly thereafter before an improvised altar, which was hastily blessed and set with candles, the Indian appeared again, dressed now in white priestly marriage vestments. (They had been carried in one of the casks, together with the sacred Host.)

The Nuptial Mass began. The bride knelt in her white ruffled cotton gown; beside her the bridegroom, in his country charro dress of homespun trousers and knotted shirt, humbly bent his knee.

The wild dance music, the screeching Mexican yodels of joy at a fiesta, and an occasional shot, continued outside while before the altar the ancient words were said and the ancient vows were taken yet once more by a boy and a girl in love.

A kilometer or two away some weary *rurales* jogged along on their tired horses and thought fleetingly of joining the fun for a bit. But they gave up the idea; they were under orders and had been searching for a priest who was said to be hiding in a village some thirty kilometers away to the south, disguised as a vendor of *aguamiel*.

After the blessing, the dancing began again in earnest. Hidden from the crowd, the priest once more dressed in civilian clothes. But not, this time, as the Indian vendor of cane juice. He emerged from his improvised vestry in gallant charro dress—a gift from the bridegroom. He wore trousers of black, with silver side lacings, a tight gray coat, red silk bow tie, and a flaring wide sombrero of black, with silver decorations. At his waist he wore the *cuarenta y cuatro* (forty-four) beloved of North Mexico riders. A fresh frisky horse was ready for him, and he swung himself up into the saddle with a joyous Mexican shout. He had been a charro in his youth, and knew all the country lore of horses, riding, and roping.

I have been told that the President who had decreed this suppression of the Church which resulted in so much bloodshed and heartache for Mexico, called for a priest and made full confession and did penance before he died. I cannot swear to this, but it would have been in character. Mexicans are notoriously dramatic, ready to risk all for their beliefs, good or bad.

The depth of the Mexican mystical feeling has been pondered by all the tourists who have come to visit in a spirit of amiable sightseeing, the Secret Convent of Santa Monica.

Guides explain that under the Reform laws it had become illegal for convents to exist in Mexico, and that all priests and nuns had been expelled from the country. Yet the Reform laws were promulgated under President Juárez in 1861, and it was not until 1928 that the Secret Convent of Santa Monica was betrayed to government inspectors. It had existed for hundreds of years, in the heart of the city of Puebla, and thousands of nuns had lived and died there and mingled their bones in a *fosa comun* (common pit). The peculiar architecture of a Mexican provincial city made it possible for the convent to continue quietly in existence, for as houses are all built flush on the street, and streets are blocked off into squares, a convent might have occupied the central section of the whole block, and be known to none but the householders there. This, indeed, had been the case, and families in the surrounding homes had brought in for the nuns the supplies they needed from the outside world. So they existed, trusting in their neighbors. The nuns heard Mass from a screened balcony onto a church in that block of houses, and all was peace in their simple cloister.

Yet they had foreseen their end, and had planned their escape. No doubt they realized that rising property values in the city, plus the rewards attendant on such a betrayal, would one day tempt someone beyond control. When the alarm was given, the nuns crept, one by one, through a hole in the wall behind their toilet, and out through a dark passage that gave into the church. There, among the women of Puebla, in their black dresses and long black veils, who would know that some of the kneeling figures were nuns from the Secret Convent? And later, as they dispersed into the streets, who would distinguish one hurrying dark figure from another in that pious city? No doubt all had memorized addresses of homes to which they might go for refuge.

I have often wondered if one or another of those nuns, perhaps weary or repentant of her vows, might not have taken the opportunity to disappear forever into "the world." Perhaps not. The strength of the Mexican mystical strain is amazing.

My own husband had an aunt, his *tia* Magdalena, who, perhaps not knowing of the Secret Convent of Santa Monica, and unwilling to leave her native country, and yet with a vocation for the conventual life, simply became a nun, in every sense except the one of living communally in an order. She fasted; she kept vigils; she dedicated herself to works of charity. She never married nor had any conversations with men and she spent no money on herself, dressing in whatever might be given her to wear out. She collected orphans, abandoned children or little ones whose two parents had to work all day, and cared for them, and her reward was that all the neighbors of her town still refer to her, with affection, as "Sister Magdalena." For this instance which I know of personally, there are hundreds, perhaps thousands more, in Old Mother Mexico.

I am not betraying anything when I say that there are still many other secret convents in Mexico, protected fiercely by neighbors and friends, sustained in their work, helped in their mission of teaching, penitence, and prayer. Many of these convents prepare young children for First Communion, and to one of them I took my two little boys.

We walked up the cobblestoned streets of San Angel, through narrow paths behind high walls. Over the walls tumble blue plumbago and purple bougainvillea, and above you can see the waving crowns of tall trees. At the address we had been given, I touched the bell beside a plain door in the towering wall. Far inside we heard a distant tinkle. Then we waited. There was no sign of life at all from within, and away down on the avenue we could hear the automobiles, whizzing by on their multitudinous errands. Where we stood there was no sound, only desultory bird song and the rustling of leaves.

At last the door opened a very little way. There I stood with my two little sons. They were in clean suits, their faces shining with soap, their wet hair showing the marks of the comb. We passed inspection, and I gave the name of the person who had told me to come. The door swung open and a little smiling nun in black, with a starched white coif framing her pink innocent face, stood inside.

We were shown into a waiting room, bare and clean, furnished only with a bench and with a very beautiful life-size crucifix. Beyond we glimpsed gardens of lawn and roses, where nuns walked two and two, reading their prayerbooks.

Then a sister rustled in to take our names and arrange hours when the little boys could come for their instruction. Upon noting that my sons' name was Treviño and they had been born in Monterrey, she looked delighted, and said, "Wait here a moment." She left, to return with another nun, much older, who instantly went down on her knees and looked into Wiki's little face.

"A grandson of Adelita Gómez!" she cried. "I would have known those eyes anywhere!"

She was indeed a cousin of Mamacita, and had come from Linares, Mamacita's birthplace.

The classes began and continued weekly until we were invited to Cuernavaca for a visit one Sunday. My husband arranged this. A business friend asked us to come to spend the day, bringing our swimming things.

Accordingly we set out, the two little boys with Teresa, the maid, on the back seat. We were happy; we sang as we drove over the mountain and then dropped down into the beautiful valley of Cuernavaca. Luis's friend had a house in a group of four cottages ranged round a communal swimming pool, where already there was a great shouting and splashing.

Our hostess came forward in resort clothes. She was cordial and kind and explained that she had been wishing to invite us for months, but that all the children in the compound had had measles.

"Can you imagine?" she asked. "I had invited another friend, who has two little girls, and she *knew* the children had been exposed to the disease, but she came along anyway and let them go in swimming and play with all the others! Every single child came down with it, and we have been more or less quarantined for months!"

I chimed in, full of indignation at this criminally thoughtless mother with her measly children, but before I could get well into my speech, I was called to the poolside to referee a fight between Guicho and two little boys. This settled, my hostess and I continued our chat, met mothers from the other cottages, and discussed drinking a cup of tea.

I had to go then and spank Guicho for ducking some little girls, who cried and pointed accusing fingers at him. As I seized him, to administer correction, I noticed that he felt rather hot, and there was a tiny red spot on his neck. Mosquitoes, I thought. Later, as husbands drank *Escotch jaibol* and talked business, and the ladies took their tea, I was sent for once again, and once again it was Guicho who was misbehaving. Wiki seemed peaceable enough. Guicho was very naughty that day, more so than usual, and I was quite mortified. No sooner had I sat down to my tea and an exchange of crocheting patterns than I was made conscious of Teresa, who was gesturing to me in silent appeal. I simply told her to go away and to entertain Guicho by himself until it was time to go home.

At last we left, after many mutual protestations of sympathy and plans to meet again. I had liked my hostess and the pretty homes around the central garden. We began the drive home.

"Señora?" began Teresa from the back seat.

"Yes, Teresa?"

"Could we stop at a drugstore perhaps and buy some talcum powder? Guicho is just covered with spots, Señora."

"Good Heavens!"

"And also Wiki has a few."

We bought the talcum and I took the children into a Pemex restroom, to powder them.

"Where could they have got all those bites?" I worried.

"Señora?"

"Yes, Teresa?"

"I think they have chicken pox, Señora. All the children in San Angel are having chicken pox."

I redressed the boys, sent Teresa into the front seat of the car, and I sat in back holding little hot hands.

They had chicken pox all right, the doctor said that night.

Somehow, I just couldn't bring myself to go back and call on the lady in Cuernavaca who had just got over the measles when the Treviños arrived. And of course, the catechism classes were suspended. I had no idea how much chicken pox we had sowed among the small aspirants at the convent, either. But, somehow, I was reluctant to go back there, to find out.

Luckily catechism classes were given at the school, and on a great day in November (not Mamacita's saint's day, but near it), together with all the others in their class, my little boys became communicating Catholics.

Mamacita arrived from Monterrey in time for this ceremony, and she cried with happiness all through it. Luis was very proud and happy. So was I.

The boys marched in. It was a long line and they were all dressed the same, in white long trousers (their first) and dark blue coats, with wide white silk arm bands. Each carried a tall white taper.

The children had been well trained, and authority had been imposed on the mischievous Guicho and the playful Wiki. For unless I looked very hard I couldn't distinguish them from among all the others, so well did they behave. The brother in charge of the little group had some sort of metal snapper in his hand, and he was a bit of a martinet. The boys performed like little soldiers. At one snap, the team which had learned the signals, dropped to their knees. Two snaps, and they stood erect. Three snaps and they were seated.

Far back in the church, with the other parents, we watched all the little heads bobbing, dipping, rising. To the smart guidance of the snaps, they filed up to the altar, they knelt, they opened their mouths, they extended their tongues. They received the holy wafer. Snap snap and they marched back to their seats, not a boy out of step, not one walking like a duck. All was dignity, order, and respect.

At home the feast was spread, *abrazos* and kisses were given, presents were passed out. The children and all their guests sat down to breakfast in the garden, while the parents, grandmother, and guests were served indoors.

There was a certain amount of shouting and fun outside, but nothing unusual. For one moment, as I glanced outside, I thought it was beginning to snow. This startled me, but I soon realized what it was. Guicho and Wiki were throwing bread balls at their friends. Back to normal.

Next day I asked Guicho the name of the priest who had been in charge of the group.

"That was Brother José," he told me. "He's not a real teacher. He just has charge of the halls and the playground."

"I want to meet him."

"Why, Mima?"

"I want to buy one of those metal snappers."

A shadow of respect passed over the small face.

"You won't have to ask him for one, Mima. I can get you one. That one he was using was mine. He took it away from me."

XIII 🦆

LOS RATEROS

Quien el peligro ama, en él acaba.
—PROVERB

Readers of *Life* magazine were entertained a few years ago by a picture of a matador being carried triumphantly out of the bullring in Mexico City, on the shoulders of his admirers, while in plain view of the camera, a pickpocket relieved one of the fans of his wallet.

Poor Mexico suffers, in more ways than one, from these troupes of trained "wallet boys" or *carteristas* who roam up and down Latin America, apparently under the command of generals who deploy them with great skill. Whenever and wherever there is a pilgrimage, an inauguration, a fiesta, a bullfight, a centennial, or any other event likely to draw crowds, there the pickpockets are busy. And during the rainy season in Mexico City, from June until mid-September, bands of them work the city streets with great success.

The newspapers are constantly carrying stories of young children who disappear from their homes, and yet the country has been singularly free from the revolting sort of kidnaping (all sorts of kidnaping are horrific enough) which bleeds anxious parents for money even after the little child has been murdered. No, the fact that in Mexico, children are likely to disappear from the most humble homes, incapable of providing ransom money, leads one to presume that they were stolen for other reasons. Mostly, they appear to be taken and trained for a life of crime, in some such school as the one Fagin conducted in *Oliverio Tweest*. Since many of these little ones are made to beg on the streets for their voracious and cruel "owners," they are constantly being gathered up and cared for in government homes. The city and state are both at war against such beggary and are trying to sort out the unfortunate children and return them to their families, and to care for the lost and homeless ones.

Tourists are advised not to give money to little boys and girls in the streets, pitifully clothed, exposed to the rain, or sleeping in corners under newspapers, but to tell the police about them. Nearly all of these children have been stolen and enslaved, and generous but misguided donations keep alive the reason for which they were taken in the first place. Undoubtedly many of these children, when too old to be useful as tear-jerkers, are taught to be pickpockets.

I am an absent-minded person, frequently composing poetry in my head, or thinking up good arguments to use when I am baited about my politics, weight, or religion. And therefore I have had my pocket picked more times than I care to remember.

The first time I was angry and I told everybody about it. The second time, I was ashamed and I concealed my losses. The third time I got mad and became vocal again.

I was reminded of my maternal grandfather, a fascinating and adventurous Dane, who traveled the length and breadth of Europe in his youth, and landed in New York in time to be hit over the head and impressed into the Union Army for the War between the States. Emerging from this struggle, after Lee's surrender, with nothing but a pair of calico trousers, a campaign jacket, a bullet in his leg and malaria, he went into the contracting and building business in New York. He did very well, married and had one son, before his health broke down, and doctors recommended that he go to live in California. He accordingly sold out his business, was carried aboard a ship bound for Panama, there crossed by rail and took ship again on the other side. He eventually reached California, docking in San Francisco. By then, Grandfather was much better and he went out for a stroll in the city. Somewhere on Market Street somebody lifted his wallet. Grandfather had an attack of rage and frustration that almost carried him off, for in all his adventurings, he had never before been humiliated to the extent of having his pocket picked. Recovering, but still furious, he bought an assortment of fishhooks, and laboriously sewed them into all his pockets. During the rest of his stay in San Francisco, before he bought a ranch and settled down in the Salinas Valley (where there were many other Danish families, among them one by the name of Steinbeck) he paraded Market Street and Embarcadero and Post and Kearney, got himself into crowds and generally passed himself around, observing the blood and skin on his fishhooks later at home, with fiendish glee.

So I seriously considered fishhooks. But women's clothes are not replete with pockets, so I gave up that inspired idea.

I then knitted myself a leg purse, with room for several bills, and with a hole in it so that it fastened over my garter and was held under my stocking. This worked very well, for as I explained to my husband, only a very good friend could pick my leg purse.

However, during the heavy summer rains, when one crosses slippery streets in crowds and is busy watching out for traffic, I have had my umbrella gently removed from under my arm, sweaters whisked from around my shoulders (if my arms were not thrust into the sleeves), and my purse relieved of everything in it that might resemble a wallet, from cardcase and Kleenex pack to little wads of tissue paper in plastic envelopes.

One continues, however, to struggle. I bought a large bag with a secret compartment and this was fine for a while, until one day I found that it had been ripped open by a sharp instrument (a razor, perhaps), while I made purchases in the market, and I was two hundred pesos poorer.

For help I turned to a lady who has always given me good advice and who can be seen daily about her multitudinous charitable enterprises in Mexico City with four or five large bags over her arm.

"Mamina Geni," I said to her, "tell me what to do!" (She is of Italian origin, though devoted to Mexico, and a long-time resident. She is very courageous and has been decorated by the Mexican government for her valor during the "Tragic Days" in the Revolution of 1910, when she, a young girl, devoted herself to dragging wounded persons out of the street to where they could be given first aid.) "It isn't the money so much—though I am always very bitter about every economy I have made when my pocket is picked. No, it isn't the money, so much. I don't carry around much cash any more. It is the way my character has been undermined. I stare accusingly into the eyes of strangers, and I snarl whenever I am jostled in a crowd. I would like to get my sweet and idiotically trusting personality back again!"

"I will give you my special design for purses that are proof against Italian pickpockets," she offered. "And the Italians," she bragged, "are the best pickpockets in the world!"

Mamina Geni's purses were made of thin strips of copper between two layers of leather, the handles being copper chains riveted on, and covered with leather, and inside they had false bill pockets and secret compartments and all sorts of other clever devices to throw thieves off the scent. Besides, she always kept in her fortress-purse a little roll of newspaper, covered with a one-peso bill and held together with a rubber band, as a decoy. Mamina Geni was way ahead of the pickpockets and they had never got their hands on one cent of the money she was always collecting for her beloved poor.

I took this idea up with Mamacita and told her I was going to order a copper-lined purse, custom-made, for myself.

"Why go to all that expense?" she asked, arching her black brows. "I thought you had a leg purse."

I blushed.

"Luis forbade me to use it, because once he saw me lift

up my skirt and take money out of it, and he said men were watching. Besides himself, I mean."

"Then he is right. That was not correct," pronounced Mamacita, who knew what was correct for all occasions. "And besides, dresses are getting shorter now. No, you must use the old-fashioned system such as I use. I have never had my pocket picked in my life."

"What do you do?"

Mamacita flipped a little silver chain she always wore around her neck, bent over slightly, and drew up from the depths of her underwear, from under her corset cover and several other garments, a little leather money bag, into which she had slipped her folded bills, with a few silver pesos to weight it. To restore this purse to its hiding place, she merely pulled forward the neck of her blouse, dropped in the purse, and let it fall into place with a dull clank.

"People think I merely have a holy medal on the end of my chain, inside my dress, and of course I do," she said. "San Antonio, who retrieves lost objects. Nobody would ever haul up my chain, because I would be looking straight at them, and I would scream. Besides, I always go to the Mass for Divine Providence on the first of every month. You should, too. One can't be too careful."

While the hazard of the pickpocket can be infuriating, it can be provided against, and a certain flavor is given one's excursions into the city, when one has worked out a system of circumventing the evil ones who lurk there, ready to despoil you of your hard-earned centavos. But there are some other peculiar dangers in Mexico, which you must simply pray may never happen to you.

We haven't any international gangs operating machine guns, nor yet any severe problem in delinquency of youth. Murders tend to be the result of alcohol or of making away with a wife not legally your own. But Mexican laws themselves, with the best will in the world, sometimes confuse the citizenry with their ample provisos for protection of supposed victims.

Take the matter of a street or highway accident, for example. Despite the wish to gather up the injured immediately and rush them to a hospital, you should be warned that the Mexican law severely enjoins everyone to report accidents at once, but in no way to disturb the injured until emergency hospital crews can reach them and care for them professionally. Relatives of a friend of mine, who found bodies strewn around a wreck on the highway, and took the dead and injured into the nearest town, found themselves spending the night in jail and in need of a good lawyer next day.

The best thing to do is to leave a member of your party with the injured, to cover them and keep them warm (to ward off shock), and drive into the nearest town or to the nearest telephone. Many of Mexico's highways now have telephone boxes at regular intervals along the way.

Another legal point of view in Mexico is that if you, as a householder, surprise somebody at the silver and shoot and kill him, you must stand trial for murder. Now this is, I believe, actually the case in many countries, including the United States, the philosophy here being that death is not quite the right punishment for thieving, in our century. In the United States, I know that some states consider burglary or breaking and entering, while armed, as tantamount to murder, since the thief was quite evidently ready to kill if stopped at his crime. Yet the burden of proof is not hard to establish, while in Mexico, where there have been revolutions and where passions wax hot over political differences, the law takes into consideration that shooting someone in your house after dark might lend itself to scheming.

And the Mexican law has much in its favor. I myself remember a case in San Angel in which a man who had enticed and seduced a young girl years before, was stalked and lured to a bloody revenge in this way. A certain man cultivated him, and ended by inviting him to his home for dinner. Now,

Mexican homes often serve an evening dinner as late as eleven, and the gentlemen may sit over their brandy and cigars until well past midnight. So, having got his victim into the right position near the sideboard where the silver was kept, the host turned out the lights and then shot him dead. He turned himself over to the police immediately as having shot a thief in his home.

Mexican police weren't born yesterday, and the secret police operate on the system of the Paris Sureté. The true facts were brought out, and the state took charge. Nevertheless, cases like this one have made law-enforcement officers careful to look into every case of a "thief" being summarily dispatched by a householder. When thieves really do break in, Papacito is usually careful to aim low. Actually, few Mexican thieves can go armed with guns. Guns are expensive and require permits, and to make sure that none are being given out without police checkups, the police regularly raid all bars and beer palaces and simply take guns away from everybody. Then persons who have legitimate permits to carry them may come and demonstrate their right. The fear of householders actually is not a pistol; it is the "white weapon," as the Spanish language so poetically describes a knife.

Moreover, it is not an easy matter to burgle a home in Mexico. Mexican homes still cherish the Spanish tradition of the household fortress, with thick walls, barred windows, and watchdogs with big white teeth. It is rigid custom that a home never be left unattended. There is always a *mozo* or a *sirvienta* in the house, as well as the loud-mouthed and hysterical dog.

Americans who arrive in Mexico for a visit are often bewildered at the way maids take telephone messages. The method derives from reasons of security. "I will see if she is in," is the usual response to a request to speak to the lady of the house, or "She will return in fifteen minutes. Please leave your telephone number."

Very often when such an answer is given, there is no

one at home at all. Maids are ordered strictly never to reveal
that the master and mistress are not at home. They are always
"about to return." Thieves may be calling to find out if they
may expect resistance. This is especially true during important
holidays, around Christmas or Easter, or during the "official
government holidays" which occur twice a year, and precipi-
tate general exodus from the city.

People who won't keep nervous dogs often depend on a
parrot. An irritable parrot is very good burglar insurance and
can be taught to scream "Thieves! Where's the gun! Shoot
him!" at any unexplained noise.

With the growth of the apartment-house dwelling in Mexico City, many of the old-time, dependable defenses have vanished. Land is at a premium, and the apartment house is the
only answer for families with moderate budgets. No longer
can these people defend their treasures with the high thick
wall, the iron-barred window, and the roaring dog.

But Mexicans will think of ways to defend themselves in
the constant war to see who will end up with the most of other
people's pesos. Thieves in Mexico also carry away such things
as the typewriter, the radio, the television, and pieces of household equipment, since these can be quickly sold for cash,
and can't be faked. Jewels are not much bothered, thanks to
the art of the fake jewelry makers.

I have lived in Mexico for one third of my normal life
expectancy and expect to stay here the remainder of my days.
Mexicans are very clever, resourceful, and resilient. They have
been trained in hard schools and have learned to survive. They
will think of new traps for the pilferers. The way of the
transgressor is hard and he has to get up pretty early in the
morning to get the better of the Mexicans I know. They have
already lived through the hungers and the revolutions.

XIV ❧

THE LAW OF THE GORGEOUS

> *Ya se cayó el arbolito,*
> *Donde durmió el pavo real . . .*
> *Ahora a dormir en el suelo,*
> *Como cualquier animal . . .*
> —MEXICAN POPULAR SONG

One day I heard the words that make any wife's heart falter and tremble.

After looking at me fixedly for a few moments, over his breakfast ranchero eggs, my husband dug down into his trousers and pulled out a fifty-peso bill, gave it to me, and said, "Why don't you go over to the beauty shop and get yourself a facial, honey? Go today."

After his departure for the battlefields of commerce, I wept. My two little boys hovered over me, eager to comfort.

"What's the matter, Mima?" they wanted to know.

"I have to go and get my face fixed," I told them.

"Why?" they both asked loyally.

"Because," was my womanly answer. You'd be surprised how good an answer it is. They accepted it immediately.

"Oh," they replied.

I went to my favorite salon and told the proprietress I had come to purchase fifty pesos' worth of beauty. She called up a couple of beautiful young Mexican girls, with clear olive skins, shining eyes, long pearly nails, and handsome hairdos, gave them white aprons, and told them to get to work on me. About two hours later I left, feeling as if my face had been washed, starched, and ironed.

That evening my husband said, "Very nice. You must go often."

"It seems," I told him, "that you have to buy me a collection of unguents to smear on between treatments. Creams that have hormones in them, and creams that are made from chicken embryos, and some other ones concocted from placentas, or fortified with wheat germ. And also I have to buy some lotions to restore lost oils, and others that put back lost moisture, and one to keep in the icebox that brings the blood up to the skin surface. I have to have a chin strap . . . that costs one hundred pesos . . . and a patter . . . that costs twenty-five . . . and . . . I forget. Here's the list."

Luis read the list, slowly turning ashen, for the total came to almost a thousand pesos.

"Those are for the face," I explained. "Then besides there are special products for the neck, and others for the eyes, and some hair lotion . . . and they think I had better have a course of static exercise on some new machine. . . . Now where did I put that other list?"

"Never mind," said Luis hastily. "Forget the whole thing, will you? I like you well enough as you are."

"But you didn't yesterday."

"Well, it isn't worth all that money!"

"You mean you would rather stand me as I am than spend the money on me?"

"Yes," he answered desperately, so after he had gone to the library to read his paper, I had to cry again. My little boys rushed to pat me and I told them I was having trouble with my face again.

"Does it hurt to fix your face?" asked the tender Wiki.

"Quite a lot."

"Then take an aspirin."

I did, but later on, I decided to struggle on toward greater beauty without the benefit of professional advice. I saw an advertisement for a beauty masque which you put on at home, and it was said to do wonders and cause husbands to salaam. I bought a package of it and read the printed directions. That afternoon I put it on.

It was a thick, gooey stuff, a revolting green in color, but the magazines I had been reading were devoting a lot of space to how important it is not to let yourself go, and how vital it is to keep young and beautiful, even if your husband has lost his hair and his waistline. I couldn't comfort myself with these words, for my husband's hair was still thick, black and wavy, and his figure was trim and slim as always, due to tennis and no second helpings.

The green goo felt fairly pleasant going on. I laid it on with a knife, leaving a rim of pink skin around my eyes and mouth. The masque was supposed to stay on for half an hour while it did its mysterious work, so I sat down with my book in the sala, to get on with my current murder.

Little Wiki came running in to find me and tell me some important bit of news or observation. He took one look at me and went into hysterics. He wouldn't let me near him, and Teresa, the maid, carried him away twitching and screaming. Guicho heard the row and came in to see what it was all about. When he saw me he laughed heartily, but when I spoke and he realized that this green frog-woman was Mima, he became completely unhinged and also began to scream. I went and washed the stuff off.

When the children had been restored to sanity, I explained that I had put on the masque to make me prettier.

"But it didn't," they told me solemnly. "It made you look terrible."

"But I have to do *something*," I tried to convince them. "I have wrinkles now, and these spots . . . see them? . . . and your Papa has begun to notice. I have to try to look better, somehow. All the other mothers do it."

I intended to tell my husband the anecdote about the beauty masque and its theatrical results, but when he came home to supper that evening he met me with a happy, far-away look in his eyes, and began an anecdote of his own.

"Do you remember Gregorio, in Monterrey?" he asked me. "Well I met him on the street today. He's just my age. But how he has gone down! I could hardly believe it. Big paunch, glasses on, hair snow white. We had a coffee together and he told me I hadn't changed at all. I look as I did twenty years ago, he said. He asked me how I did it."

I decided not to tell my story. The magazines all warn that husbands have to be kept happy, no matter what, and should never be the targets of snippy and snide remarks.

I began a little home treatment next day with lemon juice and it seemed to me that I began to look less weather-beaten. Meanwhile, I was pondering the fresh beauty of most of my Mexican women friends. There is a legend that Latins fade early; it is a calumny. They have dozens of babies, and remain smooth and creamy as to skin, and while they may be a trifle more curved as to figure, they are very much in the present-day ideal of beauty—that is slim, but definitely feminine in outline. Far more times than I can count, I have met a mother with her eldest daughter, and it would take a microscopic skin study to establish which was which.

I asked Mamacita about it.

"It's because we eat oily foods," she said. "What's the use of rubbing oil on your face, and then pushing away the butter and the cream. It doesn't make sense. Put the butter and cream *inside*, and you'll find that the outside looks better. And then too," she added placidly, "it is good for one's looks to have many babies."

"I know that you had ten, Mamacita," I admitted.

"And I have all my own teeth, and only a small wrinkle when I smile, and not many white hairs, yet I am now well into my sixties. It is because every time you have a baby, Nature works hard to make up to you for the time and trouble you are taking. I always found it so. And when I look around at my friends, all young-looking and agile after a dozen or so children, and then, you will pardon me, Eleesabet, at the young women of your country, who are worn out after two or three, it seems to me that they haven't studied their medical books very well. I once looked in Papacito's medical book, and it said that since woman is designed for childbirth, she is happiest and healthiest when she is functioning. But I understand," she concluded slyly, "that ladies in your country prefer to be on committees and work in hospitals and get worn out collecting money for political campaigns, instead of lying on a couch reading a nice romance and waiting for the sixth or seventh baby."

"I think they are changing now, Mamacita. More and more Americans are having larger families."

"A good thing too," she approved. "I always admired Americans. They will soon realize that it is better to have more of babies and less of other things."

The so-called population explosion has since proved Mamacita right on that score, as well as on several others.

I consulted her about my fading beauty and told her that I was saving up some household money to go to one of the health spas in Mexico, where you put radioactive mud on your face, and then after a while, you just peel off the old face like a glove, and toss it away.

"What you need," she told me briskly, "is a good dose of castor oil."

I took some. I was at the point where I was ready to take desperate measures. It's quite true that I felt better about all my problems, then, and for a while I forgot the whole thing.

One evening when Luis was away at some business meeting, my two little boys and I curled up on the couch in front of the fire and played one of our favorite games. We told one another what we would do some day when we were rich.

"When I am rich," I said, "I will buy us tickets on a ship and we will all go around the world. After the first day we won't see any land at all, nothing but ocean and sky all around us. Everything will be blue, above us and below us, and everything will be quiet. We won't hear anything but the whispering of the sea as it slides along the sides of the ship when we cut through the water."

Silence, and we all had visions of ourselves in a great blue bubble of sea and sky, ourselves at the heart of it.

"When I am rich," said Wiki, "I am going to buy four gorillas and I will train them for Mima. One will wear an apron and answer the front door, and one will wear a cap and set the table. One will cook . . . it might be a little hard training her . . . and the Papa gorilla I will train to cut the lawn and take the letters to the post office. Could I get four gorillas for a million pesos, Mima?"

"Three, at least," I told him stanchly. "I can always post my own letters."

"When I am rich," contributed Guicho, "I will give all the money to you Mima, so that you can have your face lifted."

There we were, back at the same old nagging problem. It continued for some time to be a leitmotiv in my life.

Once I went and had my hair washed with a new rinse guaranteeing a wealth of golden highlights. That's what the bottle said. Nobody seemed to notice, though. And once I went and had a Turkish bath which relaxed me so that I slept all next day and had to phone in sick to my office. I felt that I was on the right track here, but it cut into my working hours, and I couldn't keep it up.

Then Guicho, who is something of a house detective, came and reported mysteriously, "Mima, Wees is in the bathroom putting some black stuff on his mustache. Stuff out of a bottle. I saw him."

"Shhhh! We have to pretend we don't know," I advised him. But I felt much comforted. The last vestiges of unhappiness vanished when I caught my husband tweezing two white hairs away from his temples. They suffer too, I thought, and it seemed only fair.

Mamacita had come to visit, and I told her the secret about poor Luis.

"He will never get many white hairs," she said, unperturbed. "He takes after my people."

When I confided once more my worries over myself and what time marching on was doing to me, she said, "But *hijita*, do not disturb yourself so much. I will tell you a secret." And she did.

The next evening at dinner I said to Luis, "Isn't it time for you to buy a new suit? Tomorrow is Saturday. If you like, I will go with you, and we will select one for you."

Luis was pleased. He loves to shop and has always thought it queer and proof of some sort of mental unbalance in me, that I hate to, and that I always get psychosomatically weary unto death after an hour of fingering fabrics and asking prices.

We went and looked at dozens of suits. I didn't get tired, only needed three cups of reviving coffee all afternoon, and I told him how wonderful he looked in the gray but then also he was too, too handsome in the brown. I praised his youthful figure and his trim waist and his back and his front and the side views.

His eyes glazed slightly, but all this was, after all, the best beauty treatment I had ever had myself. He looked at me with strong admiration, and on his face was all the approval that used to shine there during our courting days.

Ever after, whenever I felt myself especially repulsive, I had only to tell Luis how beautiful he was, and life once more became easy, and all wheels whirled splendidly, greased with the oil of praise.

"You see, *hijita*," Mamacita had told me, "if you want your husband to think you are gorgeous, just tell him that *he* is gorgeous. It is curious, but this always works. Try it."

It worked conversely, too. For after all, what makes a woman better-looking than a happy husband?

I had many opportunities of confirming the wisdom of Mamacita's law. My friends Josefina and Carmen told me that in Mexico the one subject a wife must avoid at all costs is deterioration in the personal attractiveness or fascination of the gentleman.

"It is not that men are really more vain than women," they told me. "It is just that they are more sensitive. Or perhaps it is because we are allowed to make use of artifice, and they are not. But it upsets them frightfully to think that they don't always look as they did at twenty-four."

Mexican wives, tenderhearted creatures (with their practical sagaciousness, too), usually keep the bathroom scales turned down so that they register several pounds less, for Papi, and I have come upon Mexican friends carefully removing size tabs from their husband's pajamas—tabs which indicate size 42 in the heartless way of clothing manufacturers, and sewing in tabs which proclaim that the garment is a 38.

When the waistline, and the occasional bald patch are beyond explaining away, one must begin to say how distinguished the older men are, so much more attractive generally than young men, who tend to be gauche and far, *far* too thin.

There is, at around age forty-five, a tough problem which each wife must solve as she thinks best. It is whether it would be better to let the gray in her hair show, and grow old along with her husband, to comfort him, or to strive mightily for the youthful silhouette, the muscle firmer, the slim figure, and the radiant tint on the hair, indicating that while Papi may be getting on, he can still dominate the youthful creature on his arm, who looks fifteen years younger.

But of course, this has its limits too, and then there is another decision to make. (The whole thing is complicated by the fact that Papi's mother is probably telling him, every day, how young and handsome he is, and so wives have to keep up; you can't let your mother-in-law get ahead of you in the Praise and Appreciation Department.)

The final trump card, of course, is always another baby. Nothing makes a man feel more strong, proud, and resilient than passing out the cigars again.

And if there's a population explosion, so what? It's important for husbands to be happy and busy, all the books say.

If wives are sometimes a bit unhappy, that's too bad. When I took up my hems, styles having decided on shorter skirts, and then walked in front of my husband and sons to ask if the higher hemline would have their official approval, Luis was inclined to say No, being a most conservative creature in every way. But my sons defended me.

"Let her show her legs, Wees," they said. "That's all she has left!"

I was sad at this for a little while. But that's life. That's the way the cookie crumbles, as they say, or That's the way the tortilla tears.

XV ❧

LA FIESTA BRAVA

Ay, que terrible cinco de la tarde!
—FROM THE POEM OF FEDERICO GARCIA LORCA, "LAMENT
FOR SANCHEZ MEJIAS"

Luis's brother Carlos was a "loner." When they were children, despite the noisy communal activities of the other Treviños, he was usually working out elaborate schemes of his own for acquiring pocket money, which, to the frustration and envy of the others, often were productive. During the first years of the family's exile, in Victoria, Texas, while the Revolution of 1910 was still raging in the *patria*, Carlos disappeared one June day. He had run away to join the circus.

After learning where he was, Papacito dried Mamacita's tears and advised, "Let him stay with it, if he wants to. It's summer anyhow, and I will bring him back in time for school." Come September, Carlos came home voluntarily, with money jingling in his pockets, and a beautiful aura of success and adventure clinging around him. So he lived, independent and alone, making his own way, until he married. Then all the Treviño traits of fierce family devotion and protectiveness boiled up in him, and he became a sober and settled family man. But he kept one day of the week entirely for himself, and nothing—except desperate illness of one of his children or his wife—could take it from him. He kept his Domingo, his Sunday. The Domingo of the Toros. For Carlos was a fanatical *aficionado* of the Fiesta Brava.

So it was Carlos who gave me my first lessons in how I should watch the bullfight, since Luis doesn't like the fights, and never goes.

He found me thoughtfully eating a cucumber on a street corner in Mexico City one day. These cucumber stands are wonderful, especially when the weather is hot at midday. The cucumbers, peeled and slit so as to form flowerlike shapes, are kept in buckets of ice water, and when you pay your *toston* (fifty centavos), the cucumber of your choice is drawn out of the ice water, excess moisture is shaken off, and it is powdered with a mixture of salt and chile powder. It is the most delicious of foods, and has the double advantage of being cheap and non-fattening as well.

"I hope you have had your typhoid shots," murmured Carlos. (He was then representing a medical laboratory.) I told him I had.

"How's the family?"

"Fine. And yours?"

"All fine." He had three children, two sons and a daughter.

"My sister Barbara, from the States, is coming to visit me next week," I told him.

"Wonderful. I will take you both to the bullfight. There's a great *cartel.* Armillita and Pepe Ortiz and El Soldado."

I paled.

"I have never gone," I said, "and I don't know that I want to. I am so fond of animals, you know."

"Well, you eat meat, don't you?" asked Carlos, I thought, inconsequentially.

"Yes, of course."

"Do you suppose the bulls' carcasses are just thrown out, after the fight? Not a bit of it. They go to the stockyards and are sold for meat."

"But it's cruel. To make the bulls fight. To torture them that way."

"They are raised from fighting stock, bred for it. And they aren't tortured. The matador has only eight minutes in which to make his whole *faena* before he must kill," Carlos told me. "Further, the whole skill of the bullfighter is in killing clean, and instantly, with the *estocada* [sword thrust]. That's how the whole thing began. In Spain, at the slaughterhouses. The animals were killed by the sword, and gradually the whole ritual developed."

We were strolling along Insurgentes Avenue and I had spotted another cucumber stand about three blocks ahead.

"Is it better to kill the beast in a pen, with a great hammer blow on the head, or to let him charge and fight and die in the sunlight with a sword in his heart?" he asked me.

"Well, you see," I tried to explain, knowing how puerile it sounded, "I just don't think about how the animal was killed when I eat a beefsteak."

"I know. You Americans have this peculiar ability. You can close your eyes to what you don't like and pretend it isn't there. We Latins face up to it. We roar and fight, or we love and serenade, but with our eyes open. You like to think of us as romantic, but we are not. We are the true realists."

I did not answer for I was brooding about something he had said. "You claim the bullfight started at the slaughter-houses in Spain," I reminded him. "I thought it had come down via the Moors, from North Africa, and originally to them from Crete, where there was a bull God cult, and young men and maidens used to dance before the Minotaur."

"Maybe there was some memory of that when the young men began passing the bulls with the cape and killing them in Spain. It may have been mixed up with traditions of Moorish spectacles and Roman games and all that. But it is basically the killing of a food animal, and all garlanded with tradition, like the fox hunt in rural England."

"I hate the whole idea of a fox hunt. I would never go to one."

"Neither would I. Twenty people or more, all mounted, and with a great pack of dogs, all after one little fox, is not my idea of a pretty diversion. I prefer the brave little man down there on the sand, with nothing but a cape and a sword and his own guile to save him from that big black several-ton animal, raging to horn his way out of the ring."

I quickly ducked a discussion of Latin versus Saxon traits, in which I would be sure to come out badly battered, Carlos being a passionate Latin and proud of it.

"But where's the sport in watching a bull killed?" I couldn't help asking. "The men don't have to *risk* themselves. And one knows that the bull is always killed. It's not sporting to have the thing so one-sided."

"Sport? Sport?" sputtered Carlos, buying me another cucumber, and selecting for himself a big boiled ear of corn from a stand where corn was bubbling in a vat. He sprinkled salt and chile on my cucumber, peeled down the husk from his corn, and doused it with the same condiments. We munched while he thought how to instruct me.

"Of course the bullfight isn't sport! It does not pretend to be. It is a spectacle. An exhibition. An exhibition of man's tremendous courage and skill as exercised against brute force. It is the drama of our own times . . . the drama that shows us what life is. Because courage is still the supreme virtue, the quality that separates men from slaves."

"Ah. That's what you mean then, by Fiesta Brava. The Fiesta of Courage."

"That's right."

"But you mention guile. I don't especially admire guile, you know."

"Maybe you say you don't, but down inside, you certainly do. Because," declaimed Carlos, "show me the American who doesn't admire success. Guile is necessary for success! It means intelligence, really. It means outwitting your enemy. It means thinking ahead, divining what your opponent will do, and circumventing him. You have to have guile to win at chess for example!" (Carlos was a skilled player of *ajedrez*.) "Guile has been important ever since, and long before, the Trojan Horse!" He was waving his ear of corn in big gestures. "Guile is still important! God pity the diplomat who has none! He is made a fool of."

I finished my cucumber and reluctantly decided against a third.

"You let me know when your sister arrives," promised Carlos, in farewell. "I will take you to the *corrida!*"

Meanwhile I had the opportunity of seeing a fighting-bull farm . . . a *ganadería de toros de lidia.* I was asked by one of the newspapers I served to write an article on the big Madrazo Fighting-Bull farm near Aguascalientes. The owners of the ranch insisted on coming to look me over in Aguascalientes before they took me out to the *cortijo,* for they are always nervous of visitors. The bulls must never have been "passed" by a man, or in any way given an opportunity to learn to charge the man and not the cape, before they are shipped away for their star performance . . . the fight on the day they are to die. Having taken a good look at me—timid and plump and sentimental—the owners of the Madrazo ranch gave in at once. There was no danger that I might jump down into a field full of bulls, stamp my foot, and yell "*Toro.*" The contrary. I almost expired with fear when I saw the great, black, glistening creatures fairly close up, with their proud, shining white horns, their gleaming black muzzles, and small, suspicious eyes.

The Madrazo *ganadería* is, in its way, a curious and pertinent comment on the resourcefulness of men and the resilience of some families. The Madrazos were one of the rich landed families whose holdings were expropriated and divided up among the landless peons under the administration of President Lázaro Cárdenas in the late 1930s. The Madrazos found, when the final distribution of land had been made, that they had been left only a barren strip near the foothills, land useless for agriculture, where only tall cactuses grew in profusion. Like many other land-holding families, they were cash poor, and when they had counted up their remaining assets, after the expropriation, they had only a few thousand pesos. There is a saying in bridge, "Play a losing card on a losing trick," and the Madrazo brothers decided to risk all on a possibly ruinous idea.

All this was told me by the beautiful Señora Madrazo, who was showing me over the *cortijo*, a charming ranch house in the old Mexican style, low and tile-covered, decorated with replicas of famous and historic brand marks.

"My brother you know, is a *torero*," she told me. "I was born a Solórzano." Of course I had heard of the brave and handsome matador, Chucho Solórzano. "And my husband is an *aficionado*. So my husband and his brother decided that the rough land left to us might do for raising fighting bulls; in bad weather they could shelter under the cactus. They are wild creatures, you know, unused to stables or any of the softening care given dairy herds. So he and his brother pooled their assets and borrowed more money and they went to Spain to buy a bull and a few cows . . . enough to make the experiment. In Spain they decided against the Miura bulls, which are tough and strong and vicious, in favor of another nobler stock. But these bulls are big and beautiful, also black, and with great heart."

I knew that the Miura bulls had killed most of the storied and famous matadors who had died in the ring in Spain.

The Madrazos returned to Mexico and turned their animals out on their land. The Spanish stock prospered in Mexico's dry cactus country, and within a few years, the first *torillos* were separated from the cows, and fed a special diet to develop their brawn and strength.

Señora Madrazo, tying up her shining black hair in a scarf (not a red one, though she said there was no proof that red has any real effect on the temper of a bull), took me over the ranch in the feeding jeep. This machine carries a sort of truck behind, with a great drum of the mixed and powdered feed in it, and a hose by which it may be piped down into the feeding basins, without the necessity of a man descending from the vehicle.

"We use only jeeps here on the ranch," she told me. "Horses are out, of course. The bulls must never have a chance to charge one. But they seem not to fear these little cars, and nobody has ever been molested in the feeding jeep."

The ranch is divided into sections, by fences of strong barbed wire. In one section the cows roam with their calves. Another section is for the breeding bulls, one for the small bulls, and a last one for the young bulls being readied for the rings.

There were white concrete pillars, hollowed into basins at the top, into which the feed was measured from the drum on the back of our jeep. As we roved about, the animals came hurrying toward their feeding stations. The hour was near sunset, and in the failing light, their branching white horns turned pink, and reflections of blue and amethyst shone on their glistening hides. They were beautiful, and aside from seeming shy and wild, like forest creatures, they did not impress me as having ugly tempers; they seemed interested only in their food.

"We have many bulls now and a thriving business," Señora Madrazo told me. "Though of course, we have very heavy losses. Each animal is worth thousands of pesos, and costs a lot to raise. Yet if they hurt each other in fights or tear themselves on the barbed wire, there is nothing we can do for them. No man could get close enough to cure them."

"How about chloroform, to overpower them?"

"Maybe," she sighed. "If one could get enough of it near them without being rushed. And of course, the bull could never be sent to a fight. It would have to become a breeding animal. Our profits of course, are from animals sold for the *lidia,* the fight."

Fighting bulls must be of a specified weight, and the animals cross an automatic scale when they are delivered to the bullring. If they are less in weight than agreed upon in the contract of sale, the owner is fined. And the animals naturally lose a great deal of weight en route to the various *ruedas*. Mexico is a big country. Therefore, many *ganaderías* maintain feeding stations near the largest bullrings, such as the one in Mexico City. However, the Madrazos worked out a special way of keeping their animals up to weight; they fly them to the bullrings. Señora Madrazo showed me their plane, equipped with a portable ramp, into which the bulls are lured with food. A flight of an hour or two will cause far less loss in weight than a fourteen-hour journey in a closed van, for example, and trains are out of the question, for the bulls must be kept *limpio*, or clean, away from any possibility of learning the ways of men.

This visit to the fighting-bull farm, and my talks with Señora Solórzano de Madrazo had aroused a great deal of technical interest in the *corrida*, and I actually looked forward to going to the bullfight with Carlos. My sister Barbara said she wanted to go, in order to be able to tell her friends that she had gone, but she made me promise to bring her home the minute she felt that she had had enough. Agreed.

Carlos explained, as we drove to the ring, some of the "passes" and their names; he also tried to establish our allegiance toward the fighters by explaining how short a time was allowed the *torero* to "receive" the bull's first charges, a time in which he had to learn whether the bull gored to the left or right, how good his eyesight might be, how fast he was, how quick to turn and recharge.

"You will hear trumpet calls," he told us. "They tell the *torero* that his time for this *suerte*, or playing of the bull is up, and he must go on to the next part of the fight."

The traffic toward the bullring is tremendous in the last hour before the *corrida* begins. The streets and walks are close-packed with pedestrians too, who come on foot or pour out of buses. Many of these are simple working people, for whom this brilliant fiesta is the great event of the week, something they look forward to through all the hours of toil.

Mexico and Spain are the two countries in the world where the bullfight is still carried out with passionate fidelity to the Spanish tradition, and although a few South American countries have *corridas* and occasionally receive the visits of Spanish *toreros*, Mexico is, after Spain, the home of the Fiesta Brava. There could be no better proof, I think, of the homogenization of the Mexican race, in whose veins flow only a fraction of the Moorish-Arabic-Celtic-Jewish-Latin mixture which is Spanish for Mexicans are all *castizo* when it comes to the bullfight. They are experts and thrill to it in every fiber.

I cannot begin to describe the excitement which hovers in the air like smoke, in the bullring. It is almost palpable, and so is the buzz of conversation. There is a smell of hot sunlight on the wooden benches, the acrid odor of the sand, now raked smooth and as yet unstained, a smell of men already sweating with heat and nervous anticipation, and the fragrance of women's powder and perfume, for the *corrida de toros* is a great favorite of Mexican women as well as men. On the shady side, in elegant boxes down near the *barrera*, they sit waving their fans; often they dress in mantilla and high combs for the occasion. Over on the sunny side, where the *hoi polloi* go (the seats cost less, because at one point the sun will be in their eyes, spoiling their view), there are many *hembras* (females), women who come to the fight unchaperoned and tilt beer bottles with the men, and with them screech comments on each *torero's* performance and person . . . sometimes quite obscene remarks.

Refreshment and snack peddlers go about, as do the boys selling cushions for the hard benches. Carlos bought cushions for us, but we couldn't eat anything. This is the Fiesta of Death, and I felt quite solemn.

The judges appear and take their places in a box. If the *corrida* is for charity, or if it occurs during a time of great festivity, such as Carnival, or Red Cross Week, or Gaudalupe Day, a young girl of the best society may be elected queen. La Reina will undoubtedly attend, with her court. The girls settle into the box of honor, looking like full-blown roses in their big flounced skirts of pink, red, yellow, and white. There is a band that plays typical bullfight music, marches, and *paso dobles* (a quick step) with an unmistakable Spanish flavor. At exactly four o'clock, there is a thrilling clarion call from the bandstand, and the great gates open to emit a curiously stylized and medieval parade. And it is at exactly four o'clock, for as Carlos Chávez has said, "There are only two things that begin exactly on time in Mexico—the bullfight, and my symphony concerts."

First comes the *alguacil*, (Arabic-Spanish for sheriff), dressed in black and wearing a plumed hat. He is mounted on a mettlesome horse. He is to *partir plaza* (literally, to cut the plaza), or to open the show. He rides across the yellow sand and makes his horse bow on one knee before the judges and the queen. He takes off and flourishes his plumed black hat.

"He is asking permission for the fight to begin," whispered Carlos. Permission is granted, else why have we all paid our twenty or thirty pesos a seat?

Behind the *alguacil* come the matadors, the stars of the day, wearing their *trajes de luces*, or "suits of light," . . . satin knee breeches and short bolero coats in white or pink or turquoise, heavily embroidered with gold threads, pearls, and sequins; they glitter as they walk slowly in their flat shoes. They have folded their arms into their embroidered capes, holding them across their chests, and on their heads are the padded hats of black velvet, with side wings. All the *toreros* wear the *coleta*, a little pigtail of hair wadded on the neck. It is tradition to wear this, as it is supposed that it helps prevent concussion in a fall. Their walk seems stiff and awkward in comparison with their fluid poses and passes, later in the ring. Each *torero* is followed by his helpers, his *cuadrilla*, men who can rush into the ring with a cape and lure the bull away, if the matador finds himself in a position of danger, or has been gored. After these come the *picadores*, on thin old horses, which at least wear padded blankets nowadays. The *picadores* wear a costume like that of Sancho Panza in Dau-

mier's illustrations of Don Quijote, and all the horses remind
me of poor Rocinante.

Last of all are the *monos sabios* or wise monkeys; these
are merely chore boys, dressed in gray. They come romping
into the ring when the bull has been killed, and drag the
carcass away; they smooth down the bloodied sand and make
it ready for the next fight. They are supposed to be funny
in their caperings, like clowns, and I presume they represent
some sort of dance of triumph over the fallen enemy. For the
bull is referred to as the enemy by bullfight chroniclers and by
those latter-day historians who report bullfights over the radio
and television. Incidentally, these commentators have taken
over the technique of the American sports reporter, the rising
tone of excitement when a crisis is being reached, the fast-
pouring words, the occasional intimate interpolations.

After the parade, the *picadores* and the *monos sabios* and
the matadors who are not to fight the first bull retire, and the
torero who will make the first fight remains alone on the sand,
with his *cuadrilla* distributed about near the safety barriers,
which are board fences behind which they may take refuge.

On that day Armillita looked spidery and frail down there
on the sand in his bravely shining suit.

Then, to a golden trumpet call, the doors of the *toril*
swung open, and a great black beast thundered out into the
sun, enraged. He had been kept in darkness, and now, in the
sun, he shook his head, slightly blinded by it; in his hide
quivered a dart bearing the colors of the Madrazo *ganadería*.
He pawed the dust and bellowed and stared around; then he
saw something moving. Armillita's cape, being shaken toward
him, to catch his attention. He rushed toward it, heavy, fast,
his great head with the stiletto-sharp horns already lowered.

There is no terror, no thrill, quite like this first charge of
the bull. I almost fainted.

For a few minutes, as Armillita, so slim, so brave, passed
the great black locomotive of a bull, I felt as the Latins do. I
identified myself with the man down there, so alone, with

only his cape and his skill for his protection. My heart was with him, and the bull was my enemy.

There was performed for the public a curious ballet, all grace and rhythm. The bull would charge, but the cape would always be kept a few feet ahead of his horns. This is called *temple,* and a great bullfighter is one who keeps the *temple* always the same, as a great orchestra conductor dominates the tempo of the players with his beat. The *torero* led with his right arm, swinging his whole body with it, leaning toward it, and the hem of the cape just touched the sand. He performed various "passes," movements of controlled and perfect grace. The fans know all the names of each step, just as balleto-manes know a pirouette, a fouette, and a jeté. Each beautifully completed movement of man and cape, as the bull charged past, was applauded with a great "*Olé.*" Armillita was an artist, and the *Olé's* broke on the sunlit air with the regularity of waves crashing upon a beach.

At a certain moment the bull stopped, heaving still with exertion, and shook its head in bewilderment. Armillita then turned his back upon the animal, knowing with some sure instinct that it would not charge just then, and, trailing his cape on the sand, he strutted toward the judge's box, holding up his right arm, in an imperious gesture demanding applause. He got it, but right there he lost me. I shifted my allegiance, and from then on, I was with the bull.

The trumpet announced that the *tercio* was over, and the *picadores* came out, on their trembling horses, for the next act of the drama. The object of this part of the fight is to weary the bull and cause him to hold his head lower, low enough so that in the end the sword may be thrust into his heart. The horses are a frank sacrifice, to tire him out. This I could not watch, and I observed that my resourceful sister reached down into her capacious bag and drew out her knitting at this point. She knitted and purled, steadily, with lowered eyes, while our neighbors looked at us aghast and poor Carlos was humiliated almost beyond bearing.

The horses were lifted, but not killed, that day, Carlos told me. But I remembered having heard about a bull once in Monterrey which was so fierce and strong that he killed four horses and a *picador*, and the frantic impresario rushed out into the streets of Monterrey buying up pitiful old nags to throw to the bull, in an effort to exhaust him. The bull killed twenty horses that day, and in the end, when it was dark, everybody went home, and left him in command of the arena, among the corpses of the slain horses, and he tossed and threw them all night. That bull was *indultado*, or pardoned, and sent back to the bull-breeding farm, to sire many more of his heart and temper. And they tell of this legendary bull that he eventually died charging a train. This bull had a name, as they all do, but I forget it. I always think of him as the Minotaur.

After the horses have been led away (if there are any left), the *torero* places *banderillas* in the bull. Armillita is famous for doing this beautifully. He stood, with the two long decorated darts held high, his arms up, and he called the bull to him. As the bull charged, Armillita leaped up and to the side, left the darts quivering in the bull's neck just behind the hump, and ran gracefully away, out of danger. Three times he did this, to a positive roar of *Olé's*, and I could see why he was admired. It was, like any piece of acrobatics, perfect in timing and skill; and there was the ever-present danger there, to give the act a special frightening thrill.

After the darts, the trumpet sounds again, demanding the kill. Now Armillita emerged once more, his sword hidden in the *muleta* (a different cape). The bull was charging lower, sometimes almost sweeping the sand with his horns. He was slower, nearer his end. Armillita had to stamp his foot and call him, for the animal was resting longer between charges. There were more exhibitions of grace and cape play, and then, at last, the kill. With his Toledo blade glinting in the sun, Armillita rose to the tips of his toes, sighted along the steel, and then plunged it in, to the hilt, just behind the hump. It was a good kill, the *Olé's* told me. The animal stood motionless, then plummeted down, and blood gushed from its mouth. The *monos sabios* came and dragged him away, a mass of bloody flesh now, instead of a fearsome enemy. Armillita strutted around the ring, while flowers rained down on him, ladies' fans and handkerchiefs, even mantillas and fur pieces. There is a frenzy, a kind of orgiastic excitement here. The judges awarded him an ear and the tail of the bull he had killed, in token of his triumph.

Carlos was beside himself, roaring and clapping; his eyes shone behind his glasses and his white teeth were brilliant. But I felt very sad. Barbara packed up her knitting.

"I want to go home," she said.

But Carlos laid a hand on her arm, detaining her. The excitement had simmered down a little; again it was anticipatory.

"Look," said Carlos. "We are to have a Tancredo!"

A stout wooden box, about two feet high, had been set up in the exact center of the ring, and a young man, dressed in pure white, with a red sash around his waist (it is the Basque costume) mounted the box. He stood quiet there, with no sword, no cape. Then, to my horror, the doors of the *toril* opened, and another great bull shot out.

"If he is perfectly motionless, during the charge," Carlos told us, "the bull will swerve away and do him no harm. But if he loses his nerve, and moves . . . Tragedy!"

The bull, bellowing and throwing up dust with his hoofs, saw something odd in the vacancy of the ring, something white. Lowering his head, he thundered toward it like an express train. There was no movement whatever from our iron-nerved Tancredo, and the bull swerved and rushed past.

Barbara knitted, and I alternately opened and shut my eyes as Pepe Ortiz played, wore out, and dispatched the next bull. Then Barbara stood up, and said firmly, "I don't know about you, but *I* am leaving."

Carlos, courteous host, accompanied us, though it must have cost him dear to give up the last four bulls.

"I will explain something to you," he said, controlling himself with an effort, as we walked toward his car. "You two identify yourselves with the animals, not with the men."

"That's true," I admitted. "Because the men don't have to be there. The *torero* is there because he wants a lot of fame and money. But the bull is there because he can't help it."

"You have never seen a man killed in the ring. That would teach you," muttered Carlos, starting the car. "I saw Balderas killed . . . gored in the forehead. I have seen many men tossed on the horns. It changes your point of view."

"I would hate to see a man killed," said Barbara, "but I would also hate myself for having gone."

As we drove home, I was thinking of the great poem by the Spaniard, García Lorca, "Llanto por Ignacio Sánchez Mejías" (known in its English translation as "Lament for the Death of a Bullfighter"). Sánchez Mejías was a *matador* killed in the ring in Andalusia. I remembered the lines, tolling so often through the poem, "*Era las cinco de la tarde*" ("It was five o'clock in the afternoon"), and the wonderful lines, so Spanish, so vivid, used to describe Sánchez Mejías' journey to the town where the bullfight was to occur "*Y trae su muerte a cuestas*" ("And he carried his death on his back"). And then that sudden line, like a scream of pain: "*Ay, que terrible cinco de la tarde!*" ("That terrible five o'clock in the afternoon!"). When it was five o'clock on all the clocks in Spain, on the cathedral clock, and the clock in the shop and the clock in the homes . . . that terrible five o'clock! The hour when Sánchez Mejías was tossed on the horns and pierced and killed.

"I'll tell you something about you Saxons," said Carlos bitterly. "You are all babies about the idea of death. You pretend it doesn't happen. You 'pass away' or you 'pass on.' You don't wear mourning. Everything has to seem to be just as it always was. You won't look. In Mexico, and in Spain, we *die*. You can manage to squeeze out a few tears, if you see something about death in a play, when it is just mummery, but you cannot look at the moment of truth. When death is present, at the moment of truth, the moment of the great mystery." And then he dressed us down with the final scorn, "You have sugar in your heads. *Nada de sal.* No salt! No salt!" It is frightful to be without salt, in Mexico or in Spain. It means you are a goop, a square, a blob, a drip, a moron.

"But I know American girls who madly love the bullfight," I protested feebly. "They go miles to see them, and they know all about the *suertes* and the passes and everything."

The whole thing was taken up *sobre mesa* (that interval after dessert and over lots of coffee and cigarettes, elbows on the table, when Mexican guests love to sit on and talk and talk) after we had had supper. For once Carlos had given up going to the great rival bullfighter cafes, where the *aficionados* go after each fight. These are the Tupinamba and the Flor de Mexico, in the main part of Mexico City. (There are others in every district or *barrio*, where the bullfight is fought again, step by step, and fans debate acrimoniously about the merits of their favorite *toreros*.) Once the fans at Tupinamba surged out toward the Flor de Mexico, and there was a great street fight over whether Manolete was better than Silverio, and the police had to come and break it up. Mexicans are as stubborn and frenetic about their favorite bullfighters as Americans are about their political candidates during an election.

Barbara cleared her throat at our *sobre mesa* and made her final pronouncement.

"I guess it is all right for you big brave Latins that like to look at death," she said, "but as for me, I don't like to watch anything get killed, man or beast. And I will never go to another bullfight, no matter how many nasty names you call me, Carlos."

Now Carlos felt hurt in his hospitality and he rose from the table, full of injured pride. It took a little while to get everybody back on a plane of amiable family discussion.

Before he departed, Carlos turned to me, and raised his black brows at me in interrogation. They silently asked, "Well, what do you think?" One of the wonderful things about Carlos was that he could leave off speaking whenever he felt like it, and continue communicating by means of gestures, manipulation of eyebrows, shoulders, arms, hands, and fingers.

So I drew a long breath and said my piece.

"Carlos," I began placatingly, "I understand the ritual. I appreciate that the bullfight is a Fiesta Brava, the celebration of man's courage, a symbolic representation of the victory of brains over brute force, with the odds actually against the man in overwhelming number, if he lacks or loses courage. So it is a paean of praise to valor and to coolness under attack. I love the color of the costumes, and the music never ceases to thrill me. I have lived in Mexico long enough to have taken on the Mexican feeling about death; I am not indifferent to it, God knows, but I don't hide from it, and I know it is all around, all the time, part of the pattern of life.

"I realize that there is art in the improvisations of movement and plasticity carried out by the *torero*, with the plunging bulk of the bull as his partner, the man's steps, his dancing, being adjusted to the rhythms set by the bull, and always with 'death on his back,' like Sánchez Mejías, should he misjudge, or misstep.

"I know and respect all these points, intellectually. I also recognize the solemnity of the moment of truth, for the bullfight dignifies the bull's death in a way, making it into something in music, not a note, but the resolution of a chord.

"But I won't go to any more bullfights for another reason. Because the whole thing symbolizes for me, and carries out the attitude I most abhor, no matter how it is done."

"What is that?" cried Carlos, for he had thought that I was by now a convert to the glories of the Fiesta Brava.

"The thing I loathe is the violation of innocence. It is what I hate above all else, and it happens too often in our world. The martyrization of a peaceful people under Hitler was a supremely horrible example of the violation of innocence. The strafing of civilians from the air by military planes is an example of it. When horses are brutally 'broken' to the saddle, it is a violation of innocence, and I can't bear it. When little children are mistreated, or cruelly punished for things they can't understand, or made to serve adult passions, it is violation of innocence, and I believe that this is what was meant by the 'eating of the apple,' in the Bible story. It is the most utter and horrible act of pride and treachery to act violently upon any creature without warning, or which cannot avoid its fate. The violation or betrayal of innocence is a stench in the nostrils, and an abomination. And the bullfight celebrates and exemplifies what I am talking about. The bull represents brute force, yes, but also he represents innocence, a creature acting according to the laws of his being, trapped into serving man's pride. He does not know that he is to be hurt and wearied and brought to his death. That's why I will never go to another one."

"Then you hate hunting too. All the manly sports."

"I hate hunting if it is just to take specimens, or for the purpose of bragging that you 'got your deer' or your limit or whatever, yes."

"Then, to be consistent, you should not eat meat, since the animals must be killed to feed you," declared Carlos.

"From now on, I shan't."

Carlos gave up. The subject was closed. He never offered to take me to any more bullfights, and I have never gone again.

And I am now a vegetarian, though I realize how utterly illogical I am. I wear leather shoes, and carry a leather handbag, and in my closet hangs an old, somewhat moth-eaten but warm fur coat to which I am devoted. Also, I partake of chicken on occasion, and I often eat fish.

Please don't anybody ever give me any goldfish or guppies for pets, or anything else with scales or fins that I might grow fond of. For then I would be forced to live on bread—and you know how fattening that is.

XVI 🦢

"CALM YOURSELF," SAID THE MYNA BIRD

Unos nacen con estrella, y otros estrellados.
—OLD MEXICAN SAYING

School days and homework took up much of our time except over the long end-of-term holidays, which begin in late November and continue through February.

After three years at the Marmua School my little sons had to leave to attend a boys' school, for mixing of the sexes is allowed only through third grade. From then on, the black sheep are separated from the ewe lambs until in college, a few very brave young ladies, with brave parents, undertake to get a degree. (Public schools are generally coeducational, however.)

In the new school Guicho had to repeat fourth year, because I had bought him a book on astronomy. My diligent reading of American ladies' magazines had advised that children should be encouraged in their interests, if these involved learning or self-improvement in any way, and I hadn't a glimmering that astronomy was going to cause a lot of trouble. But, when we got the notice that he had to repeat his grade, and investigated, it transpired that though he could describe the movements of the planets, distances between them, duration of orbits and so on, all this was not a fourth-grade subject. As to the fourth-grade subjects, he knew nothing whatsoever about them. He had put his astronomy book in front of every book he was supposed to be studying, and had learned nothing else. Sternly lectured by the head of the school, I bought him no more extracurricular books and tried to keep my conversations from arousing in either of the children, any great thirst for general knowledge apart from school requirements.

Actually Mexican schools provide plenty of study; they do in six years what most of our primary schools take eight years to accomplish, and by the time the children are ready for *secundaria* (high school) they already have considerable knowledge of a foreign language, a year's study of algebra and a year's study of geometry, as well as advanced courses in literature.

Luis saw that the boys did their homework. This is known as the *tarea*. I could preside over history and composition, but Luis had to help with the arithmetic. In this I was useless, being a dolt in arithmetic in the first place, and ignorant of Spanish terms for procedure in the second place. Then too, I learned as the boys went into long division and fractions, that the Mexicans used systems which I understand are based on some pre-Conquest concepts of numbers. Anyway, they turned out to be faster and more logical proceedings than any I was ever taught. Every evening after dinner, when books and pencils and pads were produced, I was shunted off into a corner and told to keep quiet. Nothing could be heard but the click of my knitting needles or the twanging of my tatting shuttle, and the groans and nervous oaths of the three Treviño males as they sat struggling with their arithmetic problems.

One day, when Luis was late in arriving home, a Hungarian friend had dropped in. Observing the boys at their arithmetic *tarea* he sat down to help them until Luis appeared. It was any port in a storm, and the boys grabbed him forthwith. He and Guicho discussed the problem in Spanish, then the Hungarian did the adding, multiplying, and so on in Hungarian, which sounds especially strange when being muttered rapidly under the breath. Then the Hungarian solutions had to be translated into Spanish and explained to Wiki. All the problems were thus done in Hungarian, and such are the reflexes instilled by school systems, that the Hungarian friend rang up at noon next day to ask, with breathless interest, if he had passed.

Guicho managed to keep up with his school work, but, having been stopped in his tracks in regard to astronomy, and being frisked every morning for some book not on the school curriculum, he took to drawing again. Endless automobiles streamed out from his homework pad, and then he began drawing people. While these efforts were more or less straight portraiture, a bit in the Modigliani tradition, he soon began to develop caricatures, unerringly choosing the feature or quality in his subject, most likely to lose friends and alienate people. I felt nervous and then anxious, and with good reason. Sooner or later he tired of doing caricatures of his friends, and his sharp little green eyes rested thoughtfully on his teachers.

The school which the boys attended was a private one, run by brothers of a Catholic teaching order. Many of the monks were priests, many more were merely brothers, and there were some lay members on the teaching staff, though they were in the minority. Every night I prayed on my bended knees that Guicho would not start doing caricatures of any of the religious. It had been hard enough getting my sons into the school, for waiting lists were, and are, very long. Luis had had to go and pry out old school associates who were now prominent in civic affairs and in politics and important businesses, and get letters from them to their old school, asking that our boys be allowed to register.

I began to hold regular lectures on the importance of respect, good manners, and kindness, all of which might well take the form of refraining from making unpleasant pictures of hard-working teachers who were giving their time and energies toward educating ungrateful small persons. My talks, usually held just before serving dessert, and therefore in the star spot on the bill, were listened to. But what I suppose I had known all along in my prophetic bones would happen, broke upon me like a storm.

Guicho was sent home, suspended until further notice.

The caricatures which had caused his disgrace, he brought with him, with instructions to show them to his parents. He had portrayed one of the brothers as a myna bird, another as an aracuan (a kind of tropical cockatoo). They were, unfortunately, good caricatures, immediately recognizable.

Luis and I were horrified. We took the indicated action at home, and then we led Guicho back to school by the ear, with orders to prostrate himself and beg for forgiveness and reinstatement. If, in so doing, I hurt his little id or something, that's just too bad. It's my firm opinion that boys ought to be educated, somehow.

Our little party of three was admitted into the office of the head. The myna bird looked at me with bright black eyes in which there was more than a hint of sardonic amusement.

Guicho, prodded forward, spoke his piece, was assigned penances, and promised readmission. I sighed with relief. But I became uneasy when, on the way home, Guicho whispered, with an artist's pride, "My caricatures were good, weren't they, Mima? Didn't he look just exactly like a myna bird?"

I cannot tell a lie, and I admitted that they were good. But I made him swear by all he held dear, such as Saturday movies, swimming at Cuautla, and being allowed sometimes to drive his father's car (when his father was present), that he would not make any more caricatures to pass around among his friends, either at school or anywhere outside. I took his drawing blocks away from him, and because I was experienced in his literal translations of parental edicts, I listed every kind of paper and board I could think of, and forbade caricatures to be made on any of them, or with any pen, pencil, crayon, or water color.

Time went by, and we approached mid-terms. Both boys passed with good grades and I was able to hold my head up among my peers when, over the tea tables, the comparative intelligence of offspring was the subject under discussion.

The denouement took place in August. Guicho was expelled.

"Why? Why?" I asked, tearing my hair, when he brought me home the formal notification.

"Well, I made another caricature," he admitted.

"You *promised* me you never would!"

"Well, I didn't make it on paper. I drew on the black-board in colored chalk. You didn't say anything about the blackboard. Besides, it was just for a couple of the fellows. I was going to erase it right away when the Mamey came in and caught me."

The Mamey was his name (illustrated with caricatures before the recent expulsion act), for one of the teachers who did undoubtedly resemble this rotund reddish fruit.

"Oh Heavens! Do you realize you will lose another grade?"

"It was bad luck," insisted the culprit. "I was just about to erase it."

"We must go and apologize again. If they will listen to you."

"I don't think they will," he commented. "I think they probably don't like me much."

It seemed likely. But I insisted that he had to go to some sort of school, somewhere.

"Why can't I stay home, and you teach me?"

"I don't know enough, and besides, I have other things to do. You have been disobedient and naughty and you have broken your promise. That is the worst thing."

"I didn't promise anything about a blackboard."

"It's the same thing. You are just weaseling about the blackboard, and you know it. We *must* go back to the head and beg him to reconsider. I couldn't get you into any other school at this time of year—after mid-terms. I am disappointed in you and angry with you, and you may not speak to me again until I give you permission!"

I had learned, years before, that punishments for my older child had to be selected with great skill and ingenuity. His father had tried spanking him and even whipping him, (light on the downstroke and heavy on the upstroke), for he was always naughty and rebellious. But this never did any good at all. Guicho took pride in bearing up without tears or protests, and after all, you cannot really *hurt* a child. I was glad to know whipping wouldn't work, as I hate to see cowed children and I cannot bear to inflict physical pain on anything. As a matter of fact, spanking is only for tots in Mexico, if at all. It is a civilized country where civilized punishments are dealt out, and I have never known a Mexican parent who advocated flogging, whipping, or anything above a mild smack occasionally.

I had found that the "civil death," or being in Coventry, was the worst punishment for Guicho. After an hour or so of nobody addressing any remarks to him, or answering any questions, he would usually come and stamp his foot and shout, "Speak to me! Somebody speak to me!" And then we could take him back into communication, knowing that he would be careful not to offend for at least a half day.

It was clear now that something had to be done. I had always taught my children that there are three rules a gentleman must keep, and that all good behavior stems from them. First, he must never willingly cause pain if it can be avoided. Second, he must keep his word, once given. Third, he must never promise anything he has no intention of carrying out or cannot carry out.

I now scolded him bitterly for having broken these rules, especially the first and the second.

When his father came home and I broke the news of the expulsion, he could not eat. He was deeply shamed, and I explained to our son that besides having offended and hurt his teachers, he had made his father and me suffer.

"Well, then," agreed Guicho, "I will memorize a new apology. I didn't know this would hurt you and Wees. I'm sorry."

We made another appointment for an interview with the myna bird.

I went dressed in black and I wore all my holy medals. I had meditated the whole affair most of the night, and I was afraid that the Mexican Catholic teachers, knowing that Guicho's mother was an American from a country predominately Protestant, might think that I was not really in sympathy with them, or that I had even incited the boy to attack them. Mexican priests tend to think of all Americans as Protestants, I must point out in passing, and the Protestants have not endeared themselves to the Catholic clergy by sending down brigades of missionaries to "work among the people." Mexico is a Christian country, and does not consider herself a field for missionary endeavor. On the contrary, Mexico trains many missionaries for work in pagan lands.

Therefore, I wore the veil I always did to Mass, carried my prayerbook, and clanked with my beloved medals. The truth is, that if all went well and if Luis and I were able once more to thrust our horrible child upon the teaching brothers, I intended to go straight to church and make a heartfelt act of thanks.

But this time the myna bird stood firm. Guicho had been warned. Now he definitely was expelled.

My husband moaned in anguish that now we would not be able to get the boy into any other school. The myna bird looked impersonally sad for us, but he shrugged. There was nothing he could do. The matter was closed. We slunk out.

However, the aracuan, who had been present at this interview, rang us up that night. He asked me to drop in to his office the next day.

When I got there (again in my black, with medals, just to make my point), he received me smilingly. He was alone in his little office. He had a great frill of white hair, and a hooked nose, and indeed he looked just like a cockatoo.

"Guicho is a bright boy," he told me, wagging his head. "Talented too. But rebellious. Yes, very rebellious."

"I know," I said humbly. "But he has a good heart."

"Yes. And a sense of humor!" Unexpectedly the aracuan

gave a booming laugh. "The head and I," he told me, "were all for reinstating Guicho, after he had a good lesson, naturally. But the other caricatured person, I am sorry to say, has no sense of the comic, and no appreciation of the occasional boy who stands out from the crowd in one way or another. He was hurt. Still is. And in our order, we never act unless opinion is unanimous. And I could not bring him round. He was," the dear little cockatoo told me, "as difficult as the twelfth juror, in your country."

I felt a little quiver of hope, but this was gently but firmly quashed.

"I see that you are a good Catholic," he went on, observing my medals. He smiled understandingly at me. "So no doubt you wish that Guicho should continue in a Catholic school."

"Of course. Only now I am afraid that he will never be accepted anywhere."

Here the myna bird came in, and saw me weeping.

"Pray calm yourself!" he told me. "We asked you to call because we have talked the matter over and we have been able to persuade the head of another Catholic school—unfortunately rather far from your home—to take Guicho in to finish the year. Calm yourself, señora!"

"So we have ready a letter of recommendation for you," said the aracuan. "Take it, and the boy, over to the new school tomorrow, and he will be able to enter next Monday."

He handed me a letter, and the myna bird took his leave. But the aracuan accompanied me to the door.

"You may read it now if you like," he said, as he saw me glance at the unsealed envelope.

I looked at the note. It was short. It said only: *"The bearer of this note is the boy we told you about on the telephone. Look out, for he is a very good caricaturist, and after all, dear brother Nicolas, you do greatly resemble an old sea lion. Yours in Christ, the Myna and the Aracuan."*

It is the custom in Mexico to kiss the hand of the priest, and I was glad of it. I really wanted to hug him.

He showed me out.

"I used to do some caricatures myself, in the seminary," he told me, chuckling. "Rather good ones, too."

XVII ᔊ

MY DOUBLE LIFE AT THE BORDER

Así el mundo va andando, unos riendo y otros llorando.
—PROVERB

Whether we had had bad luck or good, whether we had paid our bills or not, whether we had made or lost money on the lottery (mostly, we lost), my husband always made it possible for me to get home to visit my parents once a year. I took both children, or one of them, or none at all, depending on how they had behaved during the year, and on who was available to look after them. Dear Mamacita, having raised nine, was perfectly willing to keep the children while Luis and I went visiting, but after taking advantage of her kindness twice, I never did it again. The first time I left the children with her, Guicho developed a mastoid, and only the sulfa drugs (then new, and very scary) kept him from an operation. The second time Wiki came down with malaria. I thought two such crises were enough for Mamacita to handle; she had raised her own children, now I would give her a rest, and raise mine.

Most often I took both little boys with me. This was not as hard as it sounds, despite the fact that Robert Benchley once wrote that traveling with small children is roughly equivalent to fourth class in Bulgaria. In those days our traveling was done mostly by train or bus. I took the children on the train, and one lower berth sufficed for the three of us. I laid Wiki across the foot of the bed, and Guicho and I lay side by side. Every day we experienced the excitement of dredging up tidbits from the enormous lunch box I had packed—chicken legs, hard eggs, or *tortas* full of beans fried with *chorizo*—and in the evening, I gave them the treat of a dinner in the Pullman dining car.

For myself, I took along a few whodunits, and I always made sure that the children would not get off the train or get lost by giving them a little speech as soon as the train had started to move.

"Now Mima is going to read," I would announce. "And what happens when Mima gets started on her book, reading?"

Both little faces opened and the right answer came out.

"You burn the coffeepot and you don't hear the telephone, and Wees comes and says 'What's your name?' and you can't remember."

"That's right. So you had better keep an eye on me, and come to make sure that I am here every little while, and watch me closely while the train is standing in the station, because I get so wrapped up in my book that I don't know what I am doing. I might even get mixed up and step off the train, leaving you two here alone with no money. So watch out for me, and don't let me do anything I shouldn't."

Thoroughly worried, the two little boys would hover fairly near me, and whenever the train slowed up, they would come and sit beside me, ready to try to recall me to the world of reality, if I got out of hand.

Once when we were in mid-career on our journey to California there was a strike on the Mexican railways. Our train staggered into a lonely village in the midst of the great windswept plain of Durango, and there we remained, motionless, for fourteen hours, until word came that the strike had been settled.

Two rather gay ladies who were traveling in order to offer their charms in fresh territory, I believe, went out to the village and bought two large bottles of rum and a package of paper cups. On their return, they stood up and announced to the Pullman-ful of glum travelers, that they were standing a shot of rum to everybody who wanted to buy his Coke, for a cuba libre. Everybody bought a few Cokes, and the bottles began going around. Before long there was cheerful laughter and merry song in the last Pullman, and the hours flew by painlessly. The two little boys, who needless to say, had only Coke in their paper cups, got into the spirit of the thing, and next year, Wiki almost got expelled, after he turned in a theme which described this revel. (He had been under the impression that there was rum in his cup, too.)

My stays at home with my parents were never of any definite time length. I always told my mother and father that I would remain as long as I could. I gauged my visit by my husband's letters.

At first they would appear, regularly, every two or three days, in English. Then, a week or ten days later, he would interpolate many Spanish phrases. When at last the letters began arriving every day, written in Spanish, I would know that it was time to pack up. My mother soon learned my husband's psychology, and she would report to her friends, via the morning telephone conversation, as follows: "Yes, my little Mexican family has been here three weeks, but they will be leaving for home soon. Luis's letters are coming in Spanish now, and that means he is growing impatient."

My trips home, besides providing me with much refreshment of the spirit, gave me opportunity to think over the home and family left behind in Mexico, and get a perspective on their specially endearing qualities, as well. It was a knitting together of two lives. I have never wanted these two lives to be cut off from each other, and I have never wanted to be a stranger in my childhood home and my home town, nor yet a foreigner in the home and within the family I hold so dear in Mexico. It has taken a bit of doing, but I thank God for the chance to travel back and forth very often.

I am sometimes chided by my mother when, recently arrived in Bakersfield and conversing in English, I slip in a word or two in Spanish, or actually (this seems incredible, but it is true) forget the English word for some object. Once I forgot how to say chandelier until I had sat and thought for a full minute.

Always, upon going upstairs to the room I have used all my life, and which I left to be married, I have found it as it was during my grammar school and high school years, during the vacations when I was home from college or home from my job in Boston. The same window to the west has a fall of pink curtains and the French door leading out to the sleeping porch (which we used in summertime, before the advent of air-conditioning) wears its pink dotted swiss ruched cover. There is the same big hand-carved walnut bed which came out to California from New York with my grandparents. And in the drawers of the walnut bureau, there are always dozens of little gifts my mother has been setting aside for me, from my last visit—little things "that had your name on them," or "a little something I found that I was sure you would like."

Occasionally there have been difficulties about bringing back into Mexico all the delightful acquisitions I have made in California. My papers now reveal that I am an American citizen resident in Mexico; as soon as it is known that I am not a tourist, I get short shrift from officers on either side of the border. For a long time I used to be able to skim off the cream, so to speak, flouncing across the border with my American citizenship papers, when I entered the United States, and skipping back into Mexico with Mexican citizenship papers. I was, for fourteen years after my marriage, considered a Mexican national by reason of my marriage to a Mexican citizen. So I crossed as an American, and came back as a Mexican, speaking the appropriate dialect on each side. When Mexico decided no longer to allow dual citizenship in 1944, I chose American, although Mexicans insist that I list myself as a *norteamericana*.

In vain have I protested that this does not identify me and confine me to any one spot on the map any more than it does to call myself an *americana*. Mexicans and Canadians, and

Cubans too, are also *norteamericanos*. In vain do I tell proud
Mexicans, who insist that they are just as much American as
I am, because they are of the American continent just as much
as I am, that legally I can call myself an American, because my
country's legal title and name is the United States of America,
just as citizens of the United States of Brazil are Brazilians,
and citizens of the Republic of Mexico are Mexicans. But I
waste my breath; nobody listens to me, and Americans who
are eager to make friends in Mexico are always careful to
identify themselves as *norteamericanos*. When, lined up for
immigration inspection, I answer and say *"americana,"* when
asked my citizenship, always an annoyed Mexican voice speaks
up to correct me "norte*americana!*"

One time my husband and I went to Monterrey for Christmas. Leaving the little boys with their aunt, he and I made a
short motor trip across the border to Laredo, Texas, to buy
clothes. My mother, to whom I have written a letter every day
of my life, from the first day I left home to attend college,
knew that I would be in Laredo, and the name of the hotel
where we would be staying. So she sent me a great box of special goodies, including all my favorite canned seafoods, and
many kinds of tinned cheese. As I unpacked this wonderful
box, beside myself with delight and anticipation, my husband
announced in sepulchral tones that I couldn't take it home.

"But I'll pay the duty on it! Gladly!" I cried.

"It isn't that. It is forbidden to import canned foods of
any kind into Mexico. Cheese is forbidden, too. I just saw
the new listing of forbidden articles. Too bad."

I was ready to burst into tears. I felt quite capable of sitting down to eat the contents of several of the cans, but I knew
I couldn't finish off the twenty-odd tins, plus all the cello-
phane-wrapped cheeses, in the box. As the first tear trickled
down Luis became agitated; tears greatly distress him, and I try
not to weep too much—only when it is really important.

"Look," he said. "Maybe I could go out and find some
doctor who would give us a signed statement that you have to

eat these things on account of the iodine. Incipient goiter!"

"We haven't time, even if we could find this hypothetical doctor. And he would have to give me a metabolism test and I would pass with honors, probably because I have *always* eaten lots of seafood to keep away incipient goiter!"

"I could try to stow all the different little tins in different places in the car."

"No. If they found one, they would naturally look for all the others. Nobody who loves lobster Newburg imports *one* tin!" Then I had a bright idea. "Wait! You know people on the railway! Maybe one of the conductors could bring the whole boxful across for us!"

"Never. They have to be awfully correct, or they lose their jobs."

I was sunk in despair.

We thought and devised plans and examined and rejected them all night. In the morning, as we got ready to leave, Luis said, "Well, who do you want to give this to? We can't take it."

"Put the box right beside me on the front seat. I have thought of something."

"It won't work," lamented Luis as we drove toward the international bridge. "Whatever it is, it won't work. These customs men have heard everything."

Somewhat depressed by his view, I nevertheless was determined to try my plan. So when we got to customs, I lugged my great box of canned seafood in and slammed it on the table in front of the inspector.

"What's this?" he barked.

"It's a box of all kinds of tinned fish and cheese," I told him. "I know it's prohibited but my mother sent it to me, and she didn't know it was against the rules. She sent it for my Christmas gift. Now what shall I do with it?"

Confronted by the simple truth, something which hadn't come his way in years, the customs inspector turned pale. He didn't know what to say.

"What shall I do with it?" I asked him again plaintively.

"Just get it out of here! Quick!" he snapped at me, stamped it hastily with an INSPECTED sign, and waved me away. He turned to the next client, and I walked out with my cans.

"You see," I bragged to Luis, as we hurtled down the road toward Monterrey, "as I lay in bed thinking up lies to tell, I felt sure they would know what to answer to every lie or variant thereof. But they might be confused by the truth. And I was right!"

"It worked once," commented my pessimistic spouse, "but it will never work again. Probably the whole border is alerted by now. 'Have no dealings with round-faced *gringas* who march in, look you in the eye and tell the truth. Dangerous.' Write to Mamacita Borton not to send us any more stuff in cans."

Changing laws with regard to customs are as nothing compared to changing regulations about the proper papers for passing the border.

At one time in my life, the El Paso *Times* contracted with me to visit every city along the recently opened Mexico City–El Paso Highway, and to write a series of articles for them. Accordingly I set out, and made my first stop in Queretaro. This is a colonial town in the midst of the section of Mexico known as "the Bajio." Here revolution was hatched, and more than once, from the days of the Corregidora, who warned the Mexican patriots that the Spanish crown officials knew of their plans, in 1810, to the days when the government of Benito Juárez tried and executed the ill-starred Maximilian and affirmed their hatred of any kind of "foreign interference" in Mexican affairs, right up to the Revolution of 1910 and the later Cristero Rebellion against the anti-church decrees of President Calles. In Queretaro, with its cobblestoned streets and many splendid churches, I lost my watch, but gained an opal ring—the gift of one of the opal merchants in the city famous for these fiery stones.

In San Miguel Allende I forgot to pack a pair of shoes that the maid had put away on a high shelf in the closet, but I rode to Celaya on a second-class bus, which taught me humility. The bus took off through uncharted country, it seemed to me, but at signals from the passengers, it would stop. They would get off and direct themselves toward the empty horizon, as if they knew just where they were going, as indeed they did.

On the second-class buses, I learned that it is wise to choose a seat next to a man. The women in Mexico carry the babies, the luggage, the chickens, and sometimes a pig. But all the passengers are kind and courteous, and once when I exclaimed over the beauties of some wild flowers, a spokesman from among the passengers ordered the bus driver to stop so that the foreign lady could pick a few of Mexico's flowers, and he did. In fact, everybody got out and picked flowers for me. I sneezed all the way to Celaya, for they gave me hay fever, but I was far too much of a lady to admit it, in the face of such warmhearted generosity.

From Celaya I went to León, and then to Guanajuato, where the *alcalde* (mayor) granted me an interview. As soon as we began to talk he invited me to dinner in his home, for he said that his wife had been to school in St. Louis, in the United States, and she longed to practice her English. I arrived for dinner, and we all became great friends, and afterward, in the silvery moonlight, we went *callejonando,* or exploring the narrow romantic alleyways of the town, one of the loveliest in Mexico. We slipped through the "Way of the Kiss," so narrow that lovers can reach each other's lips, across, each sitting in his own window, the "Way of the Severed Head," and "The Way of the Gambler's Wife," and we ended at last by the Cantaranas Fountain (where the frogs sing).

I left my nightgown in Guanajuato, but it was sent on to me, and caught up in Zacatecas. Near this center of horsemen and great cattle ranches, I reveled in the village of Mexico's exquisite poet, Amado Nervo, and was awed by the ruins of "La Quemada." In Parral, Coahulla, I had my pocket picked (for about the tenth time in my life), and in Delicias and in Chihuahua, I burst spang into a raging country fair. Passing a village late one night, I saw that every doorway was draped with a great silver rosary, many times larger than life, and I learned that these decorations (all homemade) were in honor of the visit of an image of Our Lady of Fatima, who is the apparition of Our Lady of the Most Holy Rosary. It was moving to slip through the sleeping town, by bus, in the pale moonlight, and see the holy beads, as large as street lamps, enfolding the doorway of every home, rich and humble.

When I arrived in Ciudad Juárez, I found a letter from my husband, urging me, under no circumstances, to try to cross the border, as requirements for papers had been changed since my departure from Mexico City, almost a month before.

I was disappointed, for I had purposely traveled light, hoping to shop in El Paso, and also because I wanted very much to speak to my editors at the paper.

I phoned Mayo Seamon, an old friend and manager of the advertising department of the El Paso *Times*, and told him my plight. I also advised him that I had brought in lots of material for my series of articles, and at the same time, as lagniappe, about a thousand dollars' worth of ads, paid in advance.

"Now, you haven't got your papers, you say?" he asked after a time.

"No. Luis wrote that I couldn't pass now, with the papers I brought."

"You sit tight. I'm coming for you."

In due course, he arrived driving his own car at my Ciudad Juárez hotel.

"I cross the border here all the time," he told me, "and everybody knows me on both sides. Everything will be all right."

Sure enough, he merely touched the brim of his hat and called "Howdy" as we passed. After a happy day in El Paso, writing up my first articles and conferring with friends on the paper, Mayo drove me back, touching the brim of his hat and calling "Howdy" to the Mexican authorities.

The next day, he sent somebody else, to spirit me across and back, in the same way. I had the presence of mind to change my appearance somewhat by tying a yellow scarf around my hair this time. And when, on the third day, a doctor friend who practiced in Ciudad Juárez as much as on the El Paso side and was also known to authorities on each side of the bridge, called for me, and later returned me to my hotel on the Mexican side, I wore a large black hat. Again, we whisked through with merely the friendly greeting of the raised hand, and nobody detained me and asked for my papers.

So it went, and I grew used to my double life, and even began to think I would never bother with papers and visas and permits ever any more. I would simply sail through immigration and customs calling "Howdy!" Hooray for the Yellow Rose of Texas and Viva Guadalupe!

But came the day when I had to start back home to Mexico. Having gathered all my material by slow stages, taking second- and third-class buses, I planned to go swiftly home by train, and I purchased my ticket.

Now when American (I mean norteamericana) ladies get on a train at its point of departure, such as Nuevo Laredo or Ciudad Juárez, Mexican immigration authorities board the train and ride it some miles into the interior, holding office as the train gets under way, and checking all foreigners. If I had indeed come from el otro lado, I would be expected to present my papers, all properly stamped and full of permits, and notations.

I simply did not present myself to the authority. Time passed, but I was not to escape. The authority presented himself to me. He sat and looked at me fixedly. Then, "Your papers, please," he said, holding out his hand for them.

I don't like deceit, and am generally law-abiding, but the vagaries of border officials on both sides have plagued me for years, and I was convinced, like most Mexicans, that I was

entitled to an occasional victory, having suffered so many de-
feats, delays, and frustrations at their hands.

Therefore, bracing myself, for if a lie must be told, it
should be told with conviction, I said, "No papers. I haven't
been out of Mexico."

"No, señora?"

"No, señor."

"Not at all?"

"Not at all."

He rose to his feet, shrugging, and went a few steps. Then
he returned.

"Aren't you the lady I saw in El Paso a couple of days
ago?"

"Can't be."

"Sure, señora?"

"Sure, señor."

Inside I was beginning to worry, but the hard-working
officer gave up. I suppose he has some experience with ladies
who remodel the truth. I was given up as an incorrigible liar,
I suppose. Because of course we recognized each other.

But even brave officers of the law will lie *for* a lady sometimes, God bless them.

Once I had crossed the border at Nogales on Christmas
Day, and none of the border officials on the Mexican side
wanted to bother with our carful of returning American citizens. Only I had Mexican papers and I should have had sense
enough to ask them to stamp my exit visa. But I didn't have
that much sense—as I learned when I wanted to get back *into*
Mexico a month or so later.

The Mexican immigration officer looked at my papers at
the airport, while the plane started loading luggage and I began to grow nervous.

"When did you leave Mexico?" he asked.

"On Christmas Day. At Nogales. But nobody stamped my
papers; they just waved us—there was a carful of us—through."

"But if there is no proof that you *left*, how can I stamp it that you came in?" he asked me reasonably.

I had visions of being detained while they phoned Mexico City, and then of waiting for new papers, and perhaps I would be put in jail. They would put leg irons on me, and I would catch typhus, and . . . I burst into tears.

"If you left invisibly, you came back invisibly," said the officer, thrusting my papers back into my hand. "Hurry up, or you'll miss your plane."

One of the best visas for any Mexican is Our Lady of Guadalupe, patroness and protectress of all America, but who, as everybody knows, has a special corner of her heart reserved only for Mexicans.

Once my friend, Malenita, had accompanied a friend of hers to the American border, just for the buggy ride. Without papers, Malenita remained properly on the Mexican side, in a nice boardinghouse, while her American friend crossed the border, attended to renewing her car permit, and then returned. Now, for automobile tourists into Mexico, there is an immigration inspection station some thirty kilometers down the highway toward Monterrey, and when they arrived at this station, while the friend presented papers, Malenita, good Mexican citizen, Mexican-born and proud of it, had none to show. She happens to look more like the Irish ancestors in her background than her Mexican forebears, being fair and green-eyed, with a tilted Irish nose, and a delicate air.

"I am a Mexican," she said.

"You have no proof of it," objected the immigration officer.

"Viva Santa Maria de Guadalupe!" yelled Malenita, and the gallant officer threw back his head and echoed, "Viva! Pass, friend. And may God bless you."

Not long ago it was my privilege to send a news story out of Mexico, which I obtained via some friends in diplomatic channels, which again proves that Our Lady of Guadalupe watches over her own.

Over the years many Chinese have emigrated to Mexico, and have married Mexican women. Very often, as they grew into their sixties, the Chinese returned to their homeland, taking their wives and families with them. However, children of these couples, if born in Mexico, have the privilege of Mexican citizenship. And so it was, that recently, when the Communist power grew strong in China, many of these Mexican-born children applied to return to their native country. But a very great many of them had lost all papers showing their citizenship, and had no way of proving it at all.

Then Mexican authorities did a very touching and beautiful thing. They allowed it to be known that any such person, of mixed Chinese and Mexican blood, who could produce in China, a picture, medal, or image of Our Lady of Guadalupe and present it in lieu of papers, plus his statement under oath that he was a Mexican-born citizen, would be given a visa. And so it was. Some hundreds of such persons were able to escape the Communist terror in China thus, and return to their native country.

So, it seems to me, this chapter should end with a rousing Viva!

Viva Nuestra Señora de Guadalupe!

Viva!

XVIII ❧

SUMER IS ICUMEN IN, LHUDE SING—TOURISTS!

Amigos y libros, escogidos y bien conocidos.
—PROVERB

Mexico is a marvelous vacation country, the "faraway land next door." It has seacoast like the Riviera, mountains like Scotland and Switzerland, lakes like Minnesota, and ruins like Egypt. I have been blessed by this fact, for eventually nearly all my friends from the United States turn up to take a look, or to learn how to slow down and forget the bad news on the wristwatch. Actually, if I had married a man from Idaho, say, or North Dakota, the chances are I would gradually have lost my clutch on Marian and Mona, Dorothy and Eve and Virginia, and Gladys and Genevieve and Jeane and countless others I cherish. But when people haul out their luggage and dust it off and start looking at maps, I have a fair chance of getting them in Mexico—though I have to wait for them to do Europe on alternate years.

Summer is the time of visiting firemen in Mexico. What is so rare as a day in June? Then if ever, come hordes of visitors.

Now that I am sauntering into the time of the sere and yellow leaf, I have found to my joy that many of my cronies are on an early retirement plan, and even winter has become a season for vacationing. Bless a civilization which has made it possible for ordinary and average people to say, at some point before they move into the wheelchair, "Now I'm through working, and I'm going to see the world." Also, I believe this to be one of the most effective peace plans ever devised.

Some of the visitors make amusing mistakes about the language, like the man who complained to my husband about too many of those little bureaus on the highway, and others take over Mexican customs without knowing whether they are really becoming. In this connection, I will never forget a cartoon which appeared on the cover of one of Mexico's leading magazines, one summertime. It showed two young ladies passing each other on Juárez Street (a main shopping avenue in Mexico City). One was a black-haired Mexican girl; she was wearing a tailored suit, gloves, and high-heeled slippers. She was passing an American girl (judging by the blond ponytail, freckled tilted nose and horn-rimmed glasses) who was wearing an embroidered *huipil* (three-cornered scarf) over a white cotton blouse, wide ruffled *enaguas* (or skirts) of calico, and *guaraches*, the flat Mexican sandals. The American girl was carrying a Mexican *moral*, or embroidered shoulder bag, instead of a purse.

Actually, the comfort and picturesqueness of Mexican clothes has been greeted with cries of joy by tourists, and now American magazines advertise Mexican cotton trousers for men, which tie around the waist, and *guaraches* for every member of the family. I have learned too, that Mexican baby burros are being offered as ideal playmates for children in such faraway American counties as Westchester!

Travelers to Mexico have changed with the times and with changing social patterns. Time was when people touring Mexico wanted to dine, drink, and observe the natives at work and play. Now they have become intense seekers after understanding and they tend to arrive armed with ponderous questions. In a way, it is good, and sometimes touching, that people now feel they should pay for their traveling with a little intelligent study. In another way, it occasionally works out that they take home more really erroneous ideas about the country visited than the old careless playboys and playgirls did.

A recent visitor fixed me with a stern eye and fired at me a series of questions designed to make me squirm for my dear old mañana-land.

"What is the ratio of infant mortality?" she wanted to

know. "What is the minimum wage? Is there a League of Women Voters? What is being done about the poverty?"

It is hard for me to answer all these deep questions with a few well-chosen words. For one thing, it is unfair to judge today's statistics without knowing those of twenty years ago, so that you may perceive the ratio of progress. In Mexico, it is remarkable. And whereas poverty, infant mortality, and non-participation in civic affairs may all fall short of an ideal mark, they are being combated in Mexico with many practical programs. Droughts and a difficult land program have sent thousands of country people blundering into the city where there isn't work for them all, and the result is abject poverty until they are absorbed into industry. Meanwhile, with less hands or literally "arms" (*braceros*) on the land, there is less food production, and higher prices. This is a flux that will no doubt continue for some time, but dams and waterways are being built, the land program improved, and banking facilities broadened, to help farming centers. As the situation in the country improves, people will drift back to the land, which they love best. Everything should be seen, and judged, in the light of improvement over the past, and not by comparison with some rigidly worked-out norm, I feel. But my visiting, serious-minded tourists are not always interested in my answers. I have taken to asking them a few questions in my turn.

"Why don't you ask me what is our ratio of mental illness, as compared with that in the United States? It is appreciably lower, and not only because people take care of their own *chiflados*. The general philosophy of 'God willing' seems to remove from frail shoulders the feeling that they have to carry the world's burdens alone And innocents of whatever age, whether a retarded child or an old auntie who is a bit senile and has to be given her set of blocks to play with, are looked after, at home, with practical affection, and nobody apologizes for them. Even solemn medical journals nowadays admit that there is just no substitute for love, and maybe that is why

Mexico doesn't have endless waiting lists for beds in mental hospitals.

"And, why don't you ask me," I go on, "if you can go and visit an orphanage? I would have trouble locating one, though there are a few in the country. Mostly little orphans are simply taken in, without more ado, by some member of the family, and cared for along with their own children. And so are the old people. There are no fancy 'Shady Rests' or 'Garden Villages' for senior citizens in Mexico, because their families wouldn't consider letting them go there no matter how well coated in sugar was the 'old folks' home' pill. Aging grandmas and grandpas, old aunties and uncles, are lovingly tended at home, and their later years are, like the earlier ones of their lives, surrounded by the security and warmth of home."

I have seen a happy mother of ten children turn away, in dislike, from an earnest American visitor who is exercised about the population explosion, and hide a smile behind her fan when a visiting tourist carries on about such dreadful contemporary problems as teen-age pregnancies, as if they were a matter that could be straightened out by proper legislation.

My friend Carmen likes to receive my American guests, and talk them over with me later. I correct her impression of what they said in English, and she comments on their attitudes, for she finds them as weird and exotic as they find her inexplicable and remote.

"But Eleesabet," she protested to me one day after we had had a session with an American friend who expatiated on the necessity of intelligent legal abortion for teen-age girls who just happened to find themselves pregnant. My American friend based her findings on statistic-filled articles in glossy magazines, and her concern was rooted in compassion. "But Eleesabet, does it not occur to these ladies that if they always provided a chaperone for young girls, until they were married, that they could rearrange these statistics almost at once?"

Carmen, a good mother in the Mexican Catholic tradition, never allowed Licha to go out with a young man, or even with just another young girl, without a proper chaperone. Though, once, when Licha was engaged and only a week away from the date of her religious wedding, Carmen went upstairs before the official *novio* had taken his leave.

"But of course, I spied on them!" she cried virtuously. "And Eleesabet, I am not sure I should allow Licha to marry Sidronio. Can you imagine? *All he did* was kiss her hand!" Carmen's black eyes blazed with fury and resentment.

"But Carmen, you should be pleased! What did you expect?"

"I was *not* pleased!" she cried. "He should have seized her and kissed her like a madman! He should have been like a lion uncaged!"

Now here you have the Mexican view. Danger, passion, drama, excitement—these are not things you merely watch on the silver screen. These are things you prize, and you treat with respect, as you do a fire, and if you are wise and far-seeing, you arrange your life so that your children are protected and defended until at last, with the marriage ring, you give them title to these blazing wonders. Could it be that this saves marriage from bogging down in boredom and incompatibility too soon, as well? Mamacita always told me so, and I believe her.

So my visiting firemen study the Mexican ladies and worry over them, and the Mexican ladies study the Americans, and worry over them. The Americans pity Mexicans for their poverty, their large families, their indifference to "world problems." The Mexicans grieve over the American broken marriages, the old people in "homes" because their children feel they have no room for them, the lack of romance in the lives of the young, who in the United States "go steady" and experiment with love too early, and never know the painfully sweet fear of the opposite sex, and the poetic glamour of formalized courtship.

In dealing with American visitors to Mexico, I have sometimes suffered because of things they do that irritate my Mexican friends.

Lorenzo said to me one day, "Eleesabet, I used to love the Americans. Now I have trouble liking them. *Why* are they so complacent? They act surprised if we are not immediately humble about American ways. But it never occurs to your compatriots that we *like our own ways*. And if I protest and argue a little, they become angry with me, and say menacingly, 'I wonder how you will talk the next time you Mexicans want a big American loan!' That cuts the hardest. The assumption that we can be *bought*. That breaks my heart."

In fact many Mexicans have commented to me about what they call "dollar rudeness," which they term the sort of attitude that demands special attention, special service, "because I am bringing dollars into this country!"

In general, the Mexicans (while disapproving of some phases of American statesmanship, and deploring the fact that we have too often kept a dictator in office in some Latin American country because he had promised to protect American economic interests, if otherwise allowed a free hand), like Americans, call them *bonachones* (goodhearted), and are likely to make friends with them, count their money for them, and prevent them from being cheated, as they go about their travels in Mexico.

The principal trouble is, I think, that we Americans assume that everybody reads the same history books we do, and thinks of history in the terms in which we teach it to our children. Some study of Latin American history would straighten out a lot of things. Let us take just one example.

I refer to the average *norteamericano's* idea of the Mexican Revolutions. No country has ever shed more blood, more bravely, to achieve freedom, first from Spain, then to be certain that no foreign monarchy was set up in the country, and in 1910, to effect a redistribution of land. In fact, the Revolution of 1910 should count as one of the "great revolutions" of the world, coming as it did before the Russian Revolution, and resulting as it did in a far more equitable distribution of arable land among the people who work it. And Mexico never slumped into Communism, or into a dictatorship afterward, either, but has gone steadily forward along a road leading to the freest possible democracy, within the country's economic and educational possibilities.

Pancho Villa and Emiliano Zapata were not musical comedy characters, or even local Robin Hoods. They were savage, clever, and ruthless guerrilla fighters, deserving of fearful admiration, but never of laughter—TV and movie scenarists to the contrary.

Because of this Revolution, on which the policy of the country still rests, Mexicans are not skittish about the word, but on the contrary, they all affirm, proudly, that they are *revolucionarios*, and they expect that declaration to be received with respect.

Among all my visiting firemen, over the years, the one who had the most unusual reason for traveling was the man who was eating his way around the world. Mr. Bates was not making notes for a gourmet magazine, or collecting fine recipes. He never called for the wine of the country or took on about herbs and oil and sweet butter. No, his simple desire was to eat every horrific article that had ever been consumed by man. He intended to sample every one, and was devoting the rest of his life to it. He told me he had savored rattlesnake steak in some benighted Western state of the U.S.A., birds' nest soup in China, raw fish in Japan, and that lavender goo known in Hawaii as poi and to my California family as ug. But this was only the beginning. He had got outside of fried locusts and ants, sharks' fins, and hung geese which were quite odoriferous. He had eaten raw whale blubber. When he started to tell of his travels in Africa, I stopped him, fearing to hear about barbecued missionary.

Mr. Bates was easy to entertain. First I produced *tacos* made of maguey worms. These fat little white slugs live in the heart of the maguey plant, and I suppose they are really cleaner than some of the animal flesh we eat. I tried them once, all unknowing, and they tasted rather like crisp crackling. But when I unrolled my *taco*, and looked at the little black eyes and tiny black feet of the worm I couldn't go on. Not so my gustatory friend. He enjoyed them, visibly.

I then ordered for him a north Mexican stew made of chicken entrails,—the parts tossed away when you clean a chicken. (Do housewives clean chickens any more, in this age of the oven-ready cellophane package of fowl?) I have never been able to eat this dish myself, but it has its devotees. We moved on to the tiny whitefish from Lake Chapala, which are fried entire, without gutting, and then are popped into the mouth like salted peanuts. But I ruined Mr. Bates' entire trip, when, just before he boarded his plane, I recalled that I hadn't fed him any marsh-fly caviar. This food, made by stripping the eggs of the marsh-fly off the reeds in the lakes, is pressed into a sort of cake. It is oily and salty, and is still used by some people as a seasoning for many dishes. Poor Mr. Bates left almost in tears; he was like a man on his way to Scotland to climb mountains, who suddenly catches a glimpse of Everest.

One of our hardy perennials who comes every year to Mexico is Ross Parmenter, music editor of the New York *Times*. Now Ross is a sophisticate; he has been a police reporter and a general reporter, and he was by no means born yesterday. Yet when he descends from his plane in Mexico, all his metropolitan *savoir-faire* rolls off like butter from a hot knife. He becomes a big, friendly puppy, who goes up to everyone and wags his tail. He loves everybody and thinks no evil.

We dearly love him and would not change him for the world. Yet it amuses my husband, who has been around in Mexico for a good many years now, to hear Ross tell him about how innocent and trusting Mexicans are. "Why," said Ross one day, "a man in the white cotton clothes of an Indian came up to me, obviously a foreigner, and asked me to watch his packages for him! I was so touched! He trusted me! Why,

I might have made off with all his chickens and sacks of oranges!"

"Ross, come here," said my husband. "Look in there."

Ross obediently came and looked. He looked into a mirror at his own face.

"Wouldn't *you* trust that face?" asked Luis. "Well, Mexican Indians have had centuries learning to read faces, and they almost never make a mistake. Believe me, they don't trust everybody! They are good judges."

No summer visitor has been more gorgeous in appearance than Val. Tall and blue-eyed, with a mane of curly red hair, she blew into my life when her husband, Walter Rundle, then of the United Press, was sent out to China to head up the news bureau there. Japan was invading China then, and holding part of it, and it was not considered a post to which wives could accompany their husbands. Val had come to Mexico to paint and to scheme up ways of outwitting everybody and rejoining her beloved Walt. She worked with Federico Cantú and other leading Mexican artists, and she often dropped in to my office. We would go out to have coffee together and she would read me portions of Walt's letters.

Ordinarily, painting and sketching, she wore flats, and wide skirts and blouses, and her hair hung down her back. When so attired, she was reasonably happy. But when she was worried, there was a change. When Walt's biweekly letter didn't appear on time, she would draw a large map of China from her bosom and show me the place where last he had been heard from. The next day, if there was no letter, she would be glum and silent and would smoke too many cigarettes. If another day went by she would be falsely gay, or perhaps pick a quarrel with me. I soon learned that Val never cried; she just got mad. If a few more days passed without news, she would dig down into her trunk and come up with her most glamorous outfits.

One day when she was terribly troubled and anxious, she commanded that I meet her for lunch at Ambassadeurs (a most elegant restaurant where delicate food is served from silver dishes). I waited outside until I saw her sailing toward me, tall and willowy, beautiful in a tight peacock-blue sheath, with a row of silver bracelets on her arm from wrist to elbow, and a great black cartwheel of a hat atop her high-twisted red hair.

"Excuse me, boys," I heard a man say in Spanish. "Here comes my helicopter!"

He made another admiring remark (a *piropo*) as Val drew up, but she fired a glance at him out of those blue eyes that shot him deader than a bullet.

Val's commands had to be obeyed, and therefore I was laid away in my best lilac taffeta "dressmaker" suit, and had a flowered hat on top of my braids. (In Mexico only foreign ladies wear hats, except to weddings.) We swooped into the restaurant in such hauteur that three waiters came scurrying up to seat us and take our order.

"Two double Scotches on the rocks and two sirloins, rare," commanded Val and sat back to view the other lunchers from under the three-foot wingspread of her cartwheel. I don't like Scotch nor yet rocks, and neither do I like rare meat, but with Val's eye on me, fierce with worry and bravado, I downed both, and then we swept out, I clinging weakly to her strong right arm.

I had to stagger to a phone and call in sick to my office, and be sent home in a cab. Val went on determinedly to a movie. I believe she sat through three of them that afternoon and evening, to keep from thinking.

The next day she was back, in an old painting sweater; she had on her horn-rim glasses and her hair tumbled down her back. She breezed into the office and her big hearty laugh rocketed around and ricocheted off the walls.

"Gotta letter from Walt!" she boomed, "and he's back from that trip to the front. Yesterday I was about to die. Today we can get back to normal."

Val left Mexico mysteriously one day, and I learned later

that somehow she had schemed her way into China. Years
later, when she and Walt came to visit Mexico, I asked her,
"How did you ever manage it, when they wouldn't let the
other wives in?"

Val, who loves her Scotch, has no fixed church, and is as
unconventional as any artist, told me, "Went as a missionary!
Went with a whole boatload of missionaries. Ha ha!"

Walt beamed on her with fond pride.

"I hate to think what had happened to the vocations of
the reverend brethren," he drawled, "by the time that boat
docked, having had Val aboard for a month. She likes to sun-
bathe in the nude."

"I didn't do it where anybody could see me," protested
Val. "I told the captain, and he fixed a little place for me. But
I guess the missionaries knew what I was up to, because they
all got awfully nervous!"

Another of my American friends, Irma, arrived at my
door one day in hiking clothes, with a canteen, bedroll, and
knapsack on her shoulders. "I'm seeing Mexico by mountain
trail," she told me happily, and wouldn't even stay to eat a
hot lunch. She is a learned professor, writer, and researcher on
psychology, and her hiking knickers were baggy and her glasses
kept slipping down her nose. She hiked around Mexico's
mountains for weeks, undaunted by bug, virus, suspicious Indian, or cougar, and when she had to quit and go home, she
was sorrowful. She would have hiked home via the Sierra
Madre and the Rockies, had there been time.

Another of our favorite summer visitors is Louis Mélan-
çon, official photographer of the Metropolitan Opera. He always arrives dressed in cameras from head to foot, with light
meters and tripods and flash bulbs hung on his person, and
there is always a cigarette pasted to his lower lip. A handsome
bachelor, he usually finds a couple of lone women to take pity
on. He joshes them about schoolmarm Spanish, shows them
the Mexico he loves so well, and looks after them amiably.
"Can't come to dinner," he is likely to inform us. "I found

these two hags that have never been to Puebla, so I'm taking them."

Once I asked him why he loaded himself up with strangers, while complaining that he had little time to do what he wanted to.

"It's the fruitcakes," he explained. "They always send me fruitcakes at Christmas, my hags do, and I dearly love a good fruitcake."

Louis was hag-prone, but also, we learned, he was accident-prone. One year we were expecting him to arrive in Mexico by car in the course of the month. Long before he was due, we got a long-distance call from Victoria. "Hey!" he shouted over the phone, five hundred miles away. "I was robbed last night. Can you send me a hundred dollars?" Luis assured him that we would.

Then we waited for more news. It came. A long-distance call from Morelia, about a hundred miles away.

"Hey!" shouted Louis. "I was in an accident and lost a wheel. Oh I'm fine! I'm having the wheel fixed and I'll get to Mexico City in about three days."

We waited. Then there was a call from Toluca.

"Hey!" he reported. "I'll be in as soon as I get to the top of a hill, so I can roll down the rest of the way. There's a gasoline strike here, but a man loaned me enough to get me up to the summit."

Before we could protest he had hung up. Luis then began to walk the floor, and I was tense with anxiety. We both knew how many curves there were on the road down from Toluca, and how swift was the descent from the summit. Luis listened for the screech of the Red Cross ambulance, and I for the roaring motors of the automobile-rescue units.

Then we got another phone call.

"Hey!" shouted Louis happily. "I'm here! I hit a tree, and I've got my car in a burlap sack, but I'll be out in a cab in fifteen minutes. Put the steak on!" And he arrived, gay as ever, with all his cameras and his cigarette, and with a great tray of French pastries he had bought on the way.

Many of our summer visitors complain of "the tourist disease." In vain do I tell them that I get it, when I return to the United States. I believe it is mostly a matter of changing the flora and fauna in one's insides; the battle, when the new ones take over, has its repercussions. But Luis' cousin, Dr. Pepe Gutierrez, who was house doctor at the Hotel del Prado, for years, told us that the disease known as "tourist trot" or "Montezuma's revenge" is caused, in his opinion, by a combination of nervousness, the high altitude, and the first vacationtime extra drink, and big dinner. Plus, of course, the fear of catching it. Thousands of tourists who don't think about this vacationtime diarrhea, never have a twinge.

Another summer visitor, Mercedes, who came with a tour, said to me, "I couldn't understand how this tour could be offered, everything paid, at the price it was given. But now I realize how the tour managers make money; they make their profit on the meals the tourists eat after the first two wild days of rich food and many drinks. After that, all are on tea and toast the rest of the time, and the tour can tot up a profit."

And then there was Virginia. Virginia is tall and broad-shouldered and strong and nervous. She is known to her friends as the Clinging Oak. She is almost pathologically sensitive to causing any of her friends or relatives a moment's pain or inconvenience, and so when she takes plane trips, she takes out lots of insurance in favor of them all, in case she should fall.

Once I persuaded her to come and visit me in Mexico City. After sending me four or five desperate letters telling me she wished to accept but she was afraid she might cause me inconvenience and a couple of cables, in which she advised that she was afraid I was just pretending that I wanted to see her, she bought a plane ticket, about a million dollars' worth of insurance which she ordered divided between me and the cousin who drove her to the airport, and landed in Mexico. We then proceeded to sightsee with the thoroughness typical of Virginia. Everything she does she does with all her might, and to every emotion she gives five hundred per cent of her attention.

In Oaxaca, after a twelve-hour journey there by car, we rose at dawn and visited a market where we saw native vendors of fruits and fowl and weavings; we admired the Tula tree; we entered three churches; and we "did" all the ruins at Mitla. Gulping a hasty lunch, we went to the mountaintop of Monte Alban. There we clambered upon and into every ruin and tomb. Virginia, who is tall, hit her head on the crossbeam of each. Bloody but unbowed, she paid tribute to each knock with a hoarse "My Gawd!" We staggered out and up and into the next tomb. "My Gawd!"

It was black night when at last, absolutely worn to a shred, we boarded our car and were being driven back to Oaxaca City and our hotel. I was ready to expire without giving anyone a bit of trouble. Any old corner would do. Even the Clinging Oak lay with her eyes closed and her head resting on the back of the seat, and she made tired sounds.

"Over there," recited our guide mechanically, "is the house where Benito Juárez lived."

Virginia came to. "Stop!" she roared. "I want to see the house where Juárez lived."

"We have passed it," whimpered the guide.

"Go back," ordered Virginia and we went back. Mercifully, it was closed, and we couldn't visit it.

When we got to our hotel we were too tired to eat, so, after dabbling with our soup, we sat in the lobby, panting, too much done in to climb the stairs to our room.

"They are having native dances tonight, in the lobby of the other hotel," Virginia overheard someone say. She turned to me, galvanized into energy. "Elizabeth! Native dances!" she announced, and I rose, groaning, to my feet. We went to see the native dances. How I managed to live through the chanting, stamping, and feather-waving I don't know. Virginia, even, wavered on her feet with glazed eyes, like a boxer who has just had a knockout blow but hasn't yet dived for the canvas. Nevertheless, in the morning (when I think of how we got back to our hotel and to bed, everything goes black) she danced every dance for me, accompanying herself on a drum improvised from a lampshade, and singing the tunes that went with each gyration.

On our return to Mexico City, we got tickets for the opera. Now opera is the great national diversion in Mexico, ranking second only to the bullfight. Virginia ordered me to meet her at Bellas Artes in time for us to see the famous Tiffany glass curtain, and I barely made it in through a drenching summer rainstorm. I arrived to find Virginia absolutely dancing with impatience, for fear we would miss the curtain, and seizing me by the wrist, she sprinted up the stairs to the balcony (where our seats were) almost with the speed of light. We saw the curtain just before it was lifted to vanish into the shadows above; then we had to find our seats.

Due to some aberration of the architect, the seats in the first balcony, where we were to sit, are so arranged that one's knees, when seated, press into the back of the neck of the person seated in front, so steep is the tilt of the floor. Of course this makes for wonderful visibility, but it is hard for people made dizzy by heights, as one seems to be tottering on the edge of an abyss.

We picked our way along the cliff of row G, found our seats, and subsided into them gratefully. Our seats were in the middle of a long row, and we then paid the penalty for being on time. About twenty people climbed over us in the gathering dark before the overture, causing us to lose our umbrellas, purses, and gloves. Virginia's annoyance was silent at first, but it gradually became audible, "Gawd," she gasped under her breath and later in her ringing contralto. "My Gawd, isn't there any other way into this whole balcony, than through row G?" she cried, as two more people converged on us and forced us up.

"My glasses!" shrieked Virginia. "I'll be blind!" We

clawed around beneath our seats, the people in front got down and felt under theirs. Three rows down the glasses were found and passed up toward us.

But just as we had settled down, a last seat-seeker came looming toward us through the pre-overture twilight. She was a stout young girl in white taffeta. Distracted and off in our timing, we rose just as the poor child tried to pass, and there was simply no room for our knees and all that taffeta. Down she went onto the occupants of row F. I clutched for the unfortunate child, hip and thigh, and I managed to break her fall on the woman in front. Virginia's stricken roar sounded through the whole opera house. "My Gawd, I've killed her! Is she dead? Will I be arrested?"

The poor child, weeping, with crushed white taffeta, and the lady in front, with a ruined coiffure, were disentangled, and at last peace was restored in the balcony. Just in time. The conductor had come onto the podium, rapped his baton, and the overture began.

Nobody has any idea of what opera means to Mexicans until he travels in the provinces and finds, even in small and dusty towns, the resplendent opera house, or until he attends a performance of opera in the capital. The public knows every phrase of the favorites, and it knows how they should be sung. No saving your voice in Mexico. You sing well, and take your high notes clearly, or you are hissed. But when you sing well —and what is more glorious than a human voice, trained to do the will of a passionate musician?—you are rewarded with a wave of emotion that breaks over you like a sea.

The opera was *La Bohème,* and it was the last presentation of the season. Giuseppe di Stefano was singing Rodolfo. And the Mimi was Mexico's own superb soprano, Irma Gonzalez. The public was ready to be carried away. A kind of nervous excitability, one part anticipation, and one part hysteria, hung over the packed house. The Mexican audience was all set to make some kind of a scandal, for good or ill.

It turned out that this was going to be a great night.

Both tenor and soprano were in grand voice, the orchestra played the Puccini score divinely, the conductor found the most delicious tempi. We all lived the bittersweet romance, with its tender music, the melodies so infused with nostalgia, with sensual innocence, with unsatisfied longings.

When the curtain came down and Gonzalez and di Stefano stepped out to take their bows, the people all began to scream *Bravo* and *Brava!* and I screamed too. We embraced, the girl in taffeta, the lady on whom she had fallen, Virginia and I and an unknown on my left. We all went wild. It was like election night. I bawled *Bravi* until I was hoarse. Virginia managed to ask me if she could holler too. "Of course," I answered, dashing emotional tears from my eyes and clapping and stamping.

She took a deep breath and let out an ear-splitting "*Wheeeeee!*" that was heard above the pandemonium of five thousand yelling Mexicans.

We continued to clap, bray, and screech at the end of every act, and at the final curtain the orchestra itself bestowed a special accolade. When it wants to, and not at the will of the conductor, the orchestra may play a Mexican dance tune, "The Chiapanecas," its own tribute to a musician. Sometimes they play it to honor a visiting conductor, sometimes it sounds to praise a composer whose work they have been interpreting, sometimes it is offered to the singers in an opera. Tonight it was for di Stefano and Gonzalez. This song of the orchestra, this accolade, is always introduced by a great roll on the kettle-drums, first in the high tone, and then a fifth below. At once the orchestra bursts into its Chiapanecan dance, and often the public joins in, humming or whistling. The singers stood with bowed heads, and di Stefano, perfect actor, remained with his hand on his heart. Irma Gonzalez dropped into a deep curtsy, as the last note sounded. Then, I was sure, we would bring the walls of Bellas Artes down around us, like the walls of Jericho.

But we were to be treated to one more beautiful Mexican musical custom.

While "The Chiapanecas," a fast and lively tune, is the tribute of the orchestra, sometimes—again, on its own volition, and not at the bidding of the conductor—it plays a musical farewell, a *despedida* for artists it cherishes. Tonight there was a sudden silence and the sad sweet strains of "Golondrinas," the farewell, sounded in brass, reeds, and viols.

Everybody cried.

At last it was over and we all staggered out into the fresh evening air. We were absolutely limp with tears and exultation.

"I have finally been to a five-handkerchief opera," confessed Virginia, "and I have yelled as I have really wanted to for the first time since college football. Hooray for Mexico! Hooray for *La Bohème!* Hooray for the orchestra! *Wheeeeeeeeeeeee!*"

A taxi drove right up and opened its door for us.

XIX 🦢

IT'S LOVE, OR NOTHING

A su tiempo maduran las uvas.
—OLD MEXICAN SAYING

Early on the morning of September 2, 1951, Wiki came and stood before me and announced with great joy and excitement, "Tomorrow I'll be a teen-ager!" Indeed it was so. His birthday is September 3, and he would be thirteen years old. Guicho had passed into the teens imperceptibly; for years he had been telling people he was older than he was.

For Wiki, this entering of a clearly marked new epoch was purely psychological. There are no specially teen-age activities, unless you accept the pavan of courtship, which, for the girls, often begins during their teens. A girl likes to be married by eighteen. Twenty-one will do, twenty-four is already pretty scary if you have no official *novio*. By the time you pass twenty-five in single-blessedness, you are *dejada*, or, to translate literally, you have been passed over, left.

My boys were not allowed ever to wear blue jeans in school, as is permitted in many schools my young American nephews attend. In Mexico, you would no more send your children to school in the cowboy clothing of a working vaquero than you would send them in a chef's hat and apron. Of course, if you are poor, you send them in what you have. Notwithstanding, even the poor in Mexico, prefer their own soft cotton khakis or *mezclilla* (a sort of grayish homespun cotton) to stiff dark blue jeans with copper rivets. It is a matter of opinion, but I feel personally that this reflects the Mexican taste for dress, inherent in the people. The Mexican Indians who still wear their traditional costume show extraordinary taste in design and color; who but a Tehuana would use a lace baby dress to frame her face with a starched ruffle, like the petals of a daisy, and who but a Tarrascan could have the courage to embroider her black handwoven wool with threads of magenta and orange, combined? The city people, wearing the dress of the Western world, show, on the whole, enormous taste, and without the fear of being different that seems to get so many of us, brought up in a less color-conscious world, who wear gray, beige, or navy blue almost exclusively. Shopping in the United States I have often been urged into gray or neutral shades by the remark, "In this, you can't go wrong." The sentiment reflects a fear of standing out from the others. Natural coquetry in Mexican women leads them to choose light blue and light green, to set off their black hair and eyes. Not for nothing does Maria Felix, most beautiful of Mexican movie stars, wear only white tailored suits. Her great flashing black eyes, camellia skin, and luxurious black hair are unforgettable in the setting of tailored white silk shirt and white wool suit.

Wiki inherited a flair for colors with little instinct for assembling them. As he entered his teens and developed an interest in neckties and shirts, I had to check him hastily at the door every day before departure for school. He would as likely as not have on brown trousers, red socks, a blue shirt, purple tie, and green sweater. At my protests, he always replied, "But Mima! I *love* colors!" And so he does, to this day. But now he has a little chart about how to combine them.

Schools in Mexico do very little about organized sport, and such games and teams as develop often owe their existence to the activity of some American. It was the late, much beloved Arthur Constantine, Chief of the International News Service in Mexico City, who taught some college boys to play American football, and encouraged an interest in the game.

Mexican boys and girls are kept carefully apart during their teens and the ritual of "going steady" does not exist; neither are young persons allowed to roam around in herds without adult supervision. Yet they are brought together, regularly, and I may remark in passing, interest in each other seems not to flag. But the encounters are surrounded with formality, ceremony, and respect.

The commonest of the occasions when young teen-age boy meets teen-age girl, is the ubiquitous *Baile de Quince*. In Mexico, many young girls do not continue formal schooling after they have finished the six required years of grammar school, except for special courses such as in music study, languages, and other lessons which are arranged privately. And when a girl completes her fifteenth year, she is "out," and the occasion is celebrated—when the family can afford it—with a dance.

These dances are delirious occasions, for many young people surrounded with all the magic glamour of Christmas, because there are no school dances, and the edge of enjoyment has not been blunted. When Guicho and Wiki were invited to their first *Baile de Quince*, they were quite beside themselves. First, their father had to take them to town and procure the necessary raiment, from the skin out. Nothing, absolutely nothing, Wiki felt, should be other than radiantly new, for this brilliant occasion. On the day of the dance, they were barbered and perfumed. They were conveyed to the dance by their father, who called for them once more, before it was over. In the meantime, they had to learn to dance.

Here we were in luck. Luis's brother Carlos had three children, Carlitos, Yuyú (for Lourdes), and Fernandito. Yuyú had had dancing lessons. She taught her brothers, and she was glad to teach my two. Tiny Yuyú was severe about technique; the exact amount of pressure by which Wiki was allowed to clutch his partner, was illustrated; the exact steps for a certain flair and ease, combined with dignity and style, were taught. Carlitos and Nando flew around our living room, to demonstrate, and Wiki and Guicho were made to practice. A sort of dry-run on the *baile* was held, with other cousins, Nena and Chiquis, invited. Bowing, light conversation, and how to fetch refreshments were on the agenda of subjects to be taken up. We held several of these preliminary skirmishes before the great day.

Music was no problem. We had a record player, on which my sons were wont to play their great classical favorites, but Yuyú had dance music records, and whenever they ran out of music, Luis, my husband, being a *lírico* (someone who can play the piano by ear), was pressed into service. We took up the rugs in the sala, and in the dining room, and shoved the furniture to one side and there was great activity.

Other young men came and asked to be allowed to join in. Since I was being dragon, all was correct and proper. Tavo, from two houses down, appeared, and I rejoiced to see him, for he is one of my favorites—a Don Quijote of a young man, tall and very thin and aflame with ideals. For Tavo, all women, even gray-haired mamas and grandmamas, moved in a sort of shining aura, a complete halo, so to speak. He bows deeply, kisses hands, and is full of gallantry. Despite all this, and the big spaniel-brown eyes, he had no success with women, he told me in confidence.

"I have written hundreds of letters, señora," he confessed, "to beautiful girls I have met at dances, telling them of my admiration, and not one has replied! Not one!"

"Well," I answered feebly, "you must persevere."

"Perhaps I will have more encouragement," he mused, "when I am older. I am, at present, fourteen."

Now, in this, he was absolutely right. Mexican girls may move in their own armor of light, but they are practical creatures. The merry-go-round of dances and chaperoned meetings with young men are, they see clearly, the first step in the long, hard struggle of catching a husband, and—to a girl—they hate to waste their time. Young men are expected to be able to produce proof of solvency, earning power, and prospects, and when they go courting, they are required to make it clear that they are no-nonsense fellows, and altarbound. When the day arrives—and as the Mexicans say, "Every chapel has its fiesta day"—and my sons want to have the opportunity to meet often with a certain young lady, object matrimony, Luis and I will have to dress up in our best and go to call on the parents of the young lady, to *pedir la mano*, or quite literally, to ask for her hand. The family, in other words, must know what is going on, and must give approval. The young man's parents must be prepared to answer searching questions, touching on character, finances, and health, and the parents of the young lady, though in the position of advantage (since they are being sued) have to fill out quite a questionnaire, too.

Being severely kept away from the girls, except on stated and formal occasions, the young men in their teens are forced to develop other interests. Now Mexico is not a rich country, and though there is a small very wealthy sector, which provides its sons with automobiles and wallets full of spending money, this is so small as not to count in the general social pattern. They are *Los ricos*, or *Los rancios*, and indeed, so practical (in economics) is the young Mexican, that most of them keep away from the rich boys, if they can't hope to continue on with them socially.

What about part-time jobs? There aren't any, for the reason that there is always some man, a father of a family, who will gladly do the job full time. Besides, it is only fair, one feels in Mexico, that paying jobs should be given to adults, if they want them.

I lament this, for I remember the happy activities of my brother delivering groceries during high school summers, in a fine Maxwell House apron with GOOD TO THE LAST DROP printed across his stomach. In Mexico, though, it is not even proper to require your children to cut the lawn; there is a gardener with three children who *needs* to cut your lawn. And if you are in a position to have a lawn, you are in a position to pay a gardener to cut it.

Thus, many pursuits which keep teen-agers active and out of mischief in the United States, are not possible for the average middle-class Mexican boy. And it is one of the signs of Mexico's steady progress, that the middle-class is growing —of its own accord, because the rich are dropping back down into it, and because the poor are rising quickly into it.

Well, music is one of the activities of young Mexicans which occupies them for long, excited hours. It is a musical race and a romantic one, and there is no onus attached to studying music. Quite the contrary. I am not entirely certain of the attitude of prep school boys to music study in the Eastern states of my country, but I know from experience, that in the West, boys tend to consider this something for the girls. In Mexico, it is the other way. Long before the advent of Elvis Presley, and the rise of the guitar to a position of respectability in the United States, it has been as much a part of a young Mexican gentleman's equipment as the ability to turn a *piropo*. Also great crowds of young men study the piano and the violin, and hordes of them sing.

In my household, when Guicho and Wiki were fourteen and sixteen years old, we began the tradition of the "Sunday evenings." Sunday evening was their time. They could invite as many boys as they wanted and they could play records as loudly as they wanted, until midnight, and I always had ready some sort of stretchable supper, that would feed twenty as well as ten. These evenings were a great success, and even today, when both my sons are young men, they continue, off and on, throughout most of the year. They will fall apart only when both my boys are "official" *novios*, with the date set for their wedding. Until then, they have to find ways of filling their free evenings with entertainment without any women around. Except Mima, of course. She is always around, making sandwiches, passing out Cokes or coffee, and trying to keep the hi-fi down enough so that the house doesn't fly apart from the vibrations.

Besides Tavo, Alfredo comes. He is short and round, with a round face and round eyes, and quite properly is known as "Bola," or ball. Something like what we mean by butterball. Bola is a bullfight enthusiast, and he always comes with bullfight music and Spanish flamenco records. Sometimes he brings his guitar, for he plays well. There is Mario, the pianist, and an excellent one. Profoundly musical, he took up the viola in recent years, and now plays it well. My Wiki plays his cello, with great temperament and musicality, and some difficulty with intonation in the higher registers. Then there is Carlos, a dedicated violinist, who went, not to prep school, but to the National Conservatory of Music, where high school courses are combined with music teaching for young people who wish to train to be professional musicians or music teachers.

Often Carlos, Mario, Wiki, and another friend Jorge (a little older, and working in a government office) play quartets. Even, on occasion, they bring in Dr. Sauter, an eminent eye specialist, to play the piano with them, and they work away at the Brahms Quintet, the Schumann, or the César Franck. If any one of the musicians fails, they evolve duos, or trios.

The home music group never fails of an audience. Tavo is madly enthusiastic; Juan Bosco (an organ student) is gently critical; Juanito and Guicho may sketch the musicians at their self-imposed toil, and there are others who sit around on cushions and cry *"Brutal! Que brutal!"* admiringly, at intervals.

Mexican slang tends to be as strange, mobile, and sometimes as senseless, as that of American youths, though words of admiration, like *brutal, colossal,* and *fabuloso* are similar to American use. Boys call one another Chango (monkey), Cuate (twin), and Mano (for *hermano,* or brother), while girls even address one another, under stress, as *Hombre!* (which, of course, means man). A pretty girl is called a *mango,* as our fathers and grandfathers used to speak of a peach, and there are many interesting words for automobiles, dances, and other youthful diversions. It is interesting to note here that "bad words" in Spanish are mostly blasphemies, or taking the name of the Deity in vain, while "dirty words" usually come directly from Caló or the Spanish gypsy language.

After the musicians fold their music, and polish and put away their instruments, someone is likely to call "Abelardo! A

poem!" Do you think Abelardo guffaws and acts as if this
were a joke? Do you think he deprecates? Not a bit of it. He
is on his feet at once, a solemn stout boy with a crewcut and
dreamy dark eyes. (He plans to be a priest.) He has a large
repertory of memorized poems and selections from inspiring
prose, and he recites well. Abelardo holds up a hand for silence, and then, when the last cigarette is lighted, and the last
cushion moved around, and the room is quiet, he lets the so-
norous Spanish words flow. He is sensitive and passionate, and
he knows how to use his lovely language with dramatic effect.

"*Brutal!*" they all agree, clapping, after he recites García
Lorca's "Llanto por Ignacio Sánchez Mejías," the dead bullfighter. He goes on to "Suave Patria" of López Velarde, and
then perhaps does a poem or two of Rubén Dario.

While they eat *tacos,* or move on to little iced cakes, the
boys may get Guicho to read something from *Don Quijote,*
or maybe some of the hilariously improbable dialogues of Sal-
vador Novo—like the dialogue between Diego Rivera and an
American girl reporter, or between Sister Juana Inez de la
Cruz, the great Mexican poet-nun, and Pita Amor, a Mexican
poetess of today, who is neither a nun nor nunlike. Guicho
is expert at these readings, for he is a gifted mimic, being able
to project caricature into his voice, as he does on paper. He
can duplicate any known accent, and imitate any one, in voice,
mannerisms, and tone. No doubt he inherits this gift from the
many actors in the family, but to it, he adds his own unerring
ability to discover the most peculiarly individual of any person's qualities. This stands him in good stead, now that he is
a portrait painter by profession.

Guicho's studies in the studio of José Bardasano, (a Spanish refugee, who had been trained in Spain in the traditional
Spanish school established in the seventeenth century by
Velázquez, and carried out ever since in the Royal Academy of
Painting in Madrid) began when he was sixteen. All my successful artist friends, from Wolfgang Paalen, an abstractionist
and impressionist, and Remedios Varo, a surrealist, to Juan

O'Gorman, a follower of the muralist style of Diego Rivera, and himself a painter of realistic power subjected to the transfiguration of an unfettered imagination, told me to see that Guicho had a thorough academic training, since he wanted to dedicate his life to painting.

"And," they all said to me, "insist that he learn how to draw. It's like the piano—if you want to play it, you have to learn to play scales. You must have a technique, before you can dispense with it." Every one of those successful artists, and others too, told me this, and they all told me, also, to let him break away when he wanted to, after the first three or four years.

Thus, when my sons were in their mid-teens, their ways branched in different directions. Wiki kept on with the academic school years, and Guicho trained, morning and afternoon, in the studio of a strict and demanding teacher.

Luis and I told Guicho that by going into the studio of a painter at so early an age, he would have to fill in his education by himself, through reading. This he has done, and in the way of self-educated persons, he has read widely, but following no plan. His education is spotty, but what he knows, he knows well.

Mexican children of the middle class who are being educated, generally learn to speak one or two languages besides Spanish. English is taught in the elementary grades, by law, and most educated Mexicans understand and read it, if they do not speak it easily. Very many also learn French, German, or Italian.

I had at one time some Russian friends, and they had just had a baby. Guicho came to me one day and said he would like to visit this couple daily.

"Why?" I asked.

"To learn Russian. When the baby begins to talk, I can learn each word right along with him, and in a few years I will be speaking it, just as the baby will."

It was a good practical plan, but time and politics put an end to it.

Besides the music, the young men in the teen years, have some other outlets. A few take up swimming and diving, and Mexico has produced some champions at the Olympics. Some go in for tennis. It is not expensive, and it is swift and exciting. And sometimes it is possible to catch a glimpse of the girl players, in white tennis shorts, on the strictly ladies' side of the club courts.

Another passion is the game of chess, which everyone of Spanish extraction seems to love in a special way. Perhaps the Moorish blood in them all calls it forth. Chess clubs and informal chess games are always going on. Still another favorite is dominoes; many men carry a passion for dominoes into adult years, just as they do chess.

Wiki took up mountain climbing, and practiced *roqueando* (climbing rocks with piolet and ropes), traveling over loose shale and other difficulties before the great day dawned when he was to make his first ascent of San Miguel, a high rocky peak in the Valley of Mexico. I heard later, when he came home, stood in the middle of his bedroom, and began shedding canteen, blankets, food pack, *pasamontañas* cap (mountain-pass knitted helmet, with ears and mouth covered), piolet, and all his gear that the ascent had been a great success. He frightened me with several terrible tales he had learned from other hikers on their way up, and then went on to tell me how doggedly he had managed the shale, and the snow, and how brilliantly he had affixed his pick into the holes left by the ones who climbed ahead of him, and so on. I died a thousand deaths, but I had been dying them every moment he was gone, and now these deaths were more bearable, since I had my big strong boy within touching distance.

"And when I climbed up the last rope, and pulled myself up, over the lip of the precipice, and could stand at last at the very top . . . what do you think I saw?"

"A flag?" I guessed. "A skeleton? A youth bearing a banner with a strange device, 'Excelsior'?"

"No," said Wiki. "A little old lady sitting in front of a charcoal brazier, making *tacos*."

I registered incredulity, and Wiki enjoyed my astonishment.

"She had come up the back way, on a burro, and we were certainly glad to buy a hot *taco* and a mug of scalding coffee!" he told me.

Wiki still climbs mountains, and I still worry and lie sleepless, but I am afraid he will do it all his life, as many Mexicans do. He has climbed Popocatepetl and Ixtacihuatl, the two eternally snowcapped volcanoes which guard Mexico City, many times each, and the Nevado de Toluca once. There are a great many hiking clubs, and a good many select "Alpine" clubs, and brave little knots of friends travel all over the Republic finding and climbing mountains. Some of them travel together to other countries, to indulge their special passion. It is not generally known that mountain climbing is widespread in Mexico, which is too often thought of as a sleepy country where nobody likes to exert himself.

Guicho and his cronies go in for a third popular pastime —arguments. To one who has never seen or heard young Latins in an evening argument, the sight and the sound is almost frightening, roughly equivalent, I should say, to discovering Niagara Falls. Such a roaring without cease, such vitality, such animation! It is likely to go on, for hours, or until my husband comes and starts, ostentatiously, to wind the clock and put out the cat. The same scene occurs in other Mexican homes, and in little coffee shops all over the city.

Young Mexicans are great coffee drinkers; tea (aside from the effete tea party of ladies) is considered by them all to be medicine. Over black coffee, usually heavily sugared, they take the world apart and put it together again.

I do not fare very well at these gatherings, for I represent the "Colossus of the North," one of their ideological enemies, at least in theory. (However, I understand that when "Colossus of the North" is said anywhere south of Mexico's Guatemaltecan border, it is Mexico which is being referred to.)

The young men read history, they are all bilingual and

most of them are trilingual, and politics is their passion, as football seems to be the ruling passion in my own country. Add to the delirium for football and the American college boy's interest in foreign affairs, a great dash of Latin volcanic temperament, and you have a faint picture of what young Mexicans feel about politics. It is simply the only thing in the world worth thinking about, that's all.

In vain Luis has proscribed certain subjects for discussion at the dinner table, hoping to avoid arguments, for he is a peaceful man, accustomed to allowing others to express themselves without interruption, to hear their views, and agree or disagree, or reserve judgment. But his sons raise their voices, they shout, they grow red in the face, they threaten, they beat their breasts when they speak of (in this order): Communism, Catholicism, and Mexico. Their passions rapidly reach a high boiling point, and they give off steam visibly. They are the opposite of the English university man, they tell me, whose preoccupation is never to seem excited about anything; in Mexico, young men get excited about everything because they connect everything with (again, in this order): Communism, Catholicism, or Mexico. In some way or another.

When the boys were about fifteen and seventeen, there was an occasion in which they enjoyed something of the freedom and ease in social relationships known to their American cousins. This was when the theater bared its fangs, and rushed upon the unsuspecting mothers of San Angel.

One of my friends had a talented daughter, Nina, who loved making puppet theaters, reading plays, and taking part in and directing amateur theatricals. Nina decided that since there had been a visiting theatrical company which gave plays in French, and since *Hamlet* had been given in modern dress and also in English in Mexico City, she would give it in a new way. She would present a teen-age *Hamlet*, spoken in English. That's where the bilingual Treviño boys came in.

I was sitting in my sala, calmly perpetrating some sort of knitting, when Wiki burst in on me one spring afternoon.

"Mima!" he cried. "I am going to be Hamlet! Where's your book of Shakespeare? I must start learning the lines!"

When I had been able, by pretending that I was deaf, to get him to slow down and tell me what was afoot, I learned that Nina had asked him to read for the part.

"But darling," I explained, "that doesn't mean you are going to *get* the part! I don't want you to be disappointed."

"Why, who *else* could play it?" he asked me, with the simple vanity that proclaims the born actor.

I tried to sneak in a word or two at dinner, to prepare a mattress for a possible fall, and I made a few speeches known as *indirectas*, or, as Cantinflas would say, "There is somebody here whose name I won't say, but I am looking at him. . . ."

Wiki cut classes and broke engagements and generally went wild learning the great soliloquies until the day of the reading. Guicho went along with him, in the role of an observer.

A few days later the blow fell. Wiki was not to be the melancholy Dane, after all. The part of Hamlet had gone to an English boy, a few years older, with a very dashing stage presence and very English English. I administered pain killer and stayed the rash suicidal hand until Wiki was able to accept Fate. We all spent a very bad week, and I complained to Luis that I had never been stage struck, and I had no idea why Wiki was.

"Because I was," he told me. "I was in a play in high school in San Antonio."

It seemed that this was a patriotic play about how wonderful Texans are, and Luis was offered the part of the villain . . . a Mexican, of course. He took this on, all for the rapture of being able to tread the boards. Due to his accent, he was not allowed to say much, anyhow.

Actually, he had only two appearances—once at the end of the first act, when he was to rush onstage and shout, "I demand that you surrender!" and again at the end of the third act, when he was to rush onstage, receive a bullet wound in the chest and fall dead. Fast curtain.

At all rehearsals, the general confusion and bad temper did not dismay him. He studied his line, and he rehearsed falling dead until he was wonderful at both. Came the great night of the play, and he ruined everything by rushing in, clutching his heart and falling dead in the first act, bringing the play to a premature and angry close, for lack of any plot reason to go on. Everybody hated him for weeks.

I hoped Wiki would decide to become just part of the audience at Nina's production, but ambition simmered in him, and he went back to read for the part of Claudius, the King of Denmark. The stars shone in his eyes once more, and he studied furiously. But he was crushed to earth once more. Mario got the part of the King. Poor Wiki was able to pull himself together a little sooner, this time, for after all, Mario was his best friend, and if Wiki couldn't have the part, none better than Mario.

That night, as Wiki toyed with his supper, the telephone rang. It was Nina asking him to read for the part of the Ghost. Wiki consulted with me, somewhat uncertain. "Is the Ghost a good part?" he asked me. "An important part?"

"Why, without the Ghost roaming around, egging him on, Hamlet would never have started anything," I explained stanchly. "It's the most important part in the whole play!"

So Wiki started learning lines, and trudging off daily to rehearsal. Then he was given the part of a soldier, in a later act. At first angry at the extra responsibility, later he was incensed when they decided to do without that soldier altogether and just have an off-stage voice. It seemed that every day something awful happened, to wound and humiliate him, and I was given a four-week course in the vagaries of the actor's temperament.

Guicho, declining the part of a Gravedigger, just hung around the rehearsals snickering, until someone collared him and made him help with the lights.

But Wiki, his actor's blood boiling, told me he intended to play the Ghost with such perfection that all subsequent action in the play would fall flat. I detected again the strong bent of the born actor in this, but I aided and abetted him. We consulted Uncle George, and he imparted voice lessons, so that Wiki could play the Ghost as whispering mysteriously from afar, calling sepulchrally, or groaning his message. Wiki finally decided on a combination of these three techniques. Then, about a week before the final presentation of the play, Wiki came home trembling with emotion.

"I resigned," he informed me, desperately. "They cut the Ghost's lines in two places." He went into his room and locked the door and would not come out to eat.

Nina, however, knew by instinct that her worm had turned, and she phoned to beg Wiki to come back, promising that each and every one of his lines would be restored.

Meanwhile, she began having trouble with her Hamlet. The English boy had inconsiderately moved away. One by one other hopefuls were tried and found wanting. My mother, who was visiting me, and who is as wise in her way as Mama-cita, said to me, "Mark my words. Nina will play Hamlet herself. She has probably got her black tights ordered."

And so it was. The best thing, anyhow, for nobody else could have learned all the lines. Besides, she looked charming, with her golden hair in a page-boy cut, her legs sturdy as a boy's, in the black tights. Mario was splendid as King Claudius, and Patricia, my goddaughter, was a lovely Queen Gertrude. But naturally, the Ghost was the best of all. We almost wore our arms off applauding.

Afterward, when Wiki had returned his costume to the theatrical house that had outfitted the play, I drew a long breath and thought I had got him safely past that milestone. *El teatro*, I now thought comfortably, was safely out of his system.

He pestered me for an advance on his allowance, and

after I had put up a token struggle, I gave in, and let him have it. He said it was a surprise.

I waited, counting the days to my birthday or my saint's day or Christmas. But soon I learned that the advance had been spent for photographs. Theatrical photographs, of the type sent around to agents and studios by fledgling actors.

There was one of Wiki in a loose tweed jacket, cradling a pipe in his hand. There was a close-up of him looking quizzical, one black eyebrow a half-inch higher than the other, and there was a third pose, standing with arms folded, looking sternly into the distance.

I was worried as I studied the photographs, but my husband appraised them carefully, holding them out at arm's length, setting them on the mantel and standing back a few paces, and generally according them a proper interest.

"I must show you mine," he then told the astounded Wiki, and went away to rummage in his trunk. He returned with a set of glossy stills, taken at least ten years before I had crossed his path. They revealed a hopeful young man, Luis undoubtedly, in the very same poses his son had chosen, and the same starlight shone in his dark eyes.

I was afraid my Wiki might be encouraged toward acting as a career, since it was in the family, but he grew very silent and thoughtful. I heard no more of plays, auditions, or rehearsals.

"Mima," he said one day, "I won't be in any more plays. They asked me, and I said no. For I have noticed that it is like gambling . . . if you win, you are sorry you didn't bet more, and if you lose, the money is gone. In plays, if you get the main part, nobody likes you, and if you get a poor part, you are sore. So I am giving up acting."

In no time at all, he was singing in a chorus and looking forward to taking part in a performance of the Brahms' Requiem.

XX

MUCHA MUJER, MUY MACHO

> *Aunque me visto de lana, no soy borrego.*
> —SPANISH PROVERB

When Mexican men admire a woman, they say she is "much woman," and when they admire a man, he is "much man," or a real he-man—*mucha mujer* and *muy macho*.

Since I feel that it is often possible to judge a country by what its people admire, it seems a good place to tell what I think Mexicans mean by these two expressions. They are forthright—they admire the profoundly feminine woman, and the brave and virile man. So strongly do these national ideals run through the popular ballads, the songs, the legends and stories, and even the history, that less than feminine ladies, and the occasional cowardly or limp-wristed gentleman has to pay these images the coin of imitation. And when they do, we get *machos* that are really frightening in their vigor.

The cult of the *macho* is a dangerous one, and to it we owe the *depistolización* which the government undertakes regularly. A man who is *muy macho* is braver than necessary, a pathological demonstrator of virility, a terror in the saddle, at the wheel of a car, or with his pistol. A little anecdote, which Mexicans now tell on themselves (since they have begun to realize the psychological pattern behind *machismo*) illustrates the position of the *macho*. Three men, the story goes, were riding in an airplane, when the pilot informed them that the engine had failed and they would have to jump for it. He had parachutes for four. All were willing to put on the parachute and jump but the Mexican. He jumped out without one, shouting, as he went, "I'm a real man, and I don't have to depend on any parachute! *Soy muy macho, yo!*"

The *mucha mujer* is sometimes used to mean ladies of the most opulent curves possible, but the exaggerated femininity of Mexican women tends to take other forms, now that the slender figure is admired wherever Western fashions in dress are used. The Mexican woman who wishes to impress with her sexual character, professes to be unable to stay even one hour in a house without her husband, at night. When husbands have to be away on business trips, they pack up and go to Mama's, even if the husband is away only one night, and the servants sleep in. These ladies cannot swallow a morsel of food unless their husbands are sitting opposite them at the table. They are never happy unless pregnant (perhaps this is making a virtue of necessity, in a way), and they live without any other interest whatsoever besides their families.

Now I admire Mexican women, and I feel that they are on the whole happier, more fulfilled, and wiser than their *norteamericana* sisters, who seem too often (it has appeared to me) to want to be *more* than just happy women who spread love around them. The Mexican woman sees this as her role, and she is expert at it, and it rewards her richly.

But to balance the exaggeratedly male man, the *muy macho*, there is a *mujer* who is as unbalanced as he, on the other side. Both these express some profound need in the Mexican character, and indicate a stubborn revolt against the sexes assuming the same general type of clothes and doing all sorts of work together, losing in the process some special quality that makes them need each other.

Bearing out this ideal, the roles of the two are kept strictly apart in spheres of influence. The mother, I would say, is the final authority in all matters pertaining to the home, and in this role, she has no peer. Nevertheless, Father handles the money, and he makes all major decisions. Long ago Luis told me that whenever I was asked to do anything I did not want to do, I had only to say, "My husband won't let me," and nobody would ever bother me about it any more. Being one of the independent (though never trousered) American women, I often forgot this injunction, but when I remembered to use it, it was really delightfully comfortable and easy. Nobody dared me to fight it out with him, nobody advised me to do it anyhow, and if he didn't like it, he could lump it. Nobody suggested that I do it, and lie to him. In Mexico, if your husband doesn't permit you to play bridge, you don't play bridge, and that's final. And so with anything else.

A Mexican man himself revealed to me much of the structure of the Mexican home, in his story of how he had been persuaded to let his wife return to her violin, some twelve years after their marriage.

"When we married, Eleesabet," he told me, "Josefina was a professional violinist. I didn't want her to continue; I intended to support her myself, for one thing, and for another— I'll admit it—I was jealous of that life she had had before our marriage, the friends who had meant much to her. I wanted her all to myself. So I asked her to promise that she would give up her music, and she promised.

"As you know, we have been very happy, and we have had six beautiful children. Josefina is a wonderful mother, deeply devoted to her children and to me. She is a splendid housewife, and she is still beautiful. So I am a lucky man, no? Well, I found out that I had not made my Josefina feel as lucky as I did.

"One day I came home unexpectedly from my work. Josefina did not hear me come in, and, as I heard music, I tiptoed up the stairs. The music was coming from the nursery. I went quietly and peeped in. Our youngest child was a baby, still in his cradle, and there sat my Josefina, in a housecoat, barefoot. She had the toes of one foot hooked around the leg of the cradle, and she was rocking it. And she was practicing her violin—scales, up and down, in chromatics, in thirds, in sixths.

"She looked up and saw me. She put down her violin. '*Mi vida*,' she said, 'it wasn't really music. Just scales.'

"I felt so sorry and ashamed of myself, Eleesabet, that I bought her a new, and a very fine violin next day, and I built her a house with a big music room in it.

"Now what do you think? I love music too, and I love to have her friends here to play with her."

The moral here is very clear. While music was proscribed, Josefina kept the promise she had made her husband.

I am not a bit sure I could have done it. And before my American readers bridle too much, let me report that Josefina's is one of those perfect marriages you read about and so seldom find demonstrated.

It was my enormous good luck that when I married and went to live in Mexico, people in the provinces still admired a girl whose figure was proof that her father was a man of substance who could afford to set a good table. An old country proverb says, "A horse should fill a man's legs, a fighting cock his hands, and a woman, his arms." In Mexico it was chic to have a bosom, even during the dreadful flat-chested years in the United States, and it was sensibly considered that Nature had provided ladies with a pleasant cushion to sit on, and this should be kept up, in the name of simple comfort.

Mamacita, my mother-in-law, was more than plump; she was a solid and hefty matron. She had built up her figure by a richly chosen diet which she enjoyed very much and it was her firm belief that families are held together by the tolling of the church bell and the dinner bell. She always set her table prettily, with flowers and good china, and she provided ample amounts of good soup, nutty flavorful rice, spicy *guisados* or stews or roasts, plenty of wonderful beans, and stacks of hot delicate tortillas. For dessert she usually set forth platters of beautifully arranged fruit, mounds of coconut pudding or custard or any of the Spanish-Arabic sweets made on a basis of eggs, almonds, and honey. Quite naturally, she despised people who *no saben comer*—people who didn't know how to eat.

One day, after a shopping trip to San Antonio with her daughter Adela, she called on me (bringing me a box of American chocolates) and we chatted. I knew her well, and I could tell that something was on her mind. "We had a lovely trip," she told me. "We ate in the hotel restaurant several times. The menu had all sorts of good things listed. One evening I ordered a simple, well-balanced meal. Crab cocktail to begin, then a cream of asparagus soup, roast turkey with stuffing and cranberry sauce and potatoes and gravy, and little corn muffins with butter and jam, and apple pie with ice cream. I enjoyed my little supper. But Eleesabet, I do not understand American ladies."

"How, Mamacita?"

"Well, I looked around. Not one finished her plate. They all kept looking away from their food. They would push it around with their forks, and they were all *thin*. Really thin. With bones showing. I should think their husbands would be worried about them."

"They like to be thin, Mamacita."

"Can it be? Well, perhaps. I saw one lady who came into the dining room who had just had her face and hair done; you could see that she had spent a good deal of money on both. She was dressed in a fine silk dress and she had a fur coat over her shoulders, and on her hands, two diamond rings. It was obvious that she had plenty of money, much more, for instance, than I. Yet I ate my turkey dinner and she ordered a plate of hay!"

Mamacita became very excited.

"Just lettuce and celery and cucumbers and such green things. Everybody knows all this is terribly indigestible, in the first place. In the second place, she sprinkled all this with lemon juice—not even a drop of oil. I watched. It was quite revolting. Then afterward, she had black coffee and cigarettes. It was like seeing a beggar in the street, in filthy rags, and all the while you know he has a fat bank account."

"Mamacita, she was dieting. Everybody does it. The

women in my country love to have people say, 'You look wonderful! How much have you lost?' "

"No wonder there are so many divorces over there," she
pronounced darkly. "It is unnatural."

Now this conversation took place in the late 1930s. Later
the American mania for being thin reached Mexico, and Mamacita, who had an open mind, finally decided to give it a
try. A lot of her friends were going on diets, and she liked
to be in the swim. She heard about several of the diets, and
decided at last on the banana-and-milk diet, which was popular
at the time. After three weeks on this, during which she
gained three kilos, she rejected the whole idea, and returned to
letting Nature and her own good sense take over.

"It was a great bore, eating those bananas and drinking
the milk," she told me, "and at first it really spoiled my appetite for my meals. But I got over that, for I have great will
power."

I learned a lesson, some years later. A hotel in Cuernavaca,
which was doing heavy business over the weekend, and very
little from Monday to Friday, worked out and announced a
family plan, at low rates, for people who could come with their
children at Monday noon and stay until just before noon on
Friday. I was in need of a rest, and I took my two sons, aged
twelve and fourteen at the time. I lay on a straw mat near the
swimming pool, in the sun, and my boys sported in the water.
It wasn't long before both were making spaniel eyes at a pretty
little girl, daughter of one of the resident families in the hotel.
They invented ways of being near her at table, and, against all
regulations, picked flowers for her from the hotel garden.

I pretended to be piqued. "You don't love me any more,"
I complained. "You spend all your time with Gloria. Or at
least swimming in the same pool with her. I am hurt because
you have always told me that after Maria Felix and Maureen
O'Hara, I am the most beautiful woman in the world."

Consternation was written on each small face, also the
wish to comfort.

"Why Mima," explained Guicho, "we like her because she is beautiful and also young. You are beautiful too, but you are old. You are almost forty!"

Wiki put his arms around me. "Gloria has a prettier face than you, Mima," he assured me, "but you have the fattest legs!"

I had to accept this accolade in the spirit in which it was given, but, just for the record, I then and there vowed never to allow my public to see me in slacks or shorts or Capri pants, or anything else without a nice concealing skirt over it.

Mexico, in general, feels as I do about trousers on ladies.

There is a large sign in all the churches, as follows: FE-MALES IN MALE ATTIRE WILL BE ASKED TO LEAVE THE CHURCH. And in Mexico, male attire means *pants*.

A word to the wise.

XXI

GOD WILLING

El hábito no hace el fraile . . .
—OLD SPANISH PROVERB

Whenever, on trips home to the States, or in groups of visitors, I am asked, "But what strikes you as the essential difference between the Mexicans and us?" or when I am urged to agree to the premise that "we are all basically alike, wouldn't you say?" my answer is not immediately forthcoming. I do feel that there are some essential differences between the Mexicans and the Americans and while I, of course, must agree that men and women tend to have the same problems and love the same things, yet I cannot agree that we are basically alike. The difference is a spiritual one, and not merely one evolving from the fact that Mexicans are poorer, in the individual and in the aggregate, than Americans. In other words, the non-materialistic posture of the average Mexican, as I have come to know Mexicans, is not basically a matter of making do with less because they have less. It is a spiritual attitude.

I have titled this chapter "God Willing," because it is a little phrase that occurs so often in conversations with Mexicans of every economic status, and because, quite literally, they mean it, every time they say it.

"I will meet you for lunch on Thursday, God willing," or "I shall send my son to the university, *con el favor de Dios,*" or "We are leaving on Saturday for New York. We will arrive there at five P.M., God Willing."

As I see it—as I feel it—this is not a mere figure of speech It is rooted in a great sense of fatality, of being always held in the hollow of God's hand.

"*Vaya con Dios*," friends say to one another, in farewell, and it means, "Go with God." So does goodbye, which means God be with you, but the expression in Spanish is a specific blessing, and in addition to *adiós*, which again, you will notice, means "to God," or "I commend you to God."

I have a belief that semantics have done their bit here, to fix in the national character the strong strain of mysticism which is revealed in the Mexican people. As a race, they are a fusion of Indian—with a great respect for dignity, tenderness, ritual, and devotion—and Spanish. And Spain has given us great mystics, many of them, as well as great poets. The words reminding us, at every hour of the day, that what we do is only because God has been willing—strengthen that pure stream of mystic feeling. And the Latin temperament generally (like the sensitive and stoical Indians who are part of the Mexicans) respects the mystical character, holds it dear, and defers to it.

When I first went to Mexico I ventured to discuss the mystical temperament with a Mexican friend one day, and I said, because I honestly thought so at the time, that if I had been called to a religious life, I would have wished to be useful in some direct way—in nursing, teaching, or caring for the indigent.

"Useful to people's bodies, you mean," corrected my friend. "The contemplatives are useful to the soul. Or do you deny the efficacy of prayer?"

Of course I do not deny it. I believe in it, I trust it, I turn to it with all my heart. And as the years have gone by, and as I have lived longer and longer in the country of my husband's people, I have come to turn to the contemplatives myself, and I have known days when I looked forward to the opportunity for fifteen minutes of quiet prayer, as a thirsty person does to a drink of water. I don't belittle any work to help the suffering, Heaven knows, and I am glad to see so much tremendous social uplift being done by religious charitable groups, but I have come to understand the former Mexican indifference to much of what happened to the body. Wrapped in prayer, enduring cold and hunger themselves, Mexican priests and nuns, for years, have not been terribly troubled by the physical life. Their religion teaches that God wills whatsoever He send us in this life, and that we must love His will, whether it seems to hurt or heal.

The obvious expression of the enormous difference between Mexicans and Americans is not the poverty of the Mexicans (which is disappearing slowly, as the government works to mitigate it, and the industrialization of the country brings high levels of earnings), but their attitude toward it.

I remember being received happily in the homes of friends, who, though they loved music with all their hearts, told me serenely that they would not have Symphony tickets that year because "this year we are poor." They did not repine; it was just a fact, and accepted as such. In the same manner my cook says, "My father is sick because he cannot chew his food well. He needs new teeth, but we are poor; we cannot buy them for him." When I offer to help buy them, she accepts with grace and with no false worry about what position it puts her in. In the same way, when I call to leave Symphony tickets for my friends, they are accepted as simply and happily. Obviously God wanted them to hear this concert—or he wanted Papa to have his teeth. There is a oneness in this feeling, which I admire, and which humbles me. For I tend to remember some of my built-in Americanisms . . . I have had the feeling that poverty is somehow shameful, as if I, or my husband, had refused to work, or as if we were of low mental caliber.

The Mexican is never ashamed of his poverty. He doesn't like it, and sometimes he has resented a false poverty forced upon him by selfish landlords, and he has turned against it with fury and with a passion for justice. But he is never ashamed of it.

And the same difference must be noted in the attitude toward charity. In my country, I read appeals for donations to the Community Chest "so that you need not be bothered more than once for all year," and indeed, one of the great arguments for social security and other social measures seems to be the horrific alternative of accepting charity. Everyone seems to have forgotten that if we make charity unnecessary, soon nobody will practice it, and what, I ask, would the world be without charity?

The Mexican gives and accepts charity with simplicity. "Take it, I may need you one day, as you need me today," and "Thank you, may God give you more."

These differences in point of view extend through Mexican life, and should be pondered. Mexicans revere their Constitution, but even as you and I, they feel encouraged to try to change parts of it. And all Mexicans stand together when their deepest religious ideals are set aside by law—even those Mexicans who themselves no longer communicate.

This is why there is constantly a movement toward getting the much-discussed Article III removed from the Constitution . . . the one which forbids any teaching of religion. That is why my friend Malenita's father ordered her to make him a habit.

When the government acted to arrest any priest or nun caught wearing a habit in a public place, her father, an Irishman born a Catholic but turned free-thinker, was outraged.

"My dear," he said to his daughter, "here are twenty pesos. I want you to buy an appropriate number of meters of brown serge and make me a habit."

"But father . . ." she began. He was a successful and busy mining engineer, as well as a painter of delicate and beautiful water colors. "What sort of habit?"

"Just something long and plain and full. And I will have a cowl," he told her, "for rainy days."

As soon as the habit was sewed, he put it on. And to make sure that his defiance was obvious, he made himself a large wooden cross which he wore round his neck on a length of cord. He was a tall and a very handsome man, and when he

went through the streets of Mexico to his office, he was noticed.

In due course, he was triumphantly arrested.

The police hailed him before a magistrate who demanded
to know why he was wearing a habit.

"A habit? What do you mean? This is a very comfortable
kind of a dress. I belong to no religious order."

This fact was readily proved.

"But why do you wear the cross?"

"I like it. And I made it myself. Nice piece of wood. Good
graining."

The Mexican police were dealing with an Irishman, and
they were soon fouled up in a terrific argument from which
they could find no exit.

The mining engineer was released and for some weeks
he went about in his habit until he felt that he had made his
point. Then he said, "Malenita, my dear, you may take my
habit and cut it up into a dress or dusting cloths or whatever
you like. I shan't wear it any more. I'm no longer a Catholic,
but I'm beginning to feel like Luther and I can't go on. I
shall go back to my tweeds." And he did.

In my life in Mexico I have known many men and women
of profound religious faith. One of my friends has an aunt who
gave away all her property, and who lives a life of meditation,
fasting, and mystical purity, though she belongs to no order.
Another young woman I know could not bring herself to accept any of her suitors, for she could not face surrendering
her body to any worldly passion. She avoided love as some men
avoid drink. And she was not hysterical or unbalanced; she
was loving and tender and beautiful. She belonged to no order,
but she gave her purity to God, as a devotional gift. Another
friend of mine, when he was dying, refused all sedatives,
though his disease was fatal, and it was a cruel one. "God is
permitting me to share, in an infinitesimal way, His passion,"
he said, and he took up his cross.

These were only a few of the Mexicans I knew who carried

in their spirits an instinctive turning to God, as the sunflower follows the hot yellow eye of the sun all day long. They must be multiplied by many thousands more, whose lives would not have crossed mine at any point. For they are typical. Mexicans recognize this mystical manifestation in themselves as part of their true image. The very frenzy of religious destruction, which exhibits itself occasionally in Mexico, proceeds from the same source in the spirit, for where there are great saints, there are great sinners, and vice versa. It appears that the capacity for religious feeling has no middle ground.

Here I should tell about the numerous women who dress in black and haunt the churches in Mexico, who are called *beatas* in a tone of semi-contempt by the liberals who despise this manifestation of the mystical soul, and in open admiration by those others who respect their devotion. The word means "blessed," and one is blessed before one is recognized as saint. These women have entered a state which has no name, and which has no counterpart, as far as I know, in American communities. The *beata* lives in a state complete in itself, as well-rounded with duties and joys and sorrows as the state of matrimony; these mystics give their lives to prayer and service —usually to their families and relatives—and they are engaged in constant loving sacrifice. They are seldom sad-faced, on the contrary they wear a look of innocent joy and are as ingenuous and open as eight-year-olds. Sometimes they dress in black, mourning dating from loss of a beloved one; but sometimes they are to be seen in shapeless sweaters and long skirts, or, as was the case with one of Luis's aunts, his wonderful Tía Rosa, who wore starched calico and bedroom slippers most of the time. But she was all love and service and comfort and joy, and when I think of angels, one of them must wear the calico and shapeless *pantuflas* under her wide white wings.

The *beatas*, in their black, are known and accepted for what they are, all over Mexico—as dedicated nuns, outside an order. During the Cristero Revolution, when federal troops were sent to the provinces to put a stop to the practice of the

Catholic faith and to close all the churches, orders went out to arrest every *beata* found in the streets. Since the *beata* is often in black, and this is also traditional mourning dress, flocks of black-garbed women were herded into jails, and there was great confusion sorting them out, as few indeed were the Mexican women who would betray their *beata* sisters, under this pressure. And a story is told of one confused federal general who caught a *beata* in the street, and hauled her to jail, while she protested vociferously that she was not in black but in navy blue. It was growing dusk, and nobody could prove this until the next day, so she was held, spitting with fury, in the barracks, until the morning sun came up. Then, to everybody's bewilderment, it was easily proved that she was, indeed, in navy blue, and she was perforce released. But there was a trap in the whole thing which the general brooded over for weeks. Never in his life had he seen so many women who looked and acted like *beatas*, but they were all in navy blue, and so his hands were tied.

Even today, many of the old anti-church laws have their power to worry and to sting, like angry wasps, should some federal officer wish to act upon his authority to enforce them. My friends, the Faheys, who throw open the doors of their hospitable home to visiting American priests on vacation, always keep a drawerful of red neckties, and of tan and blue shirts in which they disguise their visiting padres, should they arrive looking too obviously clerical.

This brings me to the story of my three priests.

I was instructed in the Catholic faith and baptized by a Spanish priest, member of a stern order. I had occasional letters from him after my marriage, and he told me that he had great hopes that the dream of his life, to go out to Japan to do missionary work, would soon be accomplished. Then passed several years when I did not hear from him, and my letters to the monastery where he had last been were unanswered. I supposed that Father J. was in the Orient.

Then I had a letter from a friend in Canada, asking me to

look after a French-Canadian priest, a friend of her family, who was bringing a few university students to Mexico to study the great murals.

So when I arrived home one day and Maria said, "The little *padrecito* came," I supposed it was Father A. from Canada. But Maria went on to say, "The little lame priest. He left you his card. Here it is." And behold, it was from Father J., on church business in Mexico. Luis and I went at once to find him, in the monastery where he was staying, and there we learned that he had been at the point of death for a year, with an infection in the bone of his leg, which he refused to allow amputated, until at last he was ordered to do so by his superior, in order to save his life. And so, he would never be able to go to Japan, but was to devote himself to quiet church business on this continent.

Father J. had only one evening free in Mexico City, and we had promised to attend a gathering at the home of the Faheys, so we asked if we could bring Father J. as our guest. The Faheys shouted "Of course!" over the telephone, and Father J. got permission to be with us until eleven.

Our courageous little Father J. would not change his clerical dress for any law, and when I remonstrated mildly about it, he turned his black Spanish eyes on me, and said, "I am a priest. If I am arrested, I will be arrested as a priest. No compromise." There spoke the very spirit of Spain, the Spain of the wars against the Moors, and of the Conquest—the Spain which produced men with definite defects, as we know, but men who were willing to stand up and be counted, no matter what the cost.

The party at the Faheys was in full swing. There were many delightful people there, for the Faheys are both gifted actors, and take part in many amateur plays, and they know writers and directors and singers and actors from many groups in the city. Pleasant refreshments were circulating, and over in a corner, a handsome man of thirty-odd, in loose easy tweed, was playing the piano and singing snatches from American musical comedies. "Bali Ha'i" from *South Pacific* twinkled from his fingers, then "On the Street Where You Live" from *My Fair Lady*, bits from *The King and I*, and excerpts from Gilbert and Sullivan. People would shout, "Play 'The Flowers That Bloom in the Spring!'" and the pianist, smiling, would find the right key, and launch into Koko's famous song from *The Mikado.*

We led Father J. over to the piano and Vega Fahey introduced us to the player. "Father J. meet Father R. He is visiting us for a few weeks."

Father J. stared at Father R., whose long hands roamed softly over the keys, and said sternly, "So you are a priest? You don't look like one."

Father R. said, "My order is as austere as yours, Father J., I am sure. I wear these clothes by order of my superior."

But when my little French-Canadian priest arrived with letters of introduction, he had solved the question of priestly dress while in Mexico, in the most brilliant way of all. Not like Father J. in his uncompromising clerical black, and Roman collar, nor yet like Father R. in his handsome tweeds. Father A., French to the core, was in his black suit, with clerical vest and collar, but over all he wore a Harry Truman-type of flowered sports shirt, all palm trees and hula girls, and perched on his tousled black hair, at a jaunty angle, a big Mexican straw sombrero. There is, after all, nothing like French chic.

XXII 🦢

HOME IS WHERE THE HEART IS

La vida se vive de día en día.
—OLD SAYING

"Tell me about your day," say friends of mine in the States. "How do you live from day to day? What is it like to have a home in Mexico? What do you eat? Who calls up? What goes on?"

Very well. Let us choose a day in August. Our alarm snarls at us at exactly seven A.M. Luis gets up, turns the alarm off, and goes back to bed. I rush into Wiki's room to wake him up, and he grunts and goes back to sleep. I go down the passage and outside into a brilliant morning; the trees wave lightly against a day of stretched blue satin. Not a cloud in sight, and the air feels crisply cool as I draw a long breath. I inspect the vegetable garden. Beets are coming up, string beans drip their slender green pods from the vines, and aphids have got onto my broccoli. Caramba! But there is a good crop of *brevas* (white figs) and there are plenty of plums. Something happened to the peaches this year; they all fell off the trees half ripe. We are in the tropics, and everything grows mightily, including every known type of insect pest. Plus snails. Mitchie Foo catches these sometimes, if he is bored and has nothing else to do, and pushes them around with a languid paw.

Guicho's little room and painting studio is in a corner of the garden. I waken him; he grunts and goes back to sleep. It was ever thus.

I greet Paula (the present cook, as Maria tried matrimony again, and found it a bit more supportable this time) and Elvira, the present housemaid. Elvira did not wear shoes when she came to me, but she was determined to learn how, and she practiced a lot in the garden with the first pair I bought her. Barefoot, watering the garden, she is graceful as a deer; with her feet crammed into red shoes with cuban heels, she is stiff and awkward. Both girls wear their hair in long shining black braids, and, knowing their love of color, I do not put them into uniforms, as many of my more elegant friends do. I buy them bright flowered cottons, and they have their dresses made to suit themselves, and they select bright-colored aprons. Elvira has a lovely sense of color, and often wears a pink cotton dress, with lilac apron and lilac ribbons on her hair, and Paula loves all colors, especially red. So she usually has on a red dress, a red sweater, a red apron, or red ribbons. Something red, to help her get through the day.

Elvira talks to my animals as if they were people, and she talks to the plants too, and she scolds the aphids and is severe with the snails. She loves to arrange flowers, and has vases of them in every room of the house, when we have blooms. When the garden is empty of calla lilies, tiger lilies, pansies, geraniums, and plumbago, she brings out flowers she has dried, head downward, so that the stalks are stiff and upright, and arranges them, with green leaves, in dry vases. Elvira has a mischievous sense of humor, and sometimes plays practical jokes on me. Elvira is from a small family (she has only one brother, who is a rancher in Veracruz) and so she enjoys the enormously complicated saga of Paula's people. Paula has a million relatives, and they all come to call, with their children, and tell her why they need money. Paula is always morose, thinking up new ways of getting money for them all. Some of these ways (need I point it out?) involve the señora. We keep books Paula and I; my loans and her repayments to me, involve thousands of pesos, and go for months and months. She has quite good credit in the months when she has a saint's day, or Christmas or New Year, or Guadalupe Day, or Easter, or the Day of the Holy Cross, or some other fiesta occurs.

Man or sweetheart trouble is what mows down most of

the good maids in Mexico, but I am lucky in Paula and Elvira. Paula has so many expenses with her family that she couldn't possibly take on the expense of a husband as well, and Elvira, a student of life, observed once to me tartly that she was never going to marry. "I am not such a fool," she informed me. "Girls say they are going to marry and stop working, but they all keep on working, more than ever. Not I. My money is for myself."

We set about getting breakfast and I go back to exhorting my three Treviños to wrench themselves out of the arms of Morpheus. Wiki is always last. Seizing a piece of bread from the breakfast table, he rushes off, barely in time to catch the bus to preparatory school. Guicho, in robe and slippers, calls for ranchero eggs—two fried eggs on top of a fried tortilla, the whole drenched in a fiery chile sauce. I take coffee and *cuernos* (Mexican-made croissants, and more divinely flaky and delicious than any I ate in France), and Luis, freshly shaved and neatly ready for the day (in contrast to Guicho and me, who are tousled and horrible at the breakfast table) demands his eggs in some special way.

"I want them scrambled, with just a little chopped onion," he tells Elvira, and I hear her relay the message scornfully in the kitchen. (She is scornful, because she knows he never likes anything in the morning, anyhow.) The eggs come in, with hot tortillas in a folded napkin. "Too much onion," says Luis and pushes them away. Another morning he may say, "I want my eggs fried, lightly over, with a chile chipotle on the side." He tastes them. "Cooked too much," he says, and pushes them aside. Mitchie finishes Luis's breakfast every morning, and is on hand to take care of it, sitting upright on my lap, and occasionally reaching out a paw toward a piece of buttered toast, or a bit of *cuerno*.

Guicho goes off to painting school at half-past ten. Luis leaves for his office at ten. Then Paula comes in to consult with me about lunch.

"What shall I make for lunch, señora?" she asks, in her sad voice.

"Well, I think we will have some spaghetti today, to begin."

"Sí, señora. Only I have already put the rice to soak in hot water."

"Very well. We will have rice. White rice, with peas."

"Sí, señora. And for meat?"

"Today I would like a *guisado* [stew] of beef, onions, and carrots, in gravy."

"Sí, señora. Only the señor said he wanted liver one of these days, and yesterday I asked the butcher to save me some for today."

"Oh, all right. Liver then. With vinegar sauce."

"Sí, señora. Only the señor doesn't want vinegar sauce. He said he wanted liver with onions."

"Liver with onions then," I agree irritably.

"And for dessert, señora?"

"I would like a coconut pie."

Paula has learned how to make all American hot breads and pies and cakes, and is expert at them. Usually she likes to demonstrate that she can do any of these things better than the señora. But never when I ask for them, for some strange reason of her own. She just likes to produce them unexpectedly.

"Sí, señora. Coconut pie. But there are no coconuts in the market now, and you don't like the dried coconut. So I have made a chocolate cream."

"Well, that's fine. Chocolate cream for dessert."

"But you can't eat chocolate, señora, you know you can't. It gives you a terrible headache. So I made some gingerbread for you. Just a small pan of it."

I am happy and touched.

"Why Paula, thank you."

Smiling her mysterious smile, and having bamboozled me into thinking I order lunch, she departs for the market, with her great wicker basket. She goes daily to market and buys everything fresh, from meat and fish, to fruit and vegetables, bread and tortillas. (Paula despises frozen food and fears anything not delivered with fresh dew on it. As my husband shares this feeling, we store no food in the refrigerator, and we have no deep freeze. The only thing Luis will eat that has been *trasnochada* [kept overnight] is beans; he *will* occasionally eat a dainty serving of refried beans that have been boiled and fried yesterday.) There she passes a happy morning, finding her friends and talking to them, getting rebates from her cronies on what she buys, and I don't doubt, passing over some of the señora's *mandado* to a few relatives, who just happen along, with empty baskets. I bet they all eat liver with onions, white rice with peas, and perhaps a square of gingerbread that day.

Once in a while I get mad about all this, and demand minute accounts. Then I am kept busy adding all morning, counting out the pennies for green chiles, onions, tortillas, bolillos, Mitchie Foo's meat, and so on until I write it all off to "running expenses," and get about my business.

While Paula is at the market, Elvira cleans the house, and rushes out to the truck with her daily can of garbage. Every day this upsets her. She thinks it would be so nice if we had a pig to eat the garbage. It seems a sin to throw out those tomato and potato peelings, and apple cores and old lettuce leaves. But I cannot be persuaded.

I dress and comb my hair, get Guicho off to his academy, and sit down to my typewriter. Over the gentle hum of the vacuum cleaner, I assemble my thoughts and get at my work. First, a daily letter to my mother, who likes to know the trivia of my life, rather than the great news events, and then, perhaps, I prepare an article on Tequisquiapan, where there are wonderful hot springs of interest to tourists.

Elvira breaks in on me. "Señora, the gas tank came."

We buy our cooking and heating fuel in tanks, from

Pemex, and it must be paid for on delivery. I count out the money, and endure the racket of the installation.

Back to my article.

"Señora, there is a man at the gate who says he has walked all the way from Toluca and he has no money and he is hungry. Could you give him a peso?"

"Does he smell of tequila?"

"Señora, he certainly does."

"Then, why did you bother me?"

"Because he is lame, señora. He has hurt his foot."

"All right. Give him a couple of tortillas, with beans in them, and a peso."

"Not a peso, señora. Just thirty centavos. For the bus."

So I settle that crisis. Or did I?

I write three pages in great peace and contentment, and read over my words, with a certain reluctant approval.

"Señora, Paula has come back and she needs some more money to buy cream to whip for your gingerbread."

"Here it is." I write another page.

"Señora, Mitchie Foo ate a lizard and he is being very sick."

"Where is he?"

I rush into the garden. Mitchie Foo is gagging, and convulsive movements proceed from his tail, up through his stomach, his throat and his mouth.

"Poor Mitchie! Out with it!" I pet him; there is a super-feline heave, and up comes a lizard, definitely recognizable. Elvira snatches it away, and scolds Mitchie sternly. Relieved, he lies down in the sun, and stretches himself, narrowing his eyes at me in affection. We do this lizard bit about once a week, and we both know all the lines and business.

Back to Tequisquiapan. I have almost finished the article.

"Señora, the Señora Margarita is on the phone."

A nice chat with Margarita who wants me to go shopping with her. We make a date for next morning.

Tequisquiapan. Where was I?

"Señora, the Señora Carmen is on the phone."

Carmen invites me to take tea next Friday. Her brother, the priest, is visiting from Spain. I accept with pleasure.

I believe I had better add a paragraph to the article about what hotels cost.

"Señora, there is a man at the *zaguán* selling strawberries. Big ones."

I go out to see.

"How much are the strawberries a kilo?"

"Seven pesos, Señora."

This will take time. I happen to know that they are selling for five in the market. We strike a bargain at four pesos a kilo for three kilos. Then there is a crisis about weighing them. The strawberry man has no balance. He will have to go to a little shop around the corner to weigh the berries.

"I will accompany him," says Paula darkly, not trusting him for a minute.

They go off toward the corner shop, and return, a bit later, with Paula's *casuela* full of the lovely big red berries.

I pay up, and then Paula says, "These would make nice jam, señora. The kind you make with the whole berries."

"Do you have time to make it?"

"Well, I have some shirts to wash this afternoon, but I could make the jam, afterward, if I had some sugar."

"Order some sugar from the Camelia. They will send it."

"They won't send just two kilos of sugar, señora. I will have to order some other things, too."

"What else do we need?"

"I could order some flour and oatmeal and molasses and black pepper."

"The señor doesn't want our bill in the grocery store to be more than six hundred pesos a month."

"Ay, señora, it is the twenty-fifth of the month, and already the bill is six hundred and thirteen."

I figure that when I get paid for the Tequisquiapan article, if I ever finish it, I could swing an extra fifty pesos at the grocery store.

"Go ahead and order the things."

I manage to finish the article, only to learn that I had my carbon paper in backward for the last three pages, and I have to copy them out again, if I am to remain with a copy for my files. As I am finishing the last page, my husband and Wiki arrive home for lunch.

The table is laid in the garden, and Luis, remembering the liver, has brought a bottle of red Mexican wine.

Guicho rings up to advise that he is having lunch with Juanito as Juanito's mother has made *mancha manteles*, and he is invited.

Wiki, hungry as a lion, Luis, and I sit down to lunch. We begin with the rice; this is served alone, with hot tortillas, and a side dish of chile sauce. This *salsa* differs from day to day. Sometimes it is red, sometimes green, sometimes it is made of fresh green serranito chiles, sometimes of green tomato and chile chipotle, sometimes of red tomato and quipines, sometimes of toasted black dried chile mulatto, with spices. If there isn't any salsa, my husband leaves the table. The salsa must always be served. Butter is almost never on the table, even if the family eats bread.

Afterward comes the liver, with a salad of raw onions, and of course, a dish of beans. Frijoles are served at the end of every ordinary Mexican meal (though not at parties). Frijoles are a staple, even in homes which can afford meat or fish; the idea is that they fill up any interstices left empty, and make sure that body and soul stick together until supper time, no matter what foolishness the señora has seen fit to set forth.

The chocolate cream is consumed, and Luis frugally sets aside his remaining half-bottle of wine.

Wiki departs for school again, and Luis repairs to the library, where he lies down on the couch and is instantly asleep, a piece of newspaper over his face. He is not expected back at his office until four, and so is able to indulge this most efficacious of tranquilizers—the short nap. I also lie down, well-covered with a blanket, for I am always cold at Mexico City's high altitude, and Mitchie Foo usually snuggles under the blanket with me, and sets up his steady happy purring.

When Luis rises, and brushes his teeth previous to departure, I get up too, and comb my hair again. The sky is darkening, and the first grumbles of thunder are heard. During the summer, in Mexico City, and south, we have daily tropical downpours. If I am going to play trios or quartets somewhere, or to practice in the chamber music orchestra to which I belong, I try to plan my afternoon so as to arrive well ahead of the rain. After it has started, I may be marooned for as much as an hour, because taxis mysteriously disappear, and, as the streets run with water like streams, it is foolhardy to go out in the rain. Everybody in Mexico City has an umbrella, and ladies secrete little rain caps here and there in various pockets, and have raincoats stashed at home, in the homes of relatives and best friends, so as to be ahead of Nature if possible. Nevertheless, if you venture out into a summer rain with just a transparent raincoat and hood, you will be soaked to the skin before you cross the street, so heavily does the water pour down from the sky. Rubbers? Cynical laughter. Knee boots might help, but rubbers are practically useless. Once I was caught in the rain while crossing the square in front of Bellas Artes, in Mexico City. I put a newspaper over my head and I ran for the sheltering porch of the theater, but when I got there, I was wringing wet—so wet that my husband scolded me, for the rain had plastered my clothes to my body, and my form, for good or ill, was revealed to any who cared to look.

If I am not busy with amateur or semiprofessional music, perhaps I am going to the meeting of the Damas de San Angel. These ladies, some five hundred strong, consisting of all the rich, middle-class and lower middle-class ladies of the town, who wish to help, meet once a month, and collect and administer a considerable amount of money, which they use for charity. They operate a day nursery for children of working mothers, a dining room for the poor, a school, a free clinic, and several classes . . . catechism, sewing and knitting for poor mothers, and so on, besides the yearly Christmas bazaar, flower shows, and many other events. The main distinction between the wealthy women and those with smaller economic resources in the club, is that the wealthy ladies give more of their personal time and effort to the various enterprises. Indeed, when visiting friends ask me where they can see Mexican women, I always advise visiting some charitable institution. There, when they are not in their homes, you will find them . . . nursing, teaching, keeping books, reading to the sick, or performing other tasks that need doing.

My family reunites at home around seven in the evening, and after supper (usually enchiladas or some other light Mexican dish made on a basis of tortillas—and these home dishes are not as "hot" as their counterparts served at restaurants in the United States) there may be a short family meeting.

Homework is checked. Perhaps permission is given to play some records on the hi-fi for an hour or so. Or permission is denied. Wiki hasn't practiced his cello, or Mima has to learn a new part on her violin. Luis is informed of all the various pieces of household equipment which have broken down, or come apart, or "don't want to" work. Most important of all domestic machines is the liquefier, for out of this come the sauces without which the wheels of life could not revolve. Next is the "*olla express*," or steam pressure cooker, which renders moderately priced cuts of Mexican beef fit for chewing.

There is no washing machine in the family. Paula does the laundry every day as it appears in the wash basket. I asked her one day if she wouldn't like to have a washing machine to help her with her work, and she said, politely, "Of course, if you would like one, señora, I will wash the clothes in it. But they only have to be washed again, you know, and put in the sun to get white. Those things don't *really* know how to wash."

I do not force one on her. Once I had a small washing machine for diapers, when the children were tiny, and this was moderately successful, though my maids all said the diapers had to be washed again later, to make sure. It was stolen, long since, along with two of the children's scooters; I suppose the thief thought it was some expensive sort of toy.

I recall that Luis and I went snooping one time, looking at new houses which were being offered on the market. As a last convincing argument as to why we should sell our old-fashioned cottage on Desierto and buy the new house, the agent threw open the door of a little room entirely tiled, walls and floors, with a drain in the center.

"And here," he said, warming to his subject, with shining eyes, "here is the room for the washing machine! All alone! With a key. For naturally the señora would not let the servants operate the washing machine; they break everything. She would want to run it herself. Here is the water connection, and here is where it drains out. And here you can have your drier, which you take care of youself! You need never be made altered in your nerves by having your servants operate your machinery, señora! Isn't this wonderful?"

I told him it was wonderful, and I was sure he would soon sell his house. As for me, I hate to operate machinery. It scares me, and it doesn't like me, and if I have servants, I want smart girls that like to throw the switches.

Perhaps, in the afternoon, I have decided to have my hair done. Mexico bristles with beauty shops, and even the poorest little shop girl has her hair built up into imposing edifices of curls, bangs, and puffs. I catch a bus down Insurgentes Avenue, and it is a happy day for me when some strolling musicians get aboard to serenade the passengers. Very often they are blind men, for in Mexico the tradition of the blind singer is an old one. Nearly always, they carry guitars. They elbow their way to the back of the bus and then launch into some sad song about love, using the light. high Mexican falsetto at times. This is not yodeling, as the jolly Swiss do it, but a kind of wailing, very touching and effective, and it is typical of Mexican country singing.

I am always made much of in the beauty shops, because I have long hair. It is thought that I am brave, probably dominated by a stern husband, and anyway, a bit touched. Kind Mexican ladies buy me bottles of Oranch Croosh, and offer me cigarettes. I settle down to listen to their gossip (frequently of the most absorbing interest, and I work up feelings about their sister whose husband has a *casa chica* and their daughter who wishes to marry a man who goes about advertising a bakery with a loudspeaker in his car, as intense as those of any housewife hanging over her radio, with its tearful soap opera). In between I can admire their hands. With the possible exception of the Chinese, Mexicans have the most beautifully shaped hands and nails I have ever seen. An unlovely hand, even on a servant, is exception.

Or I may make the rounds of my "little dressmaker," "shoemaker," "hatmaker," or "tailor." It is one of the blessings of Mexico that people of the middle-income group can have clothes custom-made at low cost, and I love having shoes made for my "best" costumes, hats designed specially for my long hair (at a price of ten dollars or so), dresses cut specially for me and without a pattern! (My dressmaker merely looks at pictures, and she knows my topography so well that she can cut for me, and make a lovely dress, with only one fitting.) Also, you can have anything whatsoever repaired in Mexico—from jewelry, to runs in your stockings, troubles in the works of your liquefier, and old handbags.

In the evening, perhaps Luis works out a chess problem on the dining-room table, with many muttered comments under his breath. In that case, I settle down under the lamp with Mitchie on my lap, and we read our whodunit, for I am an enthusiastic armchair detective.

Maybe the family votes for the movies. Our favorite is Cantinflas, in anything at all. Next is Danny Kaye, and after Danny, anything of Walt Disney's. (There is a steady stream of Mexican tourists to California, for the sole purpose of visiting *Disneylandia*.) Sometimes we see foreign films, and there are many in Mexico City—from Russian and Chinese films, to Yugoslav, Czech, East Indian, French, Italian, and Spanish. We get very many Japanese films here, and one Japanese actor, Mifune, is a Mexican idol. Mexican movies by law, can never cost more than four pesos a ticket; as a result, movie houses are always full. Four pesos is, at the present rate of exchange, equivalent to thirty-two cents of the dollar. Mexican films can be, and often are, very beautiful, especially with regard to photography and acting. The stories tend to be variants of the same plot, too often, and a Mexican country cowboy, or *charro*, is the favorite type of hero. The "arty" films all idealize the Indians, and are tragic in tone.

There are dozens of legitimate theaters in Mexico City, and they are a challenge to the budding playwrights, many of whom have startling and original talent. Tickets cost about twelve pesos (one dollar) usually, and there are, customarily, two presentations of the play, one at seven in the evening, and another at ten.

When there is opera or ballet, Bellas Artes is the mecca of all cars, and the great theater is always packed to standing room.

Usually, when we stay home for a quiet evening, we go to bed around eleven. At ten-thirty, Elvira brings me my cup of cinnamon tea, or *té de tila*, or some other gentle soporific.

Visitors seldom drop in unannounced in Mexico, so sacred is the idea of privacy at home, with the result that the paterfamilias of the Treviños is in robe and slippers, and the mater also likely to be laid out in nightgown, *pantuflas*, and *poncho* . . . a *sarape* with a hole in it for the head, and a very warm garment indeed.

But perhaps I am having a party, to Luis's nervous discomfiture. Like most Mexicans, he dislikes home entertainment; home should be strictly private, where a man can eat supper in his pajamas and read his chess manual in peace.

Business friends are always given lunch at restaurants in town and ladies are almost never present. But once in a while he permits me to have a family gathering, or a group of friends who are *compadres* or have been close to us for years. Then he excitedly straightens pictures, runs his finger around high pieces of furniture to see if they are dusty (for servants are short and seldom dust above shoulder level) and jitters about arranging his tray of *jaibol* or *ron* (with water) or gin and bitters. Tequila is mostly a drink for the country, for outdoors and for picnics, and is seldom served unless requested by some addict.

My dinner parties, being held in the evening, are not very long on food—there are never the seven to eight courses which would be served, on succeeding fresh plates, at a midday meal. *Merienda* is the rule in Mexico, because of the altitude, and only the diplomatic groups, the international set (to which we do not belong), or the true sophisticates, sit down to a formal evening dinner. Among my *compadres* (we baptize and confirm each other's children, and thus are on terms of affectionate intimacy for the rest of our lives), we tend to set forth one hot dish (perhaps enchiladas, or maybe a Moctezuma pie . . . a wonderful concoction made of tortillas, chicken, green chile sauce, cheese and cream baked in the oven), a salad, fruit, and coffee, with perhaps an American cake or pie, to prove that I prepared it myself.

In elegant circles, into which we sometimes stumble by mistake, cocktail parties are in vogue, but a well-laden buffet must be unveiled early in the evening, as Mexicans do not like to stand around nourishing themselves merely on *bocadas* or *bites* of things. If there is no turkey, ham, and an array of salads in view, the guests leave early to eat a proper meal. I have heard a Mexican tell his wife that he will not go to a certain cocktail party: "It is a fraud," he exclaims passionately, "to invite people out at the dinner hour, and then just give them a drink, and a little plate, and a handful of peanuts, and maybe one shrimp on a stick!"

I adore parties, and so do many of my Mexican friends. It is a chance to dress up a little, but not much, for houses are not heated and it can be cold in Mexico City in the evening. A short dark silk dress with a jacket is proper for almost any occasion except an official banquet.

After dinner, no matter how the hostess deploys her material, the men nearly always cluster in a corner and discuss politics, the bulls, and the exchange, while ladies talk over their acquaintances and perhaps touch lightly on the theater or the movies.

Mostly my entertaining, such as it is, and my reunions with my friends, takes place over the tea table. Here one can eat all sorts of wonderful little cakes, and knit and tat, and discuss husbands and children. Tea is a leisurely time, from five to seven, usually, and there is always time to get home and serve supper or *merienda* to one's family at half-past eight or nine. Ladies replete with tea very often skip supper in Mexico and this keeps them slim, though it does not do as much for me. But then, I have a hard-working metabolism, and it extracts ten calories from a lettuce leaf, and twenty from a peanut. Everybody has something terrible the matter with them, after forty, and I have my digestion. It is too good.

The telephone does not ring very often in the evening. Father, in Mexico, makes administrative rules, and Father usually decrees that the telephone shall be free for him, in case there should be a long-distance call, or some important business message, after office hours. Small fry may use the telephone during the daylight hours, and servants may answer the phone, if they are called, but they are not encouraged to do any telephone visiting.

Once in a while Wiki gets a call from a pal, to talk over a *tarea* (homework), or a friend calls to discuss the merits of some art exhibit, in Guicho's case.

Girls are not much in the day's activities. For a couple of months Guicho attended a Mass halfway across the city, in order to stare devotedly at one of the lovely communicants there, but she never seemed aware that he was alive, and after a time, he left off going. Then there were two or three mysterious phone calls for him, with no clue to the caller except a breathless feminine voice. She would not give her name. And she always asked for Guicho, but hung up when he answered. These machinations are well-known; he was to respond at once with renewed ardor, and be encouraged to take up the pursuit. But alas, his interest flags when it is not corresponded in reasonable time, and he changed back to the family church. Wiki once "made the bear," or paced steadily up and down outside the window of a girl he admired, on account of her well-rounded legs, but he too lost interest in favor of bullfights, to which he has become fiercely addicted, in true Latin fashion.

Paula does not encourage raids on the icebox, and to prevent this, she often takes the breakfast eggs and ham to her bedroom and locks them in with her. Once in a while the boys can find a bit of cheese she has overlooked, or a slab of cake. Usually they make do with a banana or a handful of peanuts. Guicho, of course, smokes. His cigarettes are the strongest and smelliest and cheapest there are, due to his poverty. Wiki sometimes smokes a little, but since the bullfight rage set in, he has gone over to the very Spanish *puro* . . . a slender cigar. I have had to have hysterics and cry and stamp my foot in order to enforce the rule that cigars may be smoked in the garden but not in the house.

Just before bed, if it is a bright evening, Luis may take out the beautiful telescope he inherited from Papacito, and invite the boys into the garden to look at the stars. Sometimes, braced and guided, even I can fix a star in the lens of the telescope and admire its color, and I can and do find the moon, where I see the rabbit which lives there. (Mexicans see the rabbit instead of the man in the moon.) We are all very fond of comets, and will get up en masse at any hour of the night to admire one streaking across the sky, with its fiery wake, and eclipses of all kinds are studied with passionate interest by all the Treviños. A recurring dream is to get hold of enough money to set up a small observatory on top of the house.

As the night grows quiet, we begin to hear the bells of Carmen Church, not often so audible during the day, due to traffic sounds. By the time they call out mellowly that it is midnight, the Treviños are all tucked into their beds—Guicho in his garden studio, Wiki in his bedroom (icy cold, with windows wide open, because he is a health fiend—except for the *puro*), Luis in his bed, and Mitchie and I in mine.

And so, Good night, and dream of the angels, as the Mexicans say.

XXIII ॐ

THE SPIDER CLUB

Nunca pegues a una mujer, ni con el pétalo de una rosa.
—PROVERB

In the course of these memoirs I may have conveyed the impression that mine has been a perfect marriage, without flaw, where never is heard a discouraging word. Let me hasten to set the record straight. In fact, I think here I will tell about the Spider Club. The spider, as everyone knows, is the only female of the whole animal kingdom who has worked out a System. She gets all the best out of marriage and fast. As soon as the honeymoon is over, she devours her spouse, thus assuring herself a life many women would find ideal, at least for short periods. She has been fulfilled, as the psychologists say, she knows all about sex, she has a family, and she hasn't any of the bother of a husband around, cluttering up the web.

My husband and I had two reliable quarrels we could always dust off and kick around, when the mood was on us. One was the horrible white sauce that Americans put on their food (he was against, I was for). The other was Brahms (he was anti, I was pro). And we could always quarrel about the Alamo. These rows could get very hot, and though each of us knew the other's dialogue, a lot of emotion could be generated and worked off. Once in a while we would have a little nostalgic fight about the *gasto* (the daily expense money, but as Luis earned more, and could bear to give a little more, this became less interesting). However, his deeply ingrained instincts of economy, born in him, and well-nurtured in money-conscious and bark-tight Monterrey, often caused the eruption of an acrimonious discussion. The Spider Club came into being shortly after the incident of the shaving water and the gas water heater.

We had been saving up our money, week by week, and at last we had been able to purchase a gas-fueled hot water heater, which was supposed to be automatic. Up to then, we had managed with one in the back patio, into which it was necessary to feed little sticks of wood for about an hour before you wanted it to give you, grudgingly, about two quarts of water a little warmer than luke, but not hot enough to make tea with. When at last our shining white water heater was trundled in and installed just beneath the bathroom window, and connected up with a tank of butane gas, I indulged in rosy dreams of hot water whenever I wanted it. To wash my hands, on icy mornings. I could even, I supposed, have a bath whenever I felt like it, instead of having to go out into the night, or even the pouring rain, and feed wood to the water heater.

However, despite the glorious new equipment, the water seemed to continue to come out of the spout marked C (for *caliente*, or hot) as cold as ever in the mornings, and the regular before-coffee vision of my husband strolling through the living room from the kitchen, with his suspenders down his back, carrying a little pan of water he had heated on the kitchen stove, was still to be seen. I am not mechanical and I thought maybe it would take a while for the automatic water heater to get used to us and like its new home. But on the fourth day, as my husband passed me, white fluff on his face, with his little steaming pan of shaving water, I detained him by one suspender end. "Hey," I said, "maybe you had better send that new water heater back to the store. There hasn't been a drop of hot water out of it since they installed it."

"Of course not," he told me. "I have not turned the indicator up to 'hot.' When you want a bath, you turn the indicator up, and it heats."

"Why can't it be up all the time, so I could have hot water all the time, whenever I want it?"

"Because," he explained patiently, "that would use up too much gas."

"Why can't we have it in the morning, to wash by, anyway?"

"Because it only takes me a minute to heat my pan of shaving water on the kitchen stove."

"So all the rest of us can wash in ice water, or go galloping around with little pans of heated water, like you?"

My husband detected signs that the little woman was working up a head of steam.

"I'll turn it on for you, if you insist, right now," he promised hastily, "but you will only waste the gas. It takes about an hour to heat up enough water for a bath."

"Then it's no better than the old wood burner," I answered bitterly.

"Now don't get excited! I'll go and turn up the indicator right now!"

I had defiant hot baths every morning (though I prefer them at night) until I began to simmer down, and finally I convinced myself that it was smarter to turn up the indicator while I ate supper, and take my bath before bed, than to wait for bath water in the morning, being late to my work, and bad-tempered all day.

Then I got a chest cold (from going out into the winter morning right after a hot bath, no doubt), and I had to stay home and nurse myself. I had a little electric heater I had bought from a friend when she broke up housekeeping to return to the States, and so I sat, sniffling in my sala, with the electric stove focused on my feet, reading Jane Austen.

"Comfortable?" my husband would ask kindly, as he left for his office, and I would nod and sneeze and cough. Almost at once the electric current would fail (as it often does in Mexico), my little stove would cool, and I would have to go back to bed, to keep warm. The third morning on which the electricity failed immediately after my husband's departure, a big ugly suspicion entered my mind. Groaning with the effort, I untangled myself from my blankets and scarfs, and went outside to look at the master switch which controls all the electricity in the house. Yes, Luis had prudently cut off the current.

My rage kept me warm all day, while I waited for him to return from the marts of trade, and I wrote and rewrote my speech in my head, making it at first hurt, then cold, and finally furious.

The quarrel got going shortly after seven, and by ten we were on the subjects of love and money.

"The trouble with you is," I accused, "that you would rather save money than make it."

"The trouble with you is that you don't love me. You knew I was a poor man when we married. But now you hate me because I am not rich."

"I don't hate you," I raged. "You are just quibbling. I could stand anything if we were really poor. But surely we can afford to run an electric stove to keep me warm when I'm sick."

The Spider Club was organized next day.

My friend Margarita and I had been planning to give a big party together to celebrate our wedding anniversaries, which occur within a week of each other. We had spent the greater part of a year preparing guest lists, figuring out menus, and going into all the extensive planning that makes parties almost more fun before than during, and this day we were to meet for tea and touch up the final blueprints.

I made a raisin cake for tea and awaited Margarita, wondering how she would take the news that I didn't want to celebrate my anniversary at all, except perhaps in sackcloth and ashes. She came in a bit late, and looking rather seedy.

"How are you?" I asked, kissing her on each cheek, and then wiping away the stain of my lipstick with my handkerchief. She did the same office for me. (This is standard procedure when Mexican ladies meet.)

"Sleepy," she answered me. "I was up all night."

"Good heavens, why? One of the children sick?"

"No. I was up all night fighting. With my husband. He is quite impossible lately. I wonder if you would mind very much if I didn't come in with you on the anniversary party. I am afraid I couldn't keep a sneer off my face."

"I don't want to give a party either. I was going to break it to you. I am not speaking to Luis, actually. He is unspeakable to. In fact, I am furious with him. I am forming a Spider Club. Care to join?"

I explained about the spiders. "They certainly have the right idea," I declaimed.

"I'll take a life membership," offered Margarita, "and I'm willing to pay my dues in advance."

My neighbor Sarita came over to borrow a cup of sugar, later, and I observed that she was breathing heavily and that there were intermittent flashes in her eyes. She agreed to sit down and take a cup of tea.

I told her we had just formed the Spider Club. "I'm acting president," I explained, "and I want to get in a few members so that we can have a regular election."

"I think I could get you a very enthusiastic member," said Sarita. "Me."

"Gosh. Rico can't possibly be as obnoxious as Luis and Carlos."

"Do you know what he did?" asked Sarita rhetorically, not waiting for my answer. "He went and joined the golf club over at Churubusco and bought himself three thousand pesos' worth of clubs. And the joining fee was a thousand pesos! Then he had the nerve to give me a lecture on how to save money and suggested that I fire the baby's Nana. I could kill him."

"I would like to run you for vice-president," I told her.

By the end of the week, we had fifteen members. Maria Luisa got wind of the club and rang up to ask how she could get in. Margarita and I prepared a splendid high tea and invited all our potential members and our pledges, to come and help draw up a constitution.

"I wonder," began one of the younger women, whose head presumably was less bloody but unbowed than ours, "if it wouldn't be a better idea just to form a new order of nuns. We could all live in the same house and divide up the work, and maybe take a nice name like 'Little Sisters of Terrible Husbands,' or something like that. I could design us a chic little habit."

Josefina was all for it. "I can do the plumbing," she offered. "You want a good plumber in the order, as the rule would be that no man could ever come into our house. Naturally. And I can fix anything with a couple of hairpins. My husband, even, says so."

Margarita said she would be the cook. I said I would be the one who went out to beg every day. I had to beg for the *gasto* every morning, and I knew all the techniques.

The upshot was we didn't come to a firm agreement, so the Spider Club remained what is known as a loose association. Once in a while, when things got just a bit too thick for somebody, we would have a meeting, and work out some agitated resolutions, and a dire program, but we could never get a quorum. Besides Mexican women are afraid to sign anything without their husband's consent. So one by one, the members fell away.

I remember how I happened to withdraw.

I had been invited one day to go and play quartets with a little group consisting of two professional musicians and one excellent amateur. A date had been set to play two Beethoven Quartets, and I had been working at my part until I knew it well. The professional musicians had canceled paying engagements for the fun of working on Beethoven, and they were coming from some distance across the city. So much for background.

That morning my Wiki "dawned" with a sore throat. I called the doctor who ordered bed, lots of lemonade, and pills and gargles, and, leaving Elvira to sit with the patient, and to provide the lemonade and pills, I packed up my fiddle and prepared to go to the quartet practice. As bad luck would have it, my husband drove up just as I was leaving.

"You mean to say that you are *leaving* your little sick child in bed to go and play music?" he asked, aghast, as he noted my fiddle case.

"The doctor says he will be all right. He's in bed, and Elvira will look after him for a couple of hours. And besides, he is eleven years old, not quite a helpless infant."

"But he has *fever!*"

"Not now. It came down."

Pale with self-righteous indignation, my husband took my fiddle case from me, and went to lock it in a closet. Shaking his finger under my nose, he ordered, "You'll stay home with your sick child. Let the music go to blazes!"

And then he got into his car and went back to work. I was put to the humiliation of phoning, at the last minute, that there would be no quartet because the least important member of the group—the one who had been honored to be invited— was sick with a violent headache. I had ruined the music the others had planned for, and I knew perfectly well that I would never be invited again. Wiki slept quietly all afternoon, and woke to ask for lemonade at the hour when I would, in the normal course of events, have been returned home anyhow.

I spent the afternoon in my room, grinding my teeth. Slowly I came to what is known as a full rolling boil. I sat down and wrote my husband a letter. I forget what I said now, but it was a well-developed essay, proceeding with re- morseless logic from point to point, and the final conclusion was that if this sort of rigid arrogance happened to me again, based on doubt of my judgment and my devotion to my chil- dren, I would simply take them and my fiddle and my cat and leave. "I am not accustomed to being treated like an imbecile, and cave men make me sick to my stomach," I think I wrote.

"You take the attitude that I am a bad mother. Well, I am a better mother than you, you hen hussy!"

"Hen hussy" is an epithet of the utmost opprobrium in my family. It has come down to us from my maternal grandmother as a term to be applied to men who nose into women's affairs.

I put this missive into an envelope, sealed it, and left it in the library where Luis would see it as soon as he arrived home for dinner, since he always went straight to the library to read his paper. When I heard his car at the gate, I went into my bedroom and locked the door.

He came in whistling happily, looked in on Wiki, who was sitting up reading *Huckleberry Finn*, and then he strolled into the library. A deep silence fell on the house and I knew that he was reading my poison-pen letter. Then, after a while, I heard the *tap-tapping* of my typewriter. He was writing me an answer!

Now I confess that I began to feel apprehensive. After all, it was nice that my husband was such a family man, I told myself. I had often bragged about this on visits home to the States. And where would I go with my kids and my cat and my fiddle, anyhow? My mother had always instructed me sternly to kill my own snakes, an old Western expression which means settling your own problems as they occur, and not going screaming around for strangers to help you. Besides, she and Daddy had brought up their own family, and were entitled to a rest. By all the rules, I should bring up mine.

I wondered if it was too late to try to effect a reconciliation. Being of a somewhat literary temperament, the writing of a hot letter usually served to work off my tantrum, and I could tear it up, feeling much better.

I wouldn't apologize, I thought. I did not feel that I had behaved badly. But peace was better than war. Anything for a quiet life. Maybe even a little Munich was better than poison gas and bombs.

Suddenly I heard Luis trying the door.

"Open up!" he shouted, and then he beat a good loud tattoo on it.

I silently opened the door.

"You wrote me a letter!" he roared. "Now I have written you one!"

He threw his letter on the bed, and rushed out, slamming every door in the house, got into his car, raced the engine, backed out and into the gatepost, cursed roundly in Spanish, tried again, made it, and disappeared into the night.

I was pretty scared by then and not at all eager to read his letter. I pottered about, rubbed Wiki's throat with balm, noting with self-justification that he was still without fever. I washed a pair of stockings. Finally I sat down and read the letter. Best to get it over with.

"*Darling,*" it began. But he always called me darling, even when furious with me. I went on. "*I know you are angry with me, and I am sorry I was so bossy. You and the children are all I love in this world. Forgive me. Your LUIS.*"

The Spider Club fell apart right there and it wasn't even thought of again for years.

XXIV 𒄷

ADIOS, MAMACITA

Cuando se quiere de veras,
Como te quiero yo a ti,
Es imposible, mi vida
Tan separados vivir. . . .
—POPULAR MEXICAN SONG

During all my years in Mexico, my husband's mother, our "Mamacita," was the foundation and the keystone of the whole family. No decision was ever made without her; she was consulted on all problems, big and little; and all family festivities centered around her.

When I first met her she was in her late fifties. She had had ten children and had gone through a Revolution. She had known poverty and exile and trouble. Yet she was plump and firm-fleshed, her beautiful black curling hair had only a few silver threads, and when she smiled her enchanting smile, she showed perfect, even white teeth—all her own. She had never been near a dentist in her life.

Mamacita was a wonderful organizer, a great planner of picnics, dinners, dances, first communions, and weddings and wedding breakfasts. For every festivity she contrived a new gown, or a new look on an old one, and the hairdresser was always summoned to build up some fresh and wonderful coiffure. Mamacita met life with sparkling eyes, well dressed and armored with the determination to cajole and flirt with it, to make it behave and hand over goods and beauties. Or, if life wouldn't behave, she laid traps for it, and fought it and outwitted it, until it came to heel again.

She loved the daily struggle, and she enjoyed the good

things with enormous gusto, and every day found her full of power and ideas. Her radiance and vitality were reflected on all her beloved family and all her friends. She was able to exert a sort of magic over us, that held us all to her vision of life as a place of joyous triumphs, in which she, Mamacita, could never be defeated. Long before everybody began talking about emotional security, Mamacita bestowed it, and with generous hands.

She had endured the deaths of many dear ones, including one infant son. Profoundly Catholic, it did not ever occur to her to oppose, in even one tiny thought, the obvious will of God. And yet, after Papacito's death, she began to change. Strong and comforting to all her children, in the first days after his passing, she began daily Rosaries for his soul, and she did not once break down. But she became distracted and restless, like someone late for an appointment, who is too polite to glance at his watch while talking to you. She often spoke now of when she would be reunited with her *viejito*, which I must explain, is a term of deep endearment, in Monterrey, though it merely means "old man." And once she said to me, rather wonderingly, "Nothing is the same, now that Papacito is gone. It is as if I ate, and was nourished, but there is no taste."

Unable to be calm anywhere, she sold her house in Monterrey and bought one in Mexico City. But she never lived in the capital. She spent a lot of time packing up, traveling, and visiting—in Mexico, in Monterrey, in Laredo, in Linares. But she would never stay anywhere very long. Naturally, her only daughter, Adela, saw her most.

Many little things she did then, I realize now, were forms of saying goodbye, of making ready to keep her appointment with Papacito. "*Cuando se quiere de veras, Como te quiero yo a ti, Es imposible, mi vida, Tan separados vivir,*" goes the song. ("When you truly love, my darling, as I love you, it is impossible to live apart.")

Once in Mexico she dug down into her trunk and brought forth a black lace mantilla and a high comb. "I will have a little picture made of myself for all my children, as a *recuerdo* [souvenir]," she said. For a moment the old enchanting, flirtatious smile showed on her aging face, and the photographer caught it. But when she saw the proofs, she began to cry. "No no. I don't feel that way any more," she protested.

Her indomitable pride and personal grooming never faltered, whether she felt well or ill. Once in my home in San Angel on a visit, she complained of not feeling well, and early next morning I went to her room to see how she had "dawned." She was still in bed, her black hair spread out on the pillow. She smiled, but she said, "*Hijita*, I feel quite weak." I phoned the doctor at once, and went to tell her he would call to see her at about ten o'clock. I urged her to rest until then and brought her a cup of tea. Yet when the doctor arrived, Mamacita was up, corseted and dressed in a proper morning costume, her hair was done, and there was a brave spot of rouge on each cheek. Only at the doctor's insistent urging, did she agree to loosen her clothes and allow him to examine her.

He found tender places and pain, but no evidence of any specific trouble. In the way of doctors, he suggested a really complete physical checkup. Mamacita said she thought that would be a good idea, and she would have it done in Monterrey, when she returned to visit Adela. But in Monterrey, she told them she would have it done in Mexico, when she went to spend Christmas with Jorge.

I think she knew her time was growing short, and she had no intention of spending any of it in hospitals. And she looked around for a few last experiences to savor, probably thinking, in her innocent, literal way, that she might tell Papacito about them. She had never flown, and she decided to return to Monterrey by air, after her Christmas visit. "I am rather frightened, but I wish to do it," she told me. "Get me a ticket, *hijita*."

But there was another indication (I see now), that she felt she might soon be keeping her appointment with Papacito. We were at supper on the day before her departure for the north. Wiki said, "Mima, please pass the *bolillos*," and

Guicho addressed a remark to his father, calling Luis, as he had always done, by their childish name for him, Wees.

Mamacita put down her fork.

"Listen to me!" she said firmly. "You must no longer call your father Wees. I forbid it. When you were little, we overlooked it, but now you are big boys. The time has gone by. From now on, you are to call him 'Papacito.' And do not call your mother 'Mima' either. I want you to call her 'Mamacita.'"

So I was promoted and given my medal, but only later did I realize that Mamacita felt she was going to resign her position so soon.

We took her to the airport and there were the usual embraces, kisses, and tears, and the promises to return quickly and to write often. Then Mamacita turned and looked steadily at the great shining steel bird that was to carry her up into the clouds. She went pale, but she threw back her head and squared her shoulders. She marched up to it like a soldier and got on board. We had one last glimpse of her, one more smile, a wave of the hand, and then she set her face forward and looked back no more, as the plane taxied out along the runway and took off into the sky.

I never saw her again.

Her illness became serious in Monterrey and the day arrived when all her children were summoned. Luis went, but I stayed home with Wiki and Guicho. She spoke of me, remembered me and blessed me, and told Luis to be good to me.

Adiós, querida Mamacita. Adiós, adiós.

THE REVOLT OF THE JOVENES

Viva México!

One Sunday, as I was busy mixing up a batch of coffee cakes for the usual evening gathering of young men, Wiki came into the kitchen.

"Mamacita," he said. "Don't call me Wiki any more. It's babyish. Call me by the glorious name of Enrique! Enrique Emperador!"

"Okay, Enrique. And what about Guicho? Does he want to be addressed as Don Luis?"

"No, he doesn't care. He is a Bohemian anyway. His friends all call him El Güero."

I had worried and agitated a good deal about the boys' citizenship, without discussing it with them. Because I am an American citizen, they had the right to choose their citizenship upon coming of age, provided Luis and I could educate them in the United States from the age of twelve to eighteen. But we could not see our way clear, economically and otherwise, to do this, and I blamed myself, sometimes, for taking away from my children, the right to choose American citizenship, should they wish it.

Then the law was revised, and any child of an American citizen, born abroad, might choose American citizenship if he wished, any time up to and including the age of twenty-five.

I told the boys about this one evening at dinner. Both stared at me incredulously.

"You mean to say we can go and become American citizens? Just by declaring ourselves?"

"No. It's the other way around. You must go and declare yourselves Mexicans, before the American Embassy authorities, if you *don't* want to be Americans."

"Now Mamacita," began Enrique, speaking to me kindly and patiently, as he has tended to do ever since entering college prep school. "Now Mama, you surely aren't serious in supposing that we would ever want to become Americans. Why?"

"Well . . ." I began. "It's a great country. I'm an American. Plenty of people would give their right arm for American citizenship right now."

"Not if they could be Mexican citizens," answered my son. "This is a new country, full of resources, with a great future ahead."

"That's no reason to be a Mexican," began Guicho, belligerently. "That's crassly materialistic. That's as materialistic as the Americans are!"

"What do you mean?" I broke in angrily. "Everybody's materialistic who wants comfort and progress and the good things of life. There's nothing against that."

"But if you put those things first," said Guicho, "then you are materialistic."

"Well, I shall go and do my military service for Mexico," announced Enrique, and he forthwith did. Guicho presented himself for military service and was turned down for flat feet.

"I don't care," he said. "I don't paint with my feet, anyhow. So let them be flat."

"You could take some exercises," I suggested timidly.

"What for? I don't want to march up and down with a gun on Sundays anyhow, I'm a pacifist."

"When did you become a pacifist? You were always a terrible-tempered fighter."

"When I thought about history. What are wars? Just exchanges of power. What do you get when it is all over, besides a lot of ruined cities and dead citizens? The same dogs, with different collars. I will never fight for anybody."

About this time he began to object to going to Mass with me, and to start arguments about his religion. I put up with this for a while, and then I told him I would not attempt to discuss anything, but that he should go and hold conversations with some learned priests we know, who were more able to answer his questions. He attended some courses on St. Thomas, and on St. Augustine's "City of God" at the University of Mexico, and found to his surprise that there was a good deal he could learn still about Catholicism. I began to feel more at ease about him and his questionings when he came one day to talk to me, and finished by saying, "I am not sure I will end up a practicing Catholic, not yet. There are some things I have to decide. But one thing *is* sure . . . I shall want to marry a Catholic girl."

I thought to myself, "Aha!" but I held my peace. Father F. had warned me to expect these questionings. In fact, he told me that usually religion was stronger after some soul searching.

In some ways, my sons have always treated me with special respect. "You can talk about *anything* with Mama," they have said. "She is never shocked. That is because she was a reporter. And an American. American girls have no illusions."

"What do you mean, no illusions? I have lots of illusions."

"No you don't. You are romantic, but you know the facts. People with illusions don't know the facts. You are just a real romantic American."

"Well, yes. But what's wrong with that?"

"Why, you romantic Americans make mistakes in your foreign policy all the time," pontificated Enrique. "The only way to be successful is to fight with the same weapons used by your enemy. With Russia, you should be secretive and hypocritical and use delaying actions, and promise things you have no intention of doing. With England, you should always put the U.S.A. first, in every situation, while remaining very polite. That's what England does, and old perfidious Albion has come out of most situations pretty well the victor, for that reason."

"Well, she has lost her colonial empire in our time. So how successful was the foreign policy there?"

"Ah," cried Enrique, the future lawyer, with immense relish. "There you have it! She lets go when she can't keep her colonies any longer, making a virtue of necessity, and immediately signs them up to good commercial treaties, while they are all softened up at her generosity. England has always been clever and wily and treacherous as a snake."

"Now you sound like a professional Irishman," I couldn't help saying snappishly.

"Irishman! I sound like a descendant of Spaniards, and that's what I am. At least, partly. I bet," he turned on me in triumph, "I bet you never heard of the Black Legend!"

"Yes I have!" I shouted. (You always shout in arguments with Latins. Nothing is ever said in a conversational tone except perhaps, "Kindly pass the *salsa*.") "I learned all about it in college. My professor of Latin American history told us how England had diffused the Black Legend throughout the English-speaking world, identifying Spain with every perfidy, and achieving the special triumph that when you speak of the Spanish Inquisition it calls up a vision of torment and cruelty such as never was on land or sea. To this day, there are people who do not know that in the England of Elizabeth's day, there were more horrid tortures than any used by the Inquisition, and more Catholics were done to death for their faith during her reign, than heretics were burned in four hundred years of the Inquisition. But the Black Legend—the constant casting of Spain as the villain in all English literature— still lives in the minds of everyone who ever was made to study English history or English literature in school. Oh, I know all about it."

I had taken the wind out of Enrique's sails, to some degree. He stood speechless, for I had uttered his lines.

I went on. "But what I can't understand," I said, "is why

you patriotic young Mexicans, all worked up about the Black Legend, that centuries-old calumny against Spain, are so against Spain nowadays."

Enrique sputtered, and his brother answered for him.

"Why, a lot of that is due to you Americans," Guicho told me. "It was your own Mr. Poinsett, Ambassador to Mexico in the 1820s, who got the so-called liberals all worked up against Spain, and who urged the intervention of the United States in Mexican affairs. Two counts we have against him."

"He was the foreigner who did most harm to Mexico, of any we ever had to put up with, Maximilian included," roared Enrique. "And never let me hear you call our beautiful *noche buena* flower by the name of that dastard, Joel Roberts Poinsett. Poinsettia indeed!"

"If you hadn't had some American intervention, you might still have had a French foreign royal house here, and how would you like that, you desperate democrats?" I cried.

"No intervention! We don't want anybody to come over and run us, and tell us how to live and think," both my young men proclaimed, as I might have known they would. This is the official view of all Mexican patriots, in government positions and out. No intervention, whatsoever. Mexico for the Mexicans!

"And," Enrique went on, "we would like to hear a lot less about all this American 'know-how.' There is nothing wrong with Mexican brains. We are perfectly capable of learning, just as Americans did, and you Americans have no corner on scientific or any other knowledge. All we lack is capital and practice."

"I realize that Mexicans resent any inference of tutelage, with its overtones of condescension. But you had better remember that capital is money and that nobody wants to risk his money until he is sure it won't be wasted by people who aren't sure of what they are doing."

"The time for all that has gone by. Capital, if it comes here, must take its risks, as elsewhere, and be satisfied with reasonable return," they proclaimed. "Why so much insistence that we guarantee everything, with payment in advance, cash against documents, and so forth? Belgium doesn't demand that from us. Neither does Germany. Neither does Japan. No wonder our trade is flowing that way. The Colossus of the North is going to price and demand herself right out of the market, and fast, by demanding extra high gains on capital because of 'risk,' while demanding so many guarantees that there really isn't any risk at all!"

"Well, I don't know about commercial treaties and trade," I muttered, "but I do know that when you say 'Colossus of the North' south of the Mexican border, it is Mexico they are talking about. A Mexican diplomat told me. So what do you think of that?"

"Fine! That means we are going to grow and to bull our way into prosperity, as others have before us. And it is about time," shouted Enrique.

Now all these arguments and altercations have not taken place at one time. They occur with regularity, and the arguments shift and change about to some degree, and if there are other young Mexicans present, new ideas are inserted. But, in general, the above is a fair chart of what young Mexicans are thinking.

With strength comes confidence. Mexico is growing strong, and at last, she is beginning to stand her ground and demand her rights before the world. Mexicans remember the ill-starred "punitive expedition" into Mexico in pursuit of Pancho Villa in 1916, commanded by Brigadier General John J. Pershing, and the shelling of Veracruz by an American naval order. Mexico forbade the showing of the movie *The Alamo* because she still bitterly resents the one-sided interpretations of that battle by American historians, and she recalls the loss of her enormous southwest territories to the United States with frustrated anger, for this territory was wrenched from Mexico because of the inept machinations of a dictator, and the Mexican people had no more say in the matter than citizens usually do under an autocrat.

There are many more arguments that rage around my supper table in San Angel, when my young sons and their preparatory school or college friends get together. In many of them, the United States is looked on as the adversary, and there am I, representing the adversary and intercepting all the looks of fiery hostility, as I pass the tamales and cut coffee cake, and pour the chocolate.

I myself, in a spirit of humility, reread a lot of Mexican history—in Spanish, and got quite a different view from the one generally accepted in my home country.

And one day Dom Grant, of the Benedictine Order, straight over from his abbey in England, to start schools in Mexico, confessed to me with a smile that he was at first startled, in talking with Mexicans, to hear them refer to Sir Walter Raleigh and Sir Francis Drake as "the English pirates."

"I had never thought of them as pirates," confessed Dom Grant in his soft Yorkshire voice, "but then of course, I had been reading *English* history. We have an old saying, you know, 'It all depends on whose ox is gored.'"

And I reflected that this upsurgence of, not exactly anti-American feeling, but of passionate defense of Mexico's position historically, is justified and likely to lose some of its urgency as Mexico grows more powerful. For what makes it possible to endure a powerful neighbor, who is able to (and occasionally did) force you to actions against your will? The way to endure him is to despise him. This is easy, and seems to put everything into balance.

So I have had to learn to put up with something I find irksome, in my own sons. When they have any reason to object to anything I say or do, it is because I am, after all, an American. But when they specially love or admire me, it is "because you are not like an American, at all, Mamacita. You are really a Latin."

Now this is not so, and I have developed a severe schizophrenic tic in my emotions. For, of course, I want to be loved and admired, and something deep in my heart wants to be revered for everything I stand for and came from, as well.

My husband, who is and always has been openly pro-American, who loves American ways and emulates many American customs, comforts me with the words so many people use in similar situations.

"They are young and full of yeast, darling," he says. "They have to feel this way. There's nothing worse than a lukewarm young man."

"I don't regret educating them here. I want them to be patriotic. I didn't want to bring up a couple of rootless exiles, men with no country and no loyalties. And yet . . ."

"Never mind. The dust will settle in time."

"But we may not be here when it settles. And I feel confused. Dust doesn't agree with me."

"The thing for us to do is to move back to the provinces," said Luis firmly. "Mexico City is too big for me, now. Five million people! My God, we might as well be in any big city anywhere in the world. I want to go back to the old Mexico."

"It is changing so fast now. Will we find it again?"

"We can look," says my husband determinedly, and we make our plans. Shall it be Puerto Vallarta, asleep by the Pacific, or Mazatlán, or La Paz? Or Manzanillo, or Colima, or maybe Topolobampo? Or Ixtapan, or Oaxaca, or Campeche?

Yes. We will look. I, too, am nostalgic for the old Mexico I knew, where I felt at home.

But this is age, I guess. One wants to go back. I am growing too old to look forward to an invigorating struggle. It is all right for the struggle to be made and I'm all for progress. But I had just as soon let it go thundering past me now.

I, too, would love to return to the provinces, to the tranquillity I love. I am willing to watch Luis parade through the sala with his little pan of hot shaving water, and I myself will water my plants in an old patio and listen to the gurgling of the beans simmering on the stove.

I want to hear slow church bells sounding through the evening air, and walk to the market with a basket over my arm, and to stroll around a plaza watching the girls and boys courting.

The time has come. I want to be a dragon chaperone, and an *abuelita*. An old lady, my work done.

The new, strong, economically and politically independent Mexico, rapidly industrializing and socializing, rapidly coming to look and feel and smell like everywhere else in the shrinking world, will grow and progress, and my young sons will grow with it. More power to them.

As for me, I want to sit behind a barred window in some gentle provincial town, and think about "the good old days."

917.2 Treviño, Elizabeth Borton
T   Where the heart is.

Wilmington Public Library
Wilmington, N. C.

RULES